Go the Way Your Blood Beats

Go the Way Your Blood Beats

EMMETT DE MONTEREY

VIKING

an imprint of

PENGUIN BOOKS

VIKING

UK | USA | Canada | Ireland | Australia
India | New Zealand | South Africa

Viking is part of the Penguin Random House group of companies
whose addresses can be found at global.penguinrandomhouse.com.

Penguin
Random House
UK

First published 2023
001

'I Got Rhythm' words and music by George Gershwin and Ira Gershwin © 1930
Ira Gershwin Music (GMR) and Chappell & Co. Inc. (ASCAP). All rights administered by
WARNER CHAPPELL NORTH AMERICA LTD.

Set in 12/14.75pt Dante MT Std
Typeset by Jouve (UK), Milton Keynes
Printed and bound in Great Britain by Clays Ltd, Elcograf S.p.A.

The authorized representative in the EEA is Penguin Random House Ireland,
Morrison Chambers, 32 Nassau Street, Dublin D02 YH68

A CIP catalogue record for this book is available from the British Library

ISBN: 978-0-241-57053-1

www.greenpenguin.co.uk

MIX
Paper | Supporting
responsible forestry
FSC® C018179

Penguin Random House is committed to a
sustainable future for our business, our readers
and our planet. This book is made from Forest
Stewardship Council® certified paper.

For Peg, with thanks for the dance

'. . . She had a perpetual sense, as she watched the taxi cabs, of being out, out, far out at sea and alone; she always had the feeling that it was very, very dangerous to live even one day . . .'

Virginia Woolf, *Mrs Dalloway*

'. . . You have to go the way your blood beats. If you don't live the only life you have, you won't live some other life, you won't live any life at all . . .'

James Baldwin, 'On Being Gay in America', *The Village Voice*, 26 June 1984

Prologue
My Mother's Jewels

My mother loses her footing on the turn of the landing in the seventh month of pregnancy. Curling herself into a tight ball around her bump – me – she rolls on to the hall tiles. It is the first of many falls, the skinned knees and gritty palms of my childhood, but I'm not shaken loose that morning.

Her waters break a few days later and, in the panic that follows, the child I was supposed to be dies. My parents had gone to a Frank Zappa concert, to celebrate the start of her maternity leave. I must have hated the music, because early the next morning I make my presence felt. Privately, my mother blames the fall, but my father can never listen to *Hot Rats* again.

I arrive feet first, after twelve hours of pain and fear. My dad, on the other side of the hospital glass, thinks he'll lose us both. Years later, when I ask to be told about that night, my mother jokes that I've always been ambivalent; I knew how hard the world would be, wanted to stay put.

My mother, Fran, is not sentimental. She doesn't save my blond curls in baby albums, keep hand-me-down first clothes, or biro my changing height on to a doorframe. Her memories are not fixed under glass, made pristine. Most of our photos are stored in bulging shoeboxes, their corners splitting, jammed with chemist's envelopes, brittle brown negatives wound tight with rubber bands.

Her jewellery is kept in an old biscuit tin, Peek Freans; a

pattern of roses, apples, on the lid. If you look closely, flowers shine with painted dew, the fruit runs with ants. I love to tip the contents out on her bed, rifling through the beads, badges and pins, the junk-shop marcasite rings I take for diamonds. Thin, pale gold bangles that rang on her dead mother's wrists.

I never like the smug boxes of real stones she acquires later half as much as this magpie's hoard. I sort through the sparkling jumble, asking the stories of each treasure: the gilded seahorse, its red glass eye, worn the weekend she met my dad. The loose opal, its colours wrapped in cotton wool, tucked into a matchbox. It had been waiting for her on a tray, in a dusty shop on Lots Road. When Dad offers to set it, mount it in a gold ring for her fortieth, the jeweller tells him its fire is fake, paste. He buys a real stone, not telling my mother.

The tin also contains a furry brown envelope; inside is what remains of my umbilical cord. A scab, a leathery nub, traces of copper blood dried in its folds. I hold it up, pressing it between finger and thumb.

When my mother explains what it is, I'm revolted, dropping it on the bedspread. I ask her to throw it out, but she won't, snatches it up angrily from the mess of beads, folding it carefully back into the envelope's soft creases. My mother does not keep my outgrown orthopaedic boots, so why keep this? She doesn't answer, just sweeps her jewels into the tin.

This scab is what remains of our physical connection. The dangerously short time when I was hers alone, when I was only an idea, a potential. More hope than flesh. When, safe in her womb, I depended on her for every breath. The dried umbilicus is a vestige of trauma, a shared ordeal, but it is a trial only my mother remembers.

I keep slipping back. The doctors snatching me up as soon as the cord is cut, the bleeding staunched. They put me in an incubator, the neonatal ICU, but my chances are as small as my ten toes. My mother looks at me from behind plastic, reaching through the porthole, brushing my fingers with her giant's hands. She hopes her huge labours, the efforts of the tight-voiced doctors, the nurses who urge her on through terrified hours, who call her Mrs Rose, though she isn't married, have been enough.

After four weeks my parents are able to bring me home, to a squat in Clapham. They put me in a cot next to their bed, tented under an Indian prayer shawl, a superstitious protection to ward off further misfortune. My parents finally breathe out. We are three, a family. After weeks of hospital, the strain of whispered conversations, squeaky-shoed nurses in neon corridors, we are alone.

Soon after that, my mother begins to suspect something is wrong. I do not roll, explore, or bend chubby legs to eat my toes. I am floppy, my large head lazy on my neck, but my eyes follow her finger, curious, and I begin to form gurgling words. At first the smiling health visitor calms her fears: I'm a happy child, gaining weight, premature babies can often be slow to develop, but I'll catch up.

I don't catch up. When I'm eighteen months old, the pinstriped consultant confirms it is brain damage. I won't walk, will have difficulties with language, won't sit up straight, but it could have been worse. My parents are young; my mother twenty-five, my father not twenty-four. The life they have imagined for themselves finally slips from their fingers, smashes. The football boots my father has imagined buying for me, since Fran was twelve weeks pregnant, are replaced by wheels he pushes. Weekend supporter-stands become hospital waiting rooms. The autumn leaves my mother and I were to scatter, to jump in, delighted, now conceal a dog turd. The plans they made, the money carefully saved, the figures mounting week by week in an embossed passbook, are useless.

They need to get away, to think what to do. They'll go to America, to visit my grandfather. They still have more love than money, so apply to a charity that grants respite funds to the parents of disabled children. Their lives have changed beyond recognition in the months since my diagnosis, the house full of new people, their mouths full of advice. My mother has a diary now, bulging with my appointment cards. She has grown up so fast, she does not recognize herself. No longer the laughing girl, blowing pot smoke-rings in her borrowed jungle-garden, worrying about tomorrow when it arrives. She is suddenly an adult with a disabled son, a label too large, too bleak, for her small, smiling child.

The grant covers our return seats on Delta. To finance the rest of the trip, they courier a car. My father drives it from Detroit to Wenatchee, Washington State, along Route 2. The journey takes six days, but they are in no hurry, stopping in Glacier National Park. They marvel at snow in the July Rockies, spitting cherry stones from a huge punnet into the scrub. The sweet juice stains their fingers.

My parents sing over the miles of Route 2, shouting their joy, a feeling stronger than relief. All the dollar hamburgers, the diner eggs, sunny-side-up, the pizzas which spill over table edges, are the best they've ever tasted.

My mother has kept one photo from that time, flattened into a junk-shop frame. The corners creased, bright colours faded to a sticky amber. She sits on the Buick's bonnet, looks past my father's lens, down the highway. Her brown hair, caught in the slipstream of passing cars, obscures her eyes. I am beside her, tiny legs stretched out on the car's hot metal, red corduroy flares, a carton of chocolate milk in my lap.

She has selected this moment from the hundreds of others forgotten in shoeboxes. Perhaps it is tangible evidence of her past happiness, a proof easily understood? I look at it whenever

4

I am in her room. Seeing myself, chubby-faced and serious, my blond curls long. The child is me, but also a stranger I don't remember.

I get my first taste of chocolate milk at a dusty roadside diner. In my parents' memory, the rest stop had been perfect, right down to the yellowed Formica tables, shiny aluminium. The bottomless lukewarm coffee was served by a smiling waitress in a checked uniform, her name – Carol – stitched pink on her breast pocket. When I was given the cardboard carton I had not recognized it as food. My breakfast milk at home wasn't thickly brown. I had to be persuaded to try it, but with my first taste of Hershey's I am hooked, and afterwards demand that all milk be chocolate.

It's a good story. The truth is, I don't remember any diner, any kind waitress, any chocolate milk. It is my parents' origin tale; I am just strapped on my mother's lap in the back seat, only a passenger.

As a teenager, I roll my eyes at the thousandth telling of my parents' great American journey. It is repeated like a prayer, the details re-ordered, endlessly embroidered. My father, red-faced and relaxed on a Friday night, the line of dented Guinness tins spilling their dregs on the varnished boards beside the sofa, tells me again how happy they were. As the years pass, there is a note of desperation, as if he is trying to convince himself. They loved each other, loved me. The love they shared, the love they sang tunelessly from the Buick's windows, as the miles unwound behind them, was enough. Surely the fierce power of that love would prove stronger than my damaged brain?

A part of them, the laughing couple who drove that Buick, a car they didn't own, has died. I come to understand that a part of me has died too. Not just my asphyxiated brain cells, the synapses of my cerebral cortex, their messages scrambled, lost; but the child I was supposed to be, the life I wanted.

My parents tell me the story again and again; they polish and pare, in order to understand their past, and the life that is left.

My father had always wanted to see America. Until he met Fran, Dad always felt that the closest he would get to its wide-open spaces, scudding clouds, narrow-eyed cowboys, their mouths bristling with matches, would be balcony seats at the Essoldo Cinema, Newcastle. When he meets her, on a Norfolk narrowboat, Dad shelves Bowie, moving on to Dylan, *Highway 61 Revisited*. Fran becomes America to him, more vivid than Technicolor. He dreams of hot asphalt, white lines that stretch forever forwards, vast skies. More sky than he has ever seen from behind the sparkling nets of a back bedroom in Benton.

When Charlie brings Fran home, his mother is shocked, but hides her dismay behind crustless sandwiches, endless cups of weak tea in her best china. Fran's smile is too wide, shows too many teeth. Her joy is obvious, uncouth. She wears jeans, out at the knee, trailing ragged hems. It's serious, Peg can see that. Why couldn't Charles marry an English girl? My grandfather disappears to the safety of his shed, his medal-winning chrysanthemums, as soon as he can.

For my mother too, Charlie offers a kind of escape. Her father, a Jewish refugee, fleeing to America, lives in fear of a second Holocaust, a spreading mushroom cloud. He builds a bunker in his New Jersey garden. Grandpa stacks the wire shelves with neat rows of canned food, against the imminent apocalypse. They will live on hot dogs, pickles, glass jars of cocktail cherries. They will be safe.

My maternal grandmother, Hilary, had had enough of living in fear. She packs up Fran, her brothers and sister, dragging them over the Atlantic to a tiny house on a back lane in Epsom. The six of them land on a penniless writer Hilary had loved before she married. Affection soon turns to bitterness, the cottage bursting at the seams. There are closed doors, raised voices. Pinched silences when the bills arrive, shoved to the back of the telephone drawer, where they turn quietly red.

My mother tells me Hilary always wanted to write, but to write you need the luxury of time, space. In the minutes she can snatch my grandmother sits in front of a blank page, the wastepaper basket filling with false starts. Her words dry up with each tuna casserole she serves. Hilary cleans endless floors, and referees the frequent screaming matches between her displaced children. She mends holes in school jumpers. The noise of her five kids, her disappointed lover, grows deafening. She smokes too much, drinks whisky with less and less water. Hilary dies suddenly, collapsing with an aneurysm on the bathroom lino.

My mother tells me often how much I would have loved Hilary. We are alike but, to me, my grandmother is only a diffident smile, a pair of beach pyjamas, a curling photograph.

Grandpa Francis flies back over the ocean, collecting his bewildered children, but my mother, at seventeen, wants to stop moving. She has friends, a boyfriend. Fran finds a job in the post office, and every Saturday journeys from the suburbs to the platform-booted pavements of the King's Road. She spends a whole week's wages on a pair of tall, brown-leather lace-ups, tight to her knee, conker-bright. She is on her own. Breathless with the freedom of her own decisions.

Fran enrols on a foundation course at Hammersmith, picking up Hilary's dream of being an artist, wanting to be a sculptor. When I'm sixteen, and she is dyeing my hair over the bathroom basin, rubber gloves stained purple, over the sound of running water she tells me about Quentin Crisp. He was a life model for her class, and his queenly manner, his lavender-rinsed bohemianism, fascinated her, but he took no notice of her shy smiles, after a lifetime of being stared at. Things might have been different if he had found out she was an American, a foreigner.

My mother tells me about Quentin Crisp over and over again, their brief acquaintance wearing thin. She understands my difference before I do, before I can form the words. She is trying to show me that convention can be a frigid trap. That it is possible to thrive outside its tight confines. To build a life worth living, full of colour, will be hard. You must be tough under your feathers and paint.

Before flying home, we travel to Michigan. Grandpa Francis picks us up in his wide Lincoln Continental, more boat than car. He drives us to his farm, with its Dutch barn, grey-green asparagus fields, fat pampered horses. I am pulled around the property in a red hay cart, too small yet for my own saddle. Francis's daily tone of wry resignation gives way to barks of laughter, as I poke fascinated fingers into his wide nostrils, pinch his long nose.

My invading finger is further proof that Hitler didn't succeed. His first daughter has had a baby. His first grandchild, born under the new name he chose for his family as he ran. They have survived. His children, theirs, will continue longer than any spitting dictator, any thousand-year Reich.

Grandpa bumps me over his asparagus, wiry arms dragging the cart. What do the doctors know? If I can't walk he will be there to push me. As soon as I am old enough, he'll put me on a horse. Tall on four legs, rather than vulnerable on my two.

My parents still have the photo, the memory of the new Buick, to remind them of who they were. They still jokingly insist that my first memory is of chocolate milk, a diner on the side of Route 2.

The memory I hide is more prosaic, more complicated than the accepted version, the American road-movie romance.

I am about four, walking to the sweet shop, my weekly fifty pence burning a hole in my pocket. A bright, hot Saturday; the school playground opposite our house is silent. The sun prints long shadows on the pavement, the sky is a boiling blue. My boots are heavy, tight, and I can feel sweat soaking the straps of my splints. I look down: my shadow stretches ahead, pinned to my scuffed feet. My mother walks a little in front. Her silhouette, the sharp outline of her skirt, is different. I am strung between new sticks, held up like laundry pinched between metal pegs. My crutches, their tall shadow, won't leave my side. My mother walks, swinging her arms loosely, the rhythm of her slapping soles precise beside the scrape of my crutches.

Panic twists my stomach; I stop. My mother is a few feet ahead, rolling, relaxed. I want to reach out, grab for her hand, but I'll lose my balance, fall on my face, if I let go of my sticks.

She cannot fix this with a kiss, the sting of iodine from a brown bottle that she paints on my skinned knees. I will always walk catching my feet on the edges of the pavement. My mother turns, smiling. I can't see her eyes, under the visor of her palm. She waits for me, but I'll never catch up.

I

Sweet Tooth

When I was a child I thought my mother was a magician. She didn't look like the other parents, crowded at the school gates. She tied her hair up with bright scarves, shrugged into dungarees, rattling with strange jewellery. A gilded chicken's foot, carved beads. I couldn't hold her hand as we walked the short distance home, but I clicked along behind, at once proud of her vivid colours and secretly wishing she looked like the other mothers.

Fran had trained as an artist before I was born, but gave it up, her ambitions drowned out by the noise of daily routine, a young son. Laundry baskets, meals. But she still drew. I would often wake up to her sketches on my pillow, my sleep-smudged face pinned to the paper in rapid charcoal. I loved finding them, knowing that she had been watching over me. I would bump down the stairs to breakfast, clutching her drawing. Chocolate milk, pancakes with broad banana grins.

On my sixth birthday, my mother flooded the house. I came down in the morning to discover that the entire ground floor was underwater. While I slept Fran had created a vast seascape. Fish darted all over the walls in quick silver-foil shoals. An octopus curled from the mantel, watched by a grinning shark. My mother had hung green streamers, soft drifts of weed, from every door. I'm sure my schoolfriends forgot the party almost as soon as they'd eaten the cake, its blue buttercream waves, the napkined slice to take home, but I never did.

Because I couldn't run after a ball, my mother would read to me, encouraging me to draw the scenes in our favourite books: *The Little Prince, Fantastic Mr Fox*. She would unroll sheets of paper, masking-tape the corners to her easel. Tip out pencils, the names of each colour tooled in tiny gold letters. I could move freely over the paper, creating any reality I chose. I was never as good as she was, but my mother always saved each drawing, a daily exhibition on the fridge door.

When I was about eight, things began to change. I was growing frustrated with drawing, watching. Becoming aware of a widening space between me and the world. I saw it in strangers' eyes as they passed, looked back. I saw it in the tight smiles of the other parents at my school.

Hearing the scuff and spin of a ball through the open window, the shouts of neighbouring children, I didn't want to listen, watch from the garden wall. I wanted to play. I assumed my disability was simply a childhood phase, a test. One Sunday, I snapped. My classmates had all gone to a party at a roller-rink, the birthday of a good friend, Simon. When the invitations went round, he mumbled an apology into his collar. I could come over for tea one day after school instead. I couldn't skate, I'd only be bored, sitting with the grown-ups. I smiled. Told him I understood, wished Simon a happy birthday.

That afternoon, nothing I tried to draw went right. I screwed up each attempt, throwing it on the floor. I heard my mother coming down the stairs; she leant over my shoulder, kissing my ear, her fingers scratching at my neck.

'What are you doing, Peach?'

'Nothing.'

My mother smiled brightly. I suddenly wanted to hurt her. Make her feel as angry as I did.

'Mum, why did you have me?'

She looked startled; her face clouding, wary. 'Well, we wanted a baby. We wanted you.'

'I hate you,' I said quietly. 'I wish you hadn't.'

My throat tightened with the shock of what I'd said. I wanted to stop, shut my mouth, but my thoughts had a momentum of their own.

'You should have got a better one, then. I'm useless, broken.'

I spat the words in her face, exhilarated by the power I felt, frightened. My mother's grey eyes widened, filmed with tears. She turned, running from the room. I wanted to follow her, but I was fixed to my seat, panicked. I'd never made her cry before. The bedroom door slammed. A moment later, her bedside radio blared through the ceiling. I swept the pencils off the table, their colours scattering in confusion.

Fifteen minutes later, my mother was back, determined. She was wearing make-up, the silk scarf my father had bought her. It was painted with shells, crabs and other sea monsters. Kept for best, which really meant she didn't like it much. My mother only wore the scarf when she needed reminding of love. She advanced carefully, touching my shoulder. Ready to withdraw her fingers if I bit again.

'Come on, Em . . . Peach. I'm sorry. Let's be friends, hey? It's a miserable day – shall we go to the Tate?'

I burst into tears.

We drove over the river in thickening rain, but as we parked in the disabled bays in Atterbury Street, it poured.

The gallery was hushed, unusually deserted. My mother went from picture to picture as though she was visiting friends. We came here so often that they almost were. I already understood that pictures were a shared, private language. One my dad didn't speak. Because I couldn't run, couldn't skate, my mother was teaching me the value of stillness, the importance of looking.

I followed her, my wet stick ends slipping on stone. I was always scared that one day I'd trip over the slim wires in front of a priceless canvas, land head-first in the screaming mouth of a Francis Bacon. I caught up with my mother in front of one of her favourite sculptures, Brancusi's *Maiastra*. I stopped, pretending to look, but really I was watching her. I could tell from the way her fingers tightened round her bag strap that she itched to touch it. The guard saw her impulse too, nodding a discouragement. He probably didn't even see the pictures any more. They were just grey units of time, another boring shift.

I liked its shine, but didn't see what my mother saw in the perching bird. Its bronze curve looked static, the folded wings stubbornly earthbound. They didn't look like they'd carry him far, weren't capable of grace or speed. At least we had that in common.

I preferred the Hockneys. I liked his beach-bleached colours, his sunny Californian optimism. The joke of *A Bigger Splash*, the coolness of *Mr and Mrs Clark and Percy*. Percy, his back to me, attention caught by something over the balustrade, reminded me of my own cat George, whose affection I'd had to earn.

My mother smiled at me, suddenly aware I was flagging. 'Have we had enough, Peach? Shall we have lunch? I think that's about the right ratio of culture to cake.'

The restaurant was rammed. A noisy knot of talk pressing on the low ceiling, Whistler's murky mural. The maître d' apologized, my mother joking with him that this was where everybody had been hiding. He raised his eyebrows, not understanding, covering his confusion with a professional grin. He seated us at the only free table. We were tight against the window, almost outside, at the very edge of the convivial hum. My mother took my sticks, stowing them under her seat. She ordered wine, only a glass; she'd have to drive us back. When it arrived she sloshed me a mouthful, topping my drink up with water until it was pale, pink. My mother smiled at me over the tall black menu. I loved her then, as much as I thought I'd hated her that morning. She looked mischievous, shiny with relief.

'You won't remember, you were too young, but this is the first restaurant I took you to – you must've been about one. My dad, your Grandpa Francis, he wanted to see us . . . he flew from Michigan. It was supposed to be a great treat, I couldn't afford to eat here then, but I was miserable, not hungry. I was so worried. I remember my dad getting annoyed. He didn't want to see it.'

By now it was long past three, the restaurant was emptying out. The staff hovered near our table. I could feel them willing us to pay. Go, so that they could get away, reclaim some weekend. My mother sipped the dregs of her coffee, signalling for another.

'You were teething, your sore gums were making you grizzle. I fed you drops of whisky from the tips of my fingers; your first drink too – you fell asleep on the banquette. My father told me that I was being stupid, that anyone with two eyes could see you were perfect, so chubby and bright, bonny. He told me I was overtired, but something about the way you sat, well, it just made my heart go cold.'

Fran was the oldest of five. Almost a second mother to her brothers and her baby sister, Vicky. She would break up their fights, spoon out frugal tuna casserole when their mother Hilary was too tired, had retreated upstairs, away from the noise. None of her siblings sat like I did. None of them had struggled to stay upright, balanced awkwardly on the base of their spine, legs out straight, stiff and immobile.

Fran would lie next to Charlie in the dark, sleepless. She would look over the rim of the cot, watching for my breathing, worrying that it might stop. Charlie's weight in the bed used to make her feel safe, but in the morning she would be sharp, turn away from his arms. Her eyes bruised, dull with fatigue.

Dad didn't want to listen, to see anything wrong, so Mum took me to the GP by herself. He barely looked up from his desk when she entered the room. In her charity-shop finds Mum looked poor, unimportant. The doctor told her it was probably nothing. Some babies were just slower to develop, that was all. He smiled, hurrying us out, said to make another appointment in a year if things didn't change.

Things didn't change. A few months later my mother got a referral to King's College Hospital, where I'd been born, and insisted Dad came with her. They wheeled me to the appointment; waiting to be called, they didn't talk. My father unzipped my coat, folding it over the handles of my pushchair. He chewed his fingers, stared at his boots. My mother remembers the scuffed walls covered in posters about childhood diseases. Mumps, rubella; dangerous but curable.

To brighten the Paediatric Department, somebody had painted a mural on the wall. Sleek, supersonic rockets; astronauts floating under yellow stars. The moon landings were only nine years before. Her whole family had gathered round the tiny set. Fran's brother Christopher didn't believe his eyes, angrily telling them that the shots were faked. That the lunar landscape was probably a backlot. A studio in Burbank, America. Home.

Seeing Neil Armstrong's first bounce on the moon's surface, Fran had felt like she was witnessing a new age in which anything was possible. She was going to be part of it. My mother was only seventeen, but had thought herself so grown up then, capable of anything.

The consultant looked up from an untidy desk. He was smoking a cigarette, a soft plume curling from his fingers. He rose, shaking my father's hand.

'He nearly dropped ash on you, but then this was 1978, every-body still smoked, even doctors – I smoked, until I found out I was pregnant with you,' Mum later said. 'He was very kind, spent time, but I remember thinking that it was rude . . . that he could deliver his verdict without even bothering to put out his fag.'

My mother unclipped my dungarees, stowed my socks in her pocket. It took the doctor less than five minutes to confirm Fran's worst fear. It was obvious that I had a neurological prob-lem, brain damage. Whether it had happened in the womb, or was a result of my being so premature, it was impossible to say. He would need to refer me for further tests, to assess the extent of my problems, but he was pretty certain. My mother tells me that the blood drained from Dad's face. That he cried, doub-ling over like he'd been kicked in the balls.

The doctor smiled sadly at them. He retrieved my slim med-ical file, pages that would fatten over the coming months. He was so very sorry, would get things rolling for them as fast as possible. They could call him anytime. My parents were too shocked to ask him questions. The doctor's cigarette was now a column of ash; realizing, he ground it out. My father stood up, shook his hand again, thanking the consultant for his time.

The doctor held the door open for my mother, reaching for her shoulder as she pushed me out. It is strange to think that I was there, in that room with my parents, but remember noth-ing. Pre-verbal, smilingly ignorant. The consultant told Charlie and Fran that they were both young, both strong. There was no reason whatever that they shouldn't go on to have a normal, healthy child.

Walking home, my father saw a neighbour's children come smiling up the road towards us. He had seen these yellow-headed boys on countless other mornings, barely noticed them. Now, the sight of them made him angry. What right had they to their ordinary, scab-kneed happiness? Why had this happened to his son, and not them?

When she first found out she was pregnant my mother would go walking. Stopping on her way home from the playgroup, the nursery in Camden where she worked, Fran would sit on a bench, look up into the trees. She would cradle her bump, imagining what fun we would have, running, scuffling in the October leaves. Fran would build me towers, golden heaps. We would hold hands, laughing, kicking them down. Throwing handfuls into the bright air.

If I was a boy she would call me Emmett; if I was a girl, Elinor. Fran was determined to make time for me, to be a better mother than Hilary had been. She had invited me into the world, after all. She wouldn't leave me, wouldn't die. We would have such a good time.

While she was waiting, my mother read a book by the French obstetrician Frédérick Leboyer, *Birth Without Violence*. It suggested that the modern medical protocols of birth were outdated, intensely traumatic for both mother and child. Reading it today it seems like pseudoscience, stanzas of barely coherent poetry. A prescriptive, patriarchal view of women's bodies hidden behind purple prose. Paternalistic and, as it turned out, dangerous. But in 1977 my mother ate up every word, making sure that the doctors knew she wanted minimal intervention, minimal pain relief, a bowl of warm water – a 'Leboyer bath' – to ease the shock of birth. The transition from her womb to a harsher world.

Because I was nearly two months premature, all these gentle, low-lit plans went out of the window. We had everything the labour ward could throw at us to keep us both alive. I was breech, tiny, jaundiced. Weighing in at one pound one ounce. A bag of sugar. My mother nearly died in the fluorescent panic

of the delivery room. After four weeks in an incubator, determined to grab my chance, I had put on enough weight to be
taken home. My parents were exhausted, bewildered, but as I
grew, smiled, they started to relax. We had all made it.

When my father had left for work Fran would cry. She had
needed to be wrong, but wasn't. It was her fault. All the fond
fantasies of the life we would have shared crowded her head.
She smothered her shouts in the bedclothes, grieving for herself, Dad, and me. The child that was gone, and the child that
remained.

Apparently, I always woke from my nap in a foul mood.
Shocked, I would scream the house down. My mother came
up with a plan. She would put me down for my afternoon sleep
in my outdoor clothes: a padded red romper suit, a gift from
Grandma Peg. Before I woke, Fran would lift me into my
buggy, wheeling me down the road to the local baker's. She
would buy us custard tarts, try to remove mine from the tight
foil case without breaking the brown frill. She would wake me
up with cake. If the plan worked, and I stayed asleep until that
moment, it was magic. Stretching for the treat, mauling it
greedily, not caring how I got outside, I would be so delighted
with the bribe that I'd forget to cry. The cool, sweet yellowness
would squeeze through my knuckles, and I'd cram my fist into
my mouth.

My mother would laugh, taking a bite of her own tart, hunt-
ing for tissues in her jeans. Walking back to St Alphonsus Road,
Fran gave me a new name: Pie-Squeezer.

We would edge the common, going home via the North
Side mansions. My mother liked looking up at the tall windows, imagining the lives that went on behind the glass. So
different from her rackety squat, kitchen suppers for twelve,
muddy lentils in chipped brown bowls. Janis Joplin singing 'Me

and Bobby McGee' at all hours. Something about their quiet permanence, polished brass, reassured her. Their bricks lent her a stability she no longer felt.

When Fran announced she was pregnant, Briony and Mary, Martin and the other squatters, all of them had told her how pleased they were, how delighted. What an adventure it was. I would be the first baby raised in the commune, brought up by all of them. I would have four mothers, not just one. Privately, my mother wasn't sure she wanted to share me, but was relieved that her news was greeted with such smiling enthusiasm. They toasted the future in warm cider, went to bed happy.

My mother needn't have worried. It turns out babies, unless they're your own, are dull. My nap-times and early nights spoiled the party. Fran was breastfeeding, not drinking any more. She would scowl at anyone for smoking near me. The promised help evaporated in daily resentments, and the three of us retreated to one room.

My mother was tired, changed. She found she no longer cared about the kitchen-table debates, the loud arguments about the broken promises of Callaghan's government, Labour's Winter of Discontent. We were on our own, needed a proper home. Money.

The diagnosis galvanized my father. After graduating from Queen Mary College, he had drifted into youth work, helping his friend Gerhard run a play centre in Camden. He liked the job, got on well with the kids. He could wear his favourite jeans to the office. But the pay was bad, and the hours worse.

Shortly before moving out of the commune, he found a better job with Lewisham Council. Young Lewisham was a community-outreach project that worked with vulnerable kids: teenagers who had been excluded from education, were in danger of drifting on to the margins. It provided industrial placements, vocational training, pastoral support. My father ran it from a tall Edwardian house near our new home. The money was good, more than he had ever earned, and now that his own son had been diagnosed with special needs, the work meant much more to my father than a weekly pay cheque.

We moved to a small cottage in Hither Green, Longhurst Road. He used all his careful savings for the deposit, borrowing some more from my Grandpa Jim. His father, who was pleased Charles had finally cut his hair, grown up, gladly lent him the cash. Jim drove six hours down the motorway from Newcastle with his toolbox. He built my parents a proper bed for their new home, putting up wooden grab rails all over the ground floor so I could pull myself off the carpet, reach my toys. Charlie sold our unreliable Morris Traveller, swapping it for a blue Cortina, the first new car he had ever owned.

My parents slept through the alarm. Pat Freeman was about to give up, go back to her car, when my dad finally opened the door. He struggled into his T-shirt, embarrassed. Pat had seen it all before. She simply smiled, followed him into the kitchen, then explained that she was a community physiotherapist, assigned to my case, me. A kind woman with a lined, deeply tanned face and a forthright compassion, Pat came to visit us every week for months. She showed my parents how to handle me, how to disguise gentle exercise as play. She scribbled on my knees, felt-tip smiles, winking eyes, trying to get me interested in my dragging legs. I watched the grins fading in the bath, pleased when she drew them again.

Pat taught my parents a new language. The three of them had tea after the first session. She was shocked to discover that none of the doctors had thought to tell Fran and Charlie what I had, the name of my condition. It was cerebral palsy. Spastic diplegia. My mother cried again hearing the words, remembering the trees on Clapham Common.

Five Hereford Gardens, Hither Green, was the second house my parents owned, but the first I really remember. It sat at the end of an ordinary terrace. The house looked like all its neighbours, with a steeply gabled slate roof, four windows facing the school, the street. It had a shallow porch, bright front door. It looked like a child's drawing of a happy home.

Our street was built on the fringes of a vast temperance estate, the result of Edwardian philanthropy, the rapid red-brick expansion of suburban London for an emerging middle class. Families like mine. Its modest lines, modest ambitions stretched as far as my eye could see.

Until the day we moved into the new house my feet had barely touched the ground. I travelled in my striped Maclaren buggy or on my mother's hip. I swayed through a crowd from the crow's nest of my father's shoulders. He would grab my ankles tightly, anchoring me, as if my feet were the tassels of his favourite Newcastle United scarf.

They unloaded the sofa first. My mother settled me on the green corduroy, cushions that were usually forts, dark caves for me to hide in. She handed me my bear, the first George, and went to get more boxes from the van. George wasn't curious about our new surroundings. His black-button eyes were blind to change. I made him comfortable against the plush, and turned, launching myself off the seat. The jute matting felt sharp, itchy on my palms. I pulled myself over the floor, out into the hall.

The front door was open. I could see my mother's brown toes, the darker leather of her sandals as she struggled with the pieces of their bed frame, stacking them against the wall, lifting a cardboard box, the carefully newspapered junk-shop willow pattern. She looked hot, worn out.

I wanted to help. There was a tin of paint on the first step of the short, steep flight. I grabbed the plastic handle, and started to climb, bumping the can behind me over the treads, a tight turn, then a fan of three final steps.

Pulling myself to the top, I sat, pleased with my effort. Looking down through the banisters, I could see my dad crossing the narrow hall, his arms stacked with more boxes. He didn't notice me. As he passed, I noticed the wide stripe of sweat printed down his back, the dust on his knees. He would be so pleased. I heard the scuff of cardboard on the kitchen tiles. The hall floor suddenly felt a long way down. It was only thirteen steps, but I panicked, realizing I didn't know how to get back. Tightening my grip on the edge of the stair, I let go of the tin. I watched it roll, bounce. The lid came off and paint spilled thickly, instantly, leaving a white arc on the carpet. It came to a stop in the hall, drooling the last of its colour on to the boards.

Hearing the sound, both my parents appeared. My father held the banisters, looking up at me. My mother stood on the threshold, her mouth open. I was sure they were going to shout, but instead they laughed. My parents seemed pleased, even delighted. As though I had christened our house, broken a bottle of champagne over the prow. My father's smile shone through the gap.

'How did you get up there, son?'

Eighteen months earlier, doctors had told my parents that such ascents would be impossible. Dad came and sat on the step below, not caring about the paint on his jeans. Mum beamed in the doorway, laughing, sagging to the floor. I didn't understand why they were so thrilled with the mess, the paint soaking into the stair carpet. I joined in, confused. I was only four. Too small to look for miracles.

A few weeks later my mother took me for another assessment at the Newcomen Centre, Guy's Hospital. Dr Baird was a paediatrician with a special interest in cerebral palsy. I watched as she built two piles on the edge of her desk, one of yellow wooden blocks, the other of fun-size Smarties. I watched her intently from Mum's lap. As soon as the doctor had finished, almost before she drew her hand back, my own shot out. I grabbed the Smarties, tearing the box. My greed made her gasp, shout with laughter. She told Mum she had never seen a child move so fast.

As she showed us out, Dr Baird said, 'Well, at least there's nothing wrong with his reflexes, his comprehension.'

My sweet tooth renewed my mother's hope. I was bright, present. Hungry.

2

Missing the Bus

Almost the first thing my mother did when we moved into Hereford Gardens was plant pumpkins. She wanted it to be a proper home, to bake her own Thanksgiving pies. A wide ribbon of grass parcelled by two gently drunk fences, the new garden was bigger than our last. It was overgrown with peony bushes, had a mature apple tree where Mum roped up a low swing. There was already a vegetable patch in the north corner. The soil was poor, South London clay, but with work, time, things would grow.

In the mornings I watched my mother from the window. Barefoot, treading lightly over the wet grass, bending to inspect the overnight gains and losses in her modest protectorate. Plucking snails from their silver progress up her raspberry canes, bowling them gently into the neighbour's flower beds. She dug in compost, sand. Lagging her pumpkins in straw, shielding the fruit from slugs, frost. Despite her care, they didn't prosper, staying stubbornly small; green, and narrow-shouldered. Canned pumpkin was hard to find in the early 1980s, but each November she would buy some, sharpening the factory-made puree with bourbon, sweetening it with brown sugar. I thought her efforts delicious, but my mother never ate much, feeding her slice to the bin.

There was a gap in the fence, two planks wide, between numbers five and six. I was reading under the tree one afternoon, when a football flew over the fence, smacking down among the pumpkins.

A shout came from the other side. 'Pass the ball over.'

I could have reached for it, but didn't. I hated mud, getting dirty. My mother made fun of my squeamishness. She would sigh, exasperated. How did she get such a cuckoo? Fran spent whole summers barefoot with her brothers. Her hair tinged green from swimming in the local lake. Diving, despite the snapping turtles.

'I can't,' I called back.

There was a scuffle in the raspberries, and Luke appeared. I knew his name already. I had heard his mother shouting, calling him to the table. Heard his boastful commentaries, his one-a-side victories. He had a sister, Emily. I had watched them from the front window; they flew up and down the pavement on matching bikes, whizzing roller skates. I thought they would find my slower games boring. They went to the primary opposite, while I still boarded a minibus each morning, driving to a special school. It was the one thing that hadn't changed when we moved. Sleeping through the alarm clock, minibus fuming at the kerb. The driver's angry blast. My mother would wrestle me into my clothes, ransacking drawers like a burglar. Dad would shout up the stairs for us to hurry, butter me a triangle of toast for the journey, then carry me out to the sullen driver. Eileen, his wife, also worked at the school. As sweet as her husband was sharp, she would smile, taking me from my father, strapping me in. My parents knew they only had three blasts. If I wasn't at the door, the bus would leave without me. When that happened, my father would shove me in our Cortina, following, swearing at every red light.

All the children at Charlton Park looked like me, and all the children at Ennersdale looked like Luke. They were fast like him. Their parents got them to school on time, lunch packed, hair brushed. I was different, so I hadn't dared to wave, squeeze through the gap.

Luke went for his ball first. He picked it up in both hands, tenderly, as if it were breakable, precious. He stretched the hem of his T-shirt, buffing the leather, like my dad polished apples, shining them on his chest before crunching. I noticed the dark smear, soil, and wondered if his mother would be angry. He turned towards me, grinning. One of his front teeth was chipped, a jagged tear in white paper. His hair was buzzed short for the summer, as bright as mine was dark.

He gestured towards my sticks, crossed in the grass near my feet. 'Can I have a go? I've seen you . . .'

When I had first brought them home from physio, wobbling along our hallway, unsteady and splay-legged as Bambi, my mother had warned me that they weren't toys. My crutches were aids. My new legs. I mustn't let them out of my sight when I was outside, lend them to anyone, my hands always full.

But I wanted my neighbour to stay, so I nodded. 'OK,' I said.

The stranger picked them up, threading his thin child's arms into the leather cuffs. He turned, walking down the garden, one stick trailing, his hand at his back. Luke mimed an old man, his grandfather? A stiff, shuffling gait which was years into the future. Millions of years, I thought. So far ahead, it seemed ridiculous then. He turned, raising both rubber ferrules, charging towards me, strafing the kitchen windows with shattering, imaginary rounds. I remember the shock of it. Seeing my crutches changed into lethal weapons. Killing machines, in other hands. It had never occurred to me that they weren't wholly benign, boringly useful. Luke stepped forward. I noticed he was wearing shiny Nikes, a fast red swoosh from toe to ankle.

I hoped he hadn't noticed my trainers, bought a size larger to accommodate sweaty plastic splints. At five, I still couldn't get the hang of laces, but Luke tied confident white bows. The physios at school had tried to teach me for several terms, with eager, encouraging eyes, using a plywood board, a cartoon boot, threaded with broad purple laces. My mother bought my shoes in bulk. Cheap, Velcro-strapped trainers from Marks and Spencer's. A sympathetic look from the cashier, who always said, 'Someone's a lucky boy,' her smile clicking off as soon as she'd handed over the receipt. Bulging green-and-gold bagfuls. Ten pairs at a time because I walked on my toes; they'd be through in a week.

'Exterminate . . . exterminate . . .'

A Dalek. The sleek Saturday-night assassins that had both me and my mother reaching for a cushion, watching *Dr Who* at Peg's. Luke must have seen the fear in my face, my flinch, because he stopped, pulling off the cuffs. Propping my crutches gently against the wide wicker seat, close to my hand. I felt suddenly angry. Stinging with jealousy. I wanted to be able to give my crutches back, to discard them when I was bored. I wanted Luke's grace for myself. Watching the way each unconscious movement led, noiseless, to the next, I was shocked again by the distance between us. I wanted to be like him, to be him, more than anything.

'Why do you need them, anyway?' His pale eyes were friendly, simply curious.

'I can't walk properly, that's all.'

I never knew what to say about my legs. How to form the words. The simple admission embarrassed me. I avoided his look, tight-faced. I felt skinned, ashamed.

'Anyway, I better go . . . Tea. I'm Luke. My mum's always on at my dad to fix the hole in the fence, but he's too busy. Is it yours or ours?'

He ran off down the garden, without waiting for an answer. Pushing aside the sharp curtain of raspberry canes, he paused, looked back, one foot in my garden, the other in his. 'Bye, then.'

We never did decide whose hole it was, and it was never fixed. After school, and most Saturdays, Luke would simply appear at the back door. My mother began to expect him, boiling extra eggs, buttering whole battalions of soldiers. She smoothed his hair, joking that he was like the neighbourhood cat. A fat ginger tom, the cat had no collar; nobody knew whose he was, too polished to be homeless. He came and went as he pleased, slinking along the fence. The cat had bowls all over Hither Green.

Because I crawled up the stairs, Luke did too. I liked it best when rain stopped play, and we spilt Lego on the carpet. Cities would spring up from the sharp, knee-jabbing mess. Improbable towers, castles from mixtures of sets. Race tracks. Cars that we would vroom and smash against the dusty skirting boards. I was Luke's equal on those wet afternoons. It was easier to pretend that there was no difference between us.

Outside, he would scuff his school sandals climbing our tree. Picking sharp apples from the highest branches, throwing them down to me. We would take one bite, screwing up our faces, leaving them for the wasps. Browning in the grass. Everywhere was Luke's natural element. When we were playing in my bedroom, I could forget his almost primate ease, and my clumsiness. The fact the tree I longed to climb was simply a ladder to him. We had midnight feasts at four p.m., wedged beside the boiler, the sour-sweet airing-cupboard dust. Luke stole some of his mother's liqueur chocolates, tiny edible bottles, wrapped in gold foil. We ate the lot by torchlight, biting off the necks, draining each, more intoxicated by the success of our crime than by the alcohol. Our delight was so loud we were found out. My mother pulled the door open, stepping on the shiny pellets, discarded wrappers. It was her duty to be cross, but her heart wasn't in it. Halfway through telling us off, her stern mask slipped. She seemed to be delighted by the ordinary naughtiness of it, the giggling transgression. The fact I had a new friend, who encouraged me in childish crimes. She shut the door again, padding downstairs. 'They were probably disgusting anyway. It'll serve you both right if you're sick,' was all she said.

Luke planned a real midnight feast. He stole the tea set from Emily's dolls, filling a pillowcase with the gold-rimmed china. Tiny cups and saucers, a pattern of rosebuds on each, laying two places on a blanket on the floor. I envied Emily the tea set almost as much as I envied Luke his Nikes. But I knew boys didn't really play with toys like hers, stayed silent.

This time we told my mother. She made us peanut butter and jelly sandwiches; neat, crustless triangles. Luke told his mum, Caroline, and at bedtime my father tied one end of a ball of string to my big toe, throwing it through the window, the short distance to Luke's sill. Caroline caught it, tied the other end to Luke's toe. She came back to the window, ducking under, grinning at me. Daft boys. My father set the alarm by my bed, its glow-in-the-dark face, for eleven-fifty p.m. We hadn't figured out how Luke would scale the bricks to eat the feast, but our alarm system was sure to work. My father kissed me goodnight. I heard Luke calling through the open window, 'Don't eat it all before I get there.'

The next morning, the sandwiches were curling, uneaten, on the carpet. The alarm hadn't gone off, tight string tugged loose by sleep.

Before Luke squeezed through the fence, I had thought of Mark as my best friend. But he wasn't as fun as Luke. Mark would be waiting for me on the minibus each morning, and I looked forward to seeing him every day. His neat copper parting, glass-green eyes. I tried not to look at the clicking silver opening in his throat, the tracheostomy that kept him alive. The hole meant Mark couldn't speak, couldn't confirm or deny our friendship. It frightened me. But he raised his head when I sat down. Always lowed a soft greeting. A kind of good morning. It was enough for me to decode. To choose for the both of us. I didn't understand, then, that this was the manner in which everything was decided for Mark.

Each day at Charlton Park started the same way. We were wheeled into assembly, parked in untidy rows under the sunny windows. The teachers, our helpers, would already be there, lined on a small stage. They would shout a good morning, and those of us that could would bellow back. Of course, Mark was silent, his head up, eyes fixed to the clock. A teacher who we all called Music-man would come to the front, a rainbow-strapped guitar hanging from his neck. He would grin down at us, beginning a song through his smile:

> He's got you and me, brother, in His hands
> He's got you and me, sister, in His hands . . .
> He's got the whole world in His hands.

I liked the singing, and I knew that Mark couldn't, so I had to make enough noise for the both of us. I didn't understand the song, though. How could one man hold up the whole world? Listening to our noise, I always thought of my Grandpa Jim. He was the tallest, the biggest man I knew. His hands were like shovels, Granny Peg said, but gentle. The fingers long, broad knuckles brown from happy hours in the garden. Those hands grew medal-winning flowers and could build anything at all out of wood, one or two nails always blackening with missed hammer-blows. He would lift me into his lap, let me play with his gold watch, as long as I was careful. It wasn't a toy. I loved Jim's hands, but even I knew that they didn't contain the whole world.

On Fridays we got to sing what Music-man called 'secular'

music. Again, I had no idea what he meant. He would wheel out a record player, tall teak-cased speakers, blow the dust off 'Brown Girl in the Ring' by Boney M. or 'Streets of London' by Ralph McTell. Occasionally, I noticed that the helpers would stop singing that one, their eyes blinking, glassy. Mark stayed quiet whatever day of the week it was.

I think I already understood that even though we were in the same class, rode the same bus, Mark was trapped in quite a different way than me. He went where he was pushed, waited for our songs to end.

Apart from singing, we painted. I wanted to know what the colours tasted like, sure the bright primaries would be as delicious as they were loud. I dipped my brush in the shallow tray. Yellow. I painted my lips with it. The taste was bitter, shockingly different to the shade. When she saw my lipstick, the teacher rushed over, scrubbing at my face with a snotty tissue. Why had I done that?

Of course, Mark couldn't hold a brush, mix his own colours, so a helper crouched beside his chair. She asked him what she should paint, her voice gentle. Mark never made a sound, so the other kids ignored him. The carer would paint flowers, writing his name underneath, Blu-Tacking the dripping paper to the wall, as though Mark had done it.

She would wheel Mark out into the garden, the weedy grass outside our classroom, knotting daisy chains for him. Looping the flowers round his neck, from the handles of his chair.

One morning I arrived to find red cardboard hearts pasted all over the walls, hanging in crêpe-paper chains from the low ceiling. The teacher, Janet, beamed at us and explained that it was Valentine's Day. She turned sideways between wheelchairs, jamming paper crowns, scissored hearts, on our heads, explaining that February the fourteenth was her favourite day of the year. It was going to be such fun.

Peg had once sent me a card, but I threw it in the bin after gutting it of the Sellotaped coins. The following year I bought one for my mother, sliding it shyly under her plate at breakfast while she stood at the kettle. She looked pained rather than pleased, tried to smile when she opened it. Muttered something about a nonsense tradition, wasting trees. It sat on the kitchen sill for a day, disappearing after that.

The teacher went round each desk, handing out blank hearts. She told us it had taken her hours, after we'd gone home yesterday. Janet wanted us to paint the name of the person we cared for most in all the world, right in the centre of our hearts. She beamed at this. When they were dry, we would make a display.

I looked over at Mark, his assistant already kneeling beside him, her brush poised. Mark looked bored. I wanted to make him smile. Dipping my own brush in the glossy black, I was just starting the 'M' when I felt a hand on my shoulder, turning to see our teacher, the sequinned hearts dangling from her ears.

'That's nice, Emmett. Is it for Mummy?'

I wanted to finish, was worried that the paint would dry before I had written the whole word. 'No,' I said. 'It's for Mark.'

Janet's face changed, snapped shut. She snatched the heart, passing me a new one from the pile at the end of my table. 'Do it again, Emmett. You can't give a Valentine's to a boy.'

On the drive home every Friday, Eileen would hand out treats. Sweet rewards for another week. I loved the striped rolls of Refreshers, chalky-sharp on my tongue. The fizzing taste so different from their soft colours. Sometimes there were Love Hearts. I would rip the silver foil, trace my thumb over the raised pink letters. Tiny endearments I was still learning to read. When we pulled up at Mark's door, and Eileen stood on the back of the rusty wheelchair lift, keeping him steady to the kerb, I noticed she always tucked a roll of sweets into his bag, the sheepskin round his narrow hips. He never ate them. He couldn't. But he was one of Eileen's kids, and so she never left him out.

One morning Mark wasn't on the bus. I asked Eileen where he was – would he meet us at school? She didn't answer, just smoothed my hair, clicking me into my belt. She went and sat at the back of the bus, close to Mark's space, the silver track that clamped his wheels to the floor.

It was a Friday, but there was no Boney M., no Music-man, and no Mark. Nobody told us where he was. The helpers all had red eyes, pulled tissues from their cuffs. We didn't paint, didn't sing, just sat in the classroom, wheeled into a loose circle around our teacher. Janet read from our story, *George's Marvellous Medicine*, sitting on her beanbag at the centre of our chairs. We usually only listened to one chapter, and she would act out the book, stirring the cauldron, changing her voice. That Friday she read until lunch, looking over our heads to the grass. Eileen wasn't on the bus home; there were no Refreshers.

My mother came up the minibus steps, lifting me into her arms. Like all the adults, her eyes were red, but she didn't tell me where Mark was, didn't say a word. By bathtime I was too frightened to speak. Mum smoothed the covers, pecking a kiss on my forehead.

'Will Mark be at school tomorrow?' I finally asked.

My mother stayed kneeling, drawing back from my bunk. 'But there isn't any school tomorrow, Peach, it's a Saturday. And I'm afraid Mark won't be coming to Charlton again. He died last night.'

I turned to the wall, turned from the sadness in her face. 'Go away. Go away, please.'

I heard her click on the nightlight, the tiny orange glow, protection against monsters.

'All right, Peach. If you need us, if you need me, I'll be right next door.'

The following Monday I didn't go to school. When my mother burst into my room, I croaked that I was ill. She played along, her cool fingers on my forehead. I didn't feel hot, no temperature, but it was only a day. After the awful shock, where was the harm? She made me hot Ribena. A nest on the sofa. Went into the kitchen, leaving the door ajar.

Charlton Park started earlier than Ennersdale, so I never saw Luke, the other kids arriving for the day. Now, I pulled myself up on the back of the couch. The bells rang, and two startled pigeons, fat commas, took off from the telephone wires. I watched a boy ducking out of his father's hug, impatient to join the games I could hear behind the high wooden fence, the shouts, spinning footballs. A woman hurrying towards the gate, late. She trailed two children, one in each hand. The boy wore an anorak, shiny green, hanging from his head like a cape. Pink bows swung from his sister's plaits; more fussed on her socks. The three of them paused at the kerb, glancing right and left for non-existent traffic. Linked like cut-out paper dolls. Looking at them, I felt angry. I wanted to hold my mother's hand. To be able to claim her on a busy street. I wanted to go to an ordinary school. A place where people were safe. Where they didn't just vanish.

They stopped at the gate, their mother pecking quick kisses on the tops of their heads. I knew I never could. That my own hands would always be full, busy with walking, my new sticks. I would always need them to hold me up. I thought of Mark, his huge wheelchair, pushed by kind strangers, his green eyes always fixed on the clock.

3
Household Gods

My mother was five, living in Speigletown, New York, when she received her First Communion. She had a new white dress for the ceremony. A stiff nylon veil pinned into her brown hair. Hilary had run out of money by the time they got to the shoes, so Fran wore her ordinary black patent pumps, buffed for the occasion. She stood in the vestibule of St Bonaventure, all smiles, lining up with the other girls, waiting to be photographed. Fran felt herself jerked out of place by an angry nun. All the others wore white shoes, didn't she see? Francesca was a wicked little girl, of course she couldn't be in the picture. She had offended Our Lord with her footwear: black, the colour of sin.

The girls laughed at her. Even as she cried, Hilary hustling her towards the car, my mother knew it was ridiculous. How powerful was God really, if he cared so much about her shoes? She rushed her prayers that night, the words running together, suddenly meaningless. The next Sunday, Fran didn't go to Mass.

Her father had been determined that his first child, his hope for better, permanence in the new world, should be protected. His daughter would be safe, an American. Francis's Viennese family, like most prosperous, bourgeois Jews, had assimilated. Swapping their mezuzahs for the rosary, challah for Communion wafers. But their observances at the Votivkirche hadn't kept them safe from Hitler. My mother's Communion was God's last chance. After Fran's humiliation, none of Francis's other children were forced into pinching Sunday shoes. Francis loved to climb, so he bought them all sturdy boots instead, pitons and ropes. Weekends were for nature, fresh air.

My father's mother, Margaret, who everybody called Peg, had raised her son to be a good Catholic, an altar boy. Sunday was her favourite day of the week. She sat at the end of the pew, buttoned into her best coat, watching as Charles rang the bell. He was bright, wanted to know the why of everything. Peg's father was in the navy, and after one leave he never wrote again, never came home. He sailed over the horizon, along with his pay. So she left school at only fourteen, had to bring in a wage, to help her mother with four younger, hungrier mouths.

Soon, she stopped being able to answer his insistent questions, so sent my dad to St Cuthbert's. The Brothers there didn't appreciate Charles's badgering either, curiosity being incompatible with faith. They thought him insolent, not clever, pulling him to the front of the class, striping his palm with a ruler. By the time the red weals had faded, so had my father's belief. He still served on Sundays, but only because he got two shillings and was saving for a bike.

I was nearly two when my parents finally got married. A matter of expediency more than romance. My mother was about to be sent back to America by Her Majesty's Immigration Services. Peg was sad that it was a civil ceremony, Epsom Registry Office, but at least the certificate conferred a kind of decency, if little else. She bought a new felt hat to dress up an old suit. In the one photo of the day she has, my mother is smiling in knee-high boots, a short flowery smock. She holds me proudly in her arms, resplendent in my own wedding best, new rainbow-striped OshKosh dungarees.

Peg thought it was a scandal that I was already there, a guest at my own parents' marriage, and tried to keep me away from the camera all day. It descended into a hissing tug of war between my grandma and her new daughter-in-law. The reception started in Fran's stepfather's cottage in Epsom, and ended at the local hospital. The small house struggled to contain two worlds: my mother's art-school bohemianism and my father's northern, net-curtain respectability. Neither side had much to say to the other, and after an awkward hour in the overheated rooms my Grandpa Jim collapsed, sliding quietly down the flowered wallpaper. When she noticed, my seventeen-year-old Aunt Marie was hysterical. She screamed that her father was dead, clambering into the back of the ambulance, ahead of a silent, grim-faced Peg.

Privately, Peg was sure that all these disasters could have been averted if her Charles had stayed in the church. Married a nice English girl. I was very sweet. She could love me, but there was no denying I was a bastard. The whole mess offended God.

The next shock for Peg was my christening. Shortly after the diagnosis, my grandparents had driven down from Newcastle. Fran and Charlie were hollow-eyed, in no state to cook or clean. Peg made thick brown stews, boiling vegetables grey. My parents ate it all, silently grateful. The morning before she was due to go home, Peg finally put her feet up. My mother made tea, strong Kenya Blend that Peg couldn't stomach. Strong enough to stand the spoon in. She didn't object, just let it go cold. My grandma looked out into the small garden, the grass cut, order restored. She spoke gently. 'It's time now, Fran, surely? After everything . . . the poor bairn. I know you don't really believe, but it would be a comfort to you.'

Seeing my mother's face cloud, Peg changed tack. 'In any case, it's a good excuse for a party.'

My mother tipped the cold tea into the sink, slamming the cups on to the draining board. 'And what has God ever done for us, for Emmett? He's done enough – we don't need it. Superstitious nonsense . . . shit,' Fran spat.

My mother scooped me up, climbing the stairs.

38

Peg couldn't sleep that night. She lay on the lumpy sofa bed, her head full of purgatory. Hearing a noise, whispers, my father found her, barefoot in the bathroom. Peg was baptizing me herself under the tap. Armitage Shanks for a font, Thames water. It had to be better than nothing.

Peg and Jim drove back to Newcastle the next morning, and we didn't see them again until Christmas, the only season God was allowed in our front door.

I was seven the first time I stayed with my grandparents alone. My parents were on their way up to Edinburgh, to visit friends, and would pick me up four days later. Peg was watching from the window when we rounded the top of The Drive. She ran from the house in her slippers, almost wrenching the door from my father's car, covering my face in sour kisses. Pretending to bite my nose, her smell a mixture of Yardley's English Lavender and menthol Steradent. Peg heaved our bags to the kerb before my father could. Realizing she was still wearing her apron, she flushed and balled it behind the tall hedge, the privet my Grandpa Jim trimmed so straight I thought he must use a ruler.

Jim was more reticent, always having the air of being a guest in his own house. He stood in the porch, his tie tightly knotted, filling the frame. He greeted us with mild surprise, unsure of his duty to these new guests, as if we were people he had once met on holiday and only dimly remembered. 'You'd better come in,' he said.

Jim pushed my father gently away. Hugging was what soft Southerners did. But then both his children lived there now. They had moved as far, as fast, as they could. He patted Charles's shoulder, edging past him.

Peg hustled us down the narrow hall, into the kitchen. She must have been baking for several days. There were two cakes on stands, paper doilies. The bleached blue Formica was crowded with china, tiny white cups with twiddly gold handles. I looked at the mountain of sausage rolls, the crisps. Mars Bars cut into slivers, presented on her best pink-flowered porcelain, as though they were fine chocolates.

The thing I always liked best about my grandmother's house was its reliability. Nothing ever changed. St Anthony of Padua watched from the sink. He stood on the windowsill, next to the wide-mouth frog, his green smile holding the scourers.

That first day, I saw my father's face as he put down my rucksack, ducking out of his mother's embrace. Noticing the saint, he smiled, not kind. 'Still surviving, is he? Still here.'

Peg swallowed her hurt at his teasing. 'But of course, Charles. Where else would he be?'

My father was all irritation. Elbows, sharp angles, suddenly too big for the space. He stood with his back to the saint, wedged between the yellowed melamine cabinets, the table. I liked the soapstone figurine of St Anthony, but my father sneered at him. He joked that the statue had been dropped so many times, slipping from Peg's soapy Marigolds, that it was held together by the power of prayer, superglue. I could tell the worn, loved things in his parents' large house annoyed him, but I liked the fact that they were always where you expected them to be. St Anthony, his palm still raised in wonky benediction. A picture, *The Spanish Dancer*, her red skirts wide, still stamping her feet above the gas fire. The horse brasses, their details smoothed by daily polishing, reduced to bright suggestions. The curved bay window, its stained-glass sunrise. That time and all the other times, there was always a cake. A sunken two-tiered sponge, the worst of the cracks mortared with buttercream icing, studded with chocolate buttons.

We bumped shoulders round the kitchen table. We were only family. Polished rosewood, the dining room, was for company, Sunday callers, the priest. I wasn't allowed these kinds of food at home, and watched my mother's face as Peg happily heaped my plate, Fran's smile fixing as she accepted a cup of tea. She blew, sipped. I saw her swallow a slight grimace at the milky-grey brew, teabag only glancing the water.

My father and Jim seemed relieved to be eating, attacking their plates with hungry focus, chewing easier than finding something to say. They had already exhausted the drive up ('We made good time after getting off the M1'), my father's work ('Busy, aye'), the weather ('Rain expected, but not arrived') and their beloved Magpies ('Peter Beardsley played a blinder, second half against Everton, Saturday last'). After five minutes they lapsed into grateful silence. Peg didn't eat anything, just hovered brightly anxious between table and kettle.

My mother pushed back her chair, with an efficient smile at Peg. She stood, bending to my ear, kissing it. 'Be good, Peach. Don't let him eat too much sugar – he won't sleep. Thanks, Peg. We'll pick him up on Wednesday night. You've got our numbers?'

Peg smiled, then blew out her cheeks. She looked relieved my parents were going, that the three of us would soon be alone. 'Of course, Fran, get along with you. He'll be no bother. We'll be champion, won't we, Em?'

We waved from the window, watching the car drive away. As soon as it had disappeared, Jim patted me on the head and went back out to his greenhouse, the fuchsias and tomato plants that filled his retirement. There was always work to do if he wanted a shot at gold next year.

Peg shut the living-room door after her husband. This was the moment I always liked best, our private welcome ritual, a treat, better than cake. 'Let's have a dance, shall we, Em?'

She knelt to pull out her records, flipping through the small collection of treasured discs until she found Slim and Slam's

'Flat Foot Floogie'. She blew the dust off. The record player was a huge teak box with a heavy-tinted plastic lid. It probably hadn't been used since my last visit. As Slim started to sing, Peg pinched at the pleats of her sensible skirt, bobbing a curtsey. She pulled me from the brown Draylon, her thin fingers, gold rings, stronger than they looked. I wrapped my other arm round her waist, as we had done hundreds of times before, my cheek tight to the rough wool.

'There now, you can do it. Put your feet on mine . . . hold on.'

My grandmother would pilot me over the paisley carpet in a jerking waltz. She would sing, always slightly behind the music, with the effort of dancing for two, of being my legs, and I would sing along. I didn't know, didn't ask, what a flat-foot floogie was. But I loved the feel of the words in my mouth. The adult non-sense that seemed to make Peg younger as she turned me round, guiding us through the furniture. The living room was big but stuffed to capacity with my grandma's treasure: mirrored display cabinets three-deep with crinolined ladies; sad-eyed dogs, Staffordshire that she believed was worth a fortune. Watched by the Spanish Dancer, her flashing ankles so much faster than my clumsy steps. A large, stern-looking Madonna, staring from her polished frame, jealous of our laughter.

Everything in Peg's crowded house was so different from my own. I didn't understand my father's embarrassment, his eager-ness to leave the rooms he'd grown up in. I was too young to comprehend the intricate shades, the rigid codes and tripwires of taste. The shame of china figurines, which my mother dis-missed as 'dust-catchers', 'knick-knackery'. I loved Peg's house, her jackdaw store, because I loved her. We never had sherry at home, so I thought that all bottles of Harvey's Bristol Cream wore felt tuxedos. To me, Peg's place was a funhouse, a palace.

I knew that I would get too old, too tall, for waltzing one day. That I would grow heavy, bruise Peg's delicate size fours. I also understood that I needed her. That I couldn't dance without my grandma's help, and that she would spin with me as long as her toes could stand it. We played the song six times before eventually collapsing on the sofa. Peg kissed me, wiping her smeared lenses on a cuff, rubbing the bridge of her nose, the red indents where her gold frames usually sat.

On rainy Sundays, after church and Yorkshire pudding, when Peg could finally be persuaded to sit still, we would watch films. Old MGM and RKO Radio Pictures were her favourites. They were black and white, but more colourful than anything I'd seen before: *Mrs. Miniver* with Greer Garson, *Top Hat* starring Fred Astaire. I wanted to dance like Astaire, pretended I was whirling my grandma over polished marble. That her carpet slippers, bald with wear, were silver kid pumps. I knew I'd never have his grace, his contempt for gravity, the brilliant, brilliantined freedom of him, but I loved my grandma for trying to give it to me, for letting me believe that one day I might.

'There now, that was fun. You can dance as well as your old gran and never let anybody tell you any different.'

The first ever evening was a Sunday. I was allowed to stay up late, as a treat. *Live from Her Majesty's* was on, and my grandparents were in opposing armchairs, their faces flushed, relaxed with laughter. They howled at Tommy Cooper. Jim had a box of toffee balanced on the soft curve of his belly. Thornton's Special Brazil Nut. It bounced with mirth, threatened to spill. Peg had her own TV treat. Jacob's Cream Crackers, thick with butter, on the arm of her chair; a bowl of salted peanuts on a card table. She moved like a bird, and ate like one too, nuts and savoury biscuits the only food she ever seemed to really enjoy.

I was on the carpet at her feet with a picnic of Smith's Salt 'n' Shake and KitKats. I was bored of Tommy Cooper, didn't understand their delight, his stupid catchphrases, ridiculous hat. Even though Jim and Peg must have been in their early

43

sixties at the time, I thought them ancient. Watching their pleasure, I reasoned that Tommy's humour must be something you only really understood when you were old. I wondered if I'd ever reach an age where I got the joke.

Tommy stepped forward in front of the curtain. His assistant helped him into an orange silk robe. She smiled right and left, red stripes of blusher like burns, her hair a lacquered, white-blonde shelf. She looked bored, exposed, in a tasselled skirt. Suddenly Tommy sank from his six-foot height, sliding to the stage. He seemed to fold up, deflate. The comedian sat a moment. He looked dejected, disappointed, rather than scared. The audience laughed. He sank further down the red velvet, a bright sack, his fez tipping forward then jerking back, as his breath escaped, rattling. His eyes widened. The audience roared. He fell backwards, falling between the heavy folds, eyes rolling upwards, disappearing. His hands flapped slowly, wounded birds. They were trying to gain purchase on the stage, push him to his feet again. There was an audible sigh, then stillness.

The audience still roared, sure that it was just part of the act, each gesture rehearsed, timed to the second. The assistant stood to one side, her arms stiff, grin slipping. A few faces in the stalls looked alarmed, at their neighbours, but most carried on laughing. Any minute Tommy would spring to his feet, with a smile and a phrase: 'Jus' like that!'

The band struck up, trying, and failing, to cover the laughter, the louder shock.

I looked at Jim. Tommy was still, his huge feet, the worn soles of his shoes, sticking out from the heavy gold fringe. Suddenly, there was a hand; somebody on the other side of the curtain pulled him back, and Tommy's legs disappeared. The programme went to a commercial break, a permed woman strolling through a yellow field, smiling sunflowers, eating a Flake.

Jim wasn't laughing any more. I looked at Peg. Her plate, the crackers, had slid off the arm of her chair, landing butter-side down in her lap.

'What's happened, Granny? Is he dead?'

Jim said, 'Don't be daft, Em. He's only messing, you'll see. You can't die on television, it isn't allowed . . .'

Peg saw the crackers, the butter on her skirt. She scooped them back on to the plate, wiping her fingers on the tea towel still draped over her shoulder. 'Come on, pet, bedtime. It's much too late for little lads to be up. Best not tell your dad what you saw. Up the dancers with you.'

I lay awake in the dark, listening to the murmur from the TV downstairs, Jim and Peg quiet now. It was the first time I had caught my grandma in a lie. They had both lied. Peg was older, wiser, even than my dad. I had trusted everything she ever said before, it was all gospel to me. I believed her when she said that I would grow out of my legs; that God was sure to fix me, with time and prayer. Peg told me the parable of the blind man – proof, she said, that the Lord can do anything. But Tommy Cooper was dead. I had seen him die, right there in the living room. Why had they lied? I was a terrible dancer, a terrible walker. Peg preferred pretty stories to difficult truths.

Next morning, the house was still. I bumped down the stairs. My sticks stood at the bottom, leaning against the telephone table, next to a trio of ebony elephants. Peg had told me they were a wedding gift, that their tusks were real ivory, but they were probably plastic. I left my sticks where they were, handing myself along the wall. Peg was in the garden, wrestling sheets over the line, pinning them briskly. Hearing me, she looked up. 'Morning, Em, sleep well? I was going to have a walk out after breakfast . . . D'you want to come, or would you rather stay with Grandpa Jim?'

I knew Jim would rather be alone in his greenhouse, and a walk with Peg always meant church, a treat on the way back.

St Mary's Church was a modest, modern building. The brick and glass looked more like a municipal office, a place to pay parking tickets, than God's house. The only clue to divine occupancy was a peeling plaster Virgin at the gate, a small white crucifix on the roof. An aerial for receiving the Lord's word. Church was our private ritual, like dancing. Just between us. As we walked up to the wide wooden doors, Peg smiled, lowering her voice. 'Imagine having all these houses to choose from, Em. Of course, he's not so keen to stop with the Anglicans.'

I smiled back, pretending to understand. I thought that if I was as powerful, as wise, as Peg's God, I would choose a grander house than St Mary's. I would want people to know, to be able to see me for miles.

Peg opened the door, and I ducked under her arm. The road outside had been deserted except for us, but the church held a deeper quiet, absorbing us like water. Peg dipped her fingers in the stoup, crossing herself automatically. As we walked up the nave, the pristine purple carpet, Peg bent her head, dipping before the high altar, the carving of Christ dying in his mother's arms. This ornate suffering was almost the only decoration in the church. I always felt awkward, watching Peg at prayer. She became a stranger. I tried to follow her movements, the muscle-memory of her daily devotions.

Looking at the statue, I thought of my next-door neighbours, of Mark's green stare. Luke and Emily, because on Sundays their mother would shout in the street, up the stairs, calling for them to hurry up. God wouldn't wait for them. When they finally appeared, she would inspect them, retying the torture of ribbons in Emily's clean hair, slapping down Luke's disobedient cowlick. I would watch them drive away, suddenly ashamed of my pyjamas, my family's slovenly weekends. Once, I asked my

46

father why we didn't go to church like our neighbours. He looked up from his paper, butter on his lips, the sagging yellow T-shirt he always slept in: 'Because in this house we prefer His name spelled backwards.'

I had laughed, because my mother had, but didn't understand, didn't ask again. I started to look out for our neighbours every Sunday, sure that they were superior to me; that church, God, was the reason they rode their bikes so fast. Luke and Emily flashed past the gate, while I just watched, couldn't walk.

There were two tall votive stands of candles before the altar, the black iron crusted with wax, an accretion of prayer. Peg rummaged in her bag, handing me over two coins, twenty pences. I dropped them in the slot, lighting my candles from the ones already lit, somebody else's hope. The flame leapt, burning my fingers.

Peg was removing her gloves. She gave me another coin, pinching the wick of another candle, handing it over. 'Pray for your mam, your father.'

As we were leaving, there was a voice behind us. 'Mrs Rose . . . who is this?'

'Oh, Father, hello. This is my grandson, Emmett, up from London.'

The man smiled, his hand in my hair. He knelt down. He had a friendly, open face, but his teeth were large, a dirty brown. His mouth too close to mine. I stepped back, seeking the safety of Peg's arm, her second-best coat.

'Say hello, now. Don't be shy, Em. This is Father Miller.'

His black suit was too tight, the knees shiny with prayer. 'Hello,' I said.

Father Miller stood, taking my grandma's hand in a proprietary way. 'Of course we'll see you at Mass tomorrow? Poor little lad, such a shame. It's a test, all right, but a sure welcome in heaven. The Lord never gives us more than we can take.'

47

I thought my grandma was going to hit him. Her mouth pressed tight, the tiny broken veins in her cheeks were suddenly livid. But all she said was, 'Yes, Father.'

Peg hurried me out, pushing me ahead of her through the doors.

On the walk into the village, she was quiet, the snatches of song that usually accompanied her neat step absent. I didn't understand what had happened. Normally, I itched with questions. Things I knew I shouldn't ask my parents. Coming home from church, Peg would tell me stories. The fall. The snake, and the apple. She would talk, breathless, about sin. The more terrible the imagined punishment, the more it made her smile. I was her little heathen, but Peg was sure God loved me all the same.

I would watch her, straight-backed at Mass, saying her creed, envious of her secret language. She knew when to stand and when to kneel. The words to all the hymns. I knew I couldn't take the magic bread, taste God's mercy, because I'd been baptized in the bathroom sink. Sitting beside her in the pew, putting my coin on the collection plate, I knew I didn't really belong there. I felt my exclusion was something to do with my sticks. People smiled at me; some of the older congregants even had sticks themselves. But none of the fidgeting, shiny-shoed children did. Somehow, the difference felt like my fault.

I wanted to pray as easily as she did, blamed my parents for not teaching me how.

Leaving church, I thought of what the priest had said about a test. I didn't understand, but wanted to please him, pass. I was too young to appreciate that Father Miller believed the way I walked was an expression of God's grace. That, in his eyes, I'd been blessed. I knew that if Peg's God was as powerful as she believed him to be, getting rid of my sticks should be simple. I just had to be good. Find the right words.

We stopped at the bakery in the parade. Normally it took forever, my grandma swapping smiles, cheerful exchanges about new ailments with every face she met. We would spend our time choosing. Pink iced buns, a stottie cake for Jim. That day she just pointed at two doughnuts, a sliced loaf. She pocketed her change without a word of thanks, shoving the brown paper in her handbag.

We sat on the bench, eating in silence. I noticed that opposite, beside the newsagent's door, the callipered boy was waiting. He had followed me to Newcastle. The Spastics Society collection box. This statue, his grey shorts, crooked gait, downcast eyes begging pensioners for coins. The same boy usually loitered outside the sweet shop at the end of my road in London. He meant that I often got a smile, free penny sweets, Cola Bottles from the man behind the till.

Peg wiped my fingers, the sugar from my lips. 'Come on, pet, Jim'll be wondering what's become of us.'

We walked home in the weak April sunshine. When I was with Peg, I never trailed behind her. She was careful to adjust her step, always walking beside me, deftly avoiding the wide splay of my sticks. My grandma gave me the illusion of speed.

At the top of the road, the black-and-white sign that marked the home straight, she stopped. 'Try something for me, Em, will you?'

I smiled at her. 'Of course, Peggy.'

My grandma liked it when I used her name; it meant we were friends, not just relations.

'Give me your sticks. If you stay close to the wall, you can reach for it. I won't let you fall. I've got you, I promise.'

I gripped the road sign, handing the sticks over without question, grinning trust. If Peg believed I could do it, then I could. When I felt steady, I let go. I walked a slow, wobbling fifty yards to her door, not stopping, not looking down, in case a pause made me fall. Peg shouted encouragement at me, my shadow teasingly always ahead. I made it. I had walked without my sticks, all that way. She handed me back my crutches, and I threaded my arms gratefully through the grey plastic cuffs. The ground solid, firm again. Peg stood in front of me, her narrow face almost eaten with smiling. She kissed me, pushing her bag up her sleeve, turning to put her key in the door.

'A miracle,' she called down the hall. 'A bloody miracle, Jimmy.'

4
Proper Names

I had to get used to sharing my father. He had more than a hundred other kids, much older than me, in his care. Young Lewisham. The weekends from June to September would be busy. Day trips to Camber Sands, Hastings. Shouting rounders games in the local park. If Dad was going to the beach, I would come too. Passed from lap to lap in the rusty minibus, its burst vinyl seats; told off for pulling out their yellow guts, stiff pinches of foam. I basked in the attention, the boss's son. Our house was never quiet. Records played, and there was laughter, but I was an only child, not used to the untidy clamour of larger families.

It was a bright blue morning in June. Barking dogs, the hum of the kitchen radio. I heard my mother singing, happily ignoring the song being played: instead she almost shouted the chorus of 'Sherry' by Frankie Valli & The Four Seasons, in a tuneless, twanging falsetto. It was our favourite song, one of our favourite games, the competition we had to see who could sing the highest. Fran exaggerated the accent she had mostly lost now, after so long in England. She became the funny American teenager she once was. Her singing reminded me of diners, drive-ins. *Happy Days.* Ice-cream sundaes taller than my head, long silver spoons.

Wanting to add my voice, I pulled on a T-shirt. A tiny boat, sailing on a padded ocean. The yellow-striped sail was only stitched on one side, free to flap. I slid downstairs, the carpet burning my back. Seeing me, my mother stopped singing, smiled. A plate and cup were already laid out. She had fired them just for me. A mug standing on moulded feet, massive trainers; white plate already painted with breakfast: bacon, egg, tomato. Her grin widened. My father had already left for work; we were alone.

'Morning, Peach. It's a beautiful day, what would you like to do with it?'

After our toast, my mother unfolded my new buggy. A wide-striped Maclaren. My chariot, she called it. It was bigger, for older children who had missed the ordinary milestone of walking. She pushed me down to the parade, but the buggy was too broad for the corner shop's crowded aisles, so she parked me outside. 'I'll just be a minute, Peach. Wait there.'

We had left my sticks at home, so I had no choice, just smiled.

A man came out of the shop opposite, crossing the zebra. I had seen him before. He lived at the far end of Longhurst Road, wore short-sleeves all year round, his slippers in the street. The man passed our window every day, getting his paper. He always smiled at me, but we had never spoken. Now he knelt by my pushchair, too close, reaching to steady himself on my knee. A sword inked on his forearm. Large, lettered knuckles, faded, green-black. I leant forward, trying to read them.

'You're much too old to be riding around in that.'

The man gestured towards the shop window, my mother. Handwritten adverts, a bucket of exhausted flowers, carnations.

'You should get out, give your mum a push. Stop being so lazy.'

Just then, my mother came back. She roared towards us, dropping her bag – Mother's Pride, for the ducks. 'You get away from him!'

We should have known. My mother couldn't leave me any-where. I was too trusting. Only recently she had parked me outside the greengrocer's: five minutes, no more. She came back to find an old man feeding me sweets. He pushed them into my mouth, unwrapping Opal Fruits with dirty fingernails. The man had looked shocked, stammered away, hadn't meant any harm.

This man stood, in no hurry, a slow smile spreading over his face. He reached for my mother's shoulder, and she jerked back, grabbing my handles, wheeling me safely away. Her anger meant we forgot the bread, that the ducks would go hungry. The stranger called after us, 'Look, I didn't mean anything by it. He's a little spastic, is he?'

My mother didn't answer, didn't stop. She started to sing. Frankie Valli, 'Sherry' again.

But this time I didn't join in. The lyrics were exactly the same, but sharpened, defensive. Their loudness on the quiet pavement was meant to scare people away.

We didn't stop until we reached the park. Our favourite bench, at the edge of the small lake, the weeping willow. The ducks came up expectantly to the low wire fence, their black eyes questioning why we had dared to turn up empty-handed.

What did it mean, that word? I wasn't stupid, knew I was different from other children on my street, but 'spastic' wasn't something I had ever heard used at Charlton Park, only seen on dusty collection boxes. At school I was Emmett, or Little Rascal. I had learnt to pretend deafness to the Saturday-morning questions of children, out with their parents. Feign blindness to their frank stares, the way I caused panic. Some would answer as if I was invisible, explaining in stage whispers that I was crippled, handicapped. I was an unlucky boy. But most parents were silent, hurrying their kids in front of them. Glancing back over shoulders with silent, crimson apology. I might have pretended blindness, deafness, but I wasn't dumb.

Years later, grown up, I still had to feign deafness. To the shouts from out-of-office drunks, their ties loose, pint glasses in one hand, a fag in the other. One evening, a man in a regimental blazer – it was always men – was smoking outside a pub as I walked past. He caught my eye, smiled, told me to hurry up. He barked at me to get moving. I've learnt it's safer to keep your head down. Keep going, say nothing. When I didn't respond the stranger laughed, called me a spastic, a fucking mong. I hated him. Hated my vulnerability. I wanted to tell him I wasn't laughing. I wanted to tell him my name. But I kept my mouth shut, carried on.

Even though I'm a man, the names I'm called have given me some understanding of what pavements can be like for women. Fair game for any beery comment, any intrusion. A joke that isn't funny. Watchful for any smile that turns.

What does a name mean to the person, the thing, it describes? My mother was silent on our bench, looking out over the green water, one hand still on my pushchair.

She called me Peach, Pie-squeezer, Bean, and Sunshine. She had to be cross to call me by the name on my birth certificate. My father called me Son, just that. I liked them all, knew how to respond to each one. The hiss of 'spastic' sounded unkind somehow, a dismissive spit. I didn't understand what about it described me. I couldn't recognize myself in the sound. You could always depend on my mother for a straight answer; she hated euphemism, sugared evasion. When I shared a bath with Luke, he called it a winkie. My mother told him crisply that in our house, our bath, he had a penis.

'Well, Peach, "spastic" describes your medical condition, the reason your hands are stiff, need the chariot for long distances. Some people – that man – use it unkindly. But it isn't all that you are.'

In 1974 the philosopher Mary Warnock was invited by Margaret Thatcher, then Secretary of State for Education, to chair an inquiry into current provision for children with special needs. The Warnock Report was published in 1978, when I was a year old. The paper argued for greater integration, recommending that, wherever possible, disabled kids should attend mainstream schools. Each eligible child was to go through a process of 'statementing' by the local authority. Tests to assess individual suitability, abilities and opportunities. In the language of the time, I would probably be classified as 'handicapped, physically impaired, not mentally deficient'.

I was an experiment. But I didn't know any of this, didn't care, when we piled into the car on a cold March morning. I was just happy that I wasn't on the minibus, smiling at the thought of missing school.

We drove into central London, pulling up at a grand house in Fitzroy Square. It wasn't an area I'd been to before. The street was quiet, and even though the sky was grey, the houses shone. White-iced, proud as wedding cakes. Dad leant across to unclip my belt, rummage in the glovebox for my new orange badge. It was a superpower, an advantage he hadn't expected of fatherhood. It meant we could park anywhere. He slapped the magic disc to the windscreen, opening his door. I looked up at the tall windows. My mother's fingers pushed round the headrest, grabbing my shoulder.

I always liked to know where my sticks were, preferred to travel with them under my feet in the back seat. If my father was driving, and I was in the front, they went in the boot. My mother jumped out, smoothing her skirt, bringing my crutches. She was wearing her favourite necklace, a long string of beads, Baltic amber. Sometimes she let me play with it. I liked to sit on her bed, holding the beads up to the light. They were smooth, irregular, solidified honey. The largest bead had an ant inside, stopped in its busy tracks, tiny antennae stilled.

'Come on, Peach, don't dawdle. We'll be late.'

My father pressed the buzzer. The brass plaque above it read THE SPASTICS SOCIETY in sure black letters. There it was, engraved on the door. Bold as brass. The stranger had been right.

The buzzer clicked, and my dad held the door open for me to pass under his arm. The splendour of the facade stopped at the street. The hall had a false ceiling of stained styrofoam tiles, its walls thick with yellowed leaflets. It looked like our GP's waiting room, and it read like it too: *MMR Vaccine: The Safest Way to Protect Your Child*; *Mother and Toddler Play Clinic, Thursdays 4.30 p.m., Third Floor.*

Dad unfolded a piece of paper from the back pocket of his jeans, looking for the lift. It was narrow, wood-panelled, old-fashioned. My father pressed the button. I hate lifts, anywhere small. Even the tight darkness of a jumper over my head, itchy wool, is enough to make me shout. I listened to the lift as it descended, trying to tell from the sound if it might break. A wheeze and a clank. I wished my mother would carry me up the stairs instead.

When I had gone to my last review at Guy's Hospital, three months before, we had got stuck on the seventh floor of Guy's Tower. It was only a matter of minutes, but it had felt like days. I had charged the metal doors, desperate to get out. We were never going to run out of air, but I was choked with fear, sure my cat would die. That I would never see George again. Who would feed him if I was stuck in here? The lift smelt like a sour mouth. My mother tried to calm me down, tickling my neck, telling me to fix on her, to breathe. But I didn't want to. Her face looked sallow, waxy in the trapped light.

The next week she took me to the GP. Was it normal, that kind of panic? A comorbidity with my condition? It was hard to say exactly. The doctor thought my claustrophobia could be a vestige of birth trauma, the urgent delivery. I stopped wearing jumpers, but lifts were harder to avoid.

My dad rattled back the inner grille, smiling. He imitated a tannoy, a supercilious department-store voice. 'Going up. Second floor: fancy goods, ladies' hosiery . . .'

I loved that word. Hosiery. It made me think of painted, out-for-the-evening ladies, the smart rhythm of their heels, legs coiled with lengths of green garden hose. I laughed, forgot to be scared.

'Idiot!' My mother grinned at him.

A man was already waiting for us by the lift. He had thick white hair brushed back from a lined, smiling face. I remember his polka-dot tie, a rusty tweed jacket. He shook my father's hand, my mother's, then said, 'Good, you found us all right?'

My father seemed nervous, as if this man was a teacher. He answered quickly, pleased to take refuge in traffic-talk. 'No, it was easy – quick. We only had to come from Lewisham.'

The man knelt at my level. I thought he looked like Grandpa Joe Bucket; we had been reading *Charlie and the Chocolate Factory*. Too-short bedtime episodes. So of course I liked him.

'And you must be Emmett? I'm Mr Gardner . . . Leslie.'

'I am,' I said, agreeing emphatically.

I forgot my parents. Clicking down the hall, over the bald carpet, behind Mr Gardner. He pulled a chair out in front of his crowded desk, steadying it while I dropped my sticks.

My mother said, 'Don't leave your traps for Mr Gardner, Emmett. Sorry . . .'

Mr Gardner waved away her apology, smiling round the office.

There was a tall filing cabinet in one corner. The drawers open, bursting with files, records of other children. A spider plant spilled from Mr Gardner's desk. It looked neglected.

Parched and dusty, the leaf-points browning. I knew my mother would want to rescue it, take it home. Mr Gardner leant back in his chair, steepling long fingers. His teeth were large, white and regular, like sugar-shelled gum.

He reached behind him for a binder, sliding it over to me, flipped it open. Pages of patterns. Red and white. Triangles, rectangles. Short flights of stairs, going nowhere. He emptied a carton of blocks on to the desk. More blocks. Play, easy. They clattered towards me over the wood. I put my arm out to stop them, picking one up. It was precisely painted along the diagonal, one half red, the other white.

'You see those patterns, Emmett? I'm going to time you. I want you to match as many as you can in five minutes. D'you think you can do that?'

I nodded, wanting to please him.

Mr Gardner glanced at the clock over my dad's head. 'Go . . .'

The patterns formed easily, even though I was nervous, my fingers stiff. I didn't hear him say stop. The other tests weren't so simple. Mr Gardner asked me to draw a square. The sides wobbled, my pencil skidding, tight in my hand. I was embarrassed by this failure after the success of the blocks. My attempt looked nothing like Mr Gardner's precise blue line, his ballpoint leaving swift indents on the pad.

'Do you see the difference?' he smiled.

'I decided I wanted to draw a circle instead. Why don't you do it for me?'

This made all three of them bark with laughter, but it seemed like the right answer. We went on like this for an hour, Mr Gardner making discreet notes. He thought I didn't notice his furrowed observations, busy pen. Finally, he said, 'Considering the spasticity in his left hand, that he only really uses his right, Emmett has done very well indeed. Bright boy . . . cheeky. I'll send you a copy of my report, in support

58

of his statement, but I think he'd thrive in a more normal setting.'

He walked us back to the lift. When it arrived he took my father's hand in both of his. Dad's face was flushed. When he thanked Mr Gardner, his voice was tight. The consultant put his hand on my mother's shoulder, opening the lift door with the other, sliding back the grille. 'Thanks for coming. We'd like to see him again in six months, if you agree. And at regular intervals after that. He'll be one of the first. If you need anything, be in touch.'

He grinned at me through the cage. 'Bobby-dazzler, good luck.'

I had never heard the expression before. I was a spastic, but also a bobby-dazzler. Another new name.

My mother was quiet all the way back to Lewisham. She seemed neither happy nor sad, staring out of the window at the still, leafless trees. At every red light, my father felt for my hand.

Near the end of term, after storytime but before the bus, my teacher gave me a present. A black-and-white photo. A handsome, wistful-looking man, the sharp points of his collar splaying over a tight jumper, so large they almost speared his narrow shoulders. The photo was signed in a small, looping hand: *For Emmett, best wishes, Chris Timothy, X*.

Even after reading the inscription, it took me a moment to realize that the image was Christopher Timothy. My favourite TV actor, I was more used to seeing him in Peg's living room. Watching in my pyjamas, squeaky-haired from the bath, as the vet dumped his jacket on a bale of straw, rolling up his sleeve, putting his hand into a patient cow. I smiled up at Janet, thanking her. Not understanding why she'd given me the photo, how she had arranged such a magical thing.

'Can I keep it?' I asked.

'Of course you can, dafty. I got it for you. Have a great time tonight. I'll miss you.'

Normally, Fridays meant pocket money. As soon as my father came through the door, he put out his fists, always making me guess which one contained the bright fifty-pence piece. The ritual as important as the reward. Dad passed it behind his back, palm empty, the coin vanishing. Eventually I managed to prise it from his fingers, rolling on the Persian carpet in the front room, breathless, shrieking with joy, sharp tickles. He walked me down the street to spend my fortune. Waxed-paper bags of Cola Bottles, sweet-stale fudge. Fifty pence could buy you a huge black gobstopper. They were pure sugar, I didn't often get the chance, but sometimes my father decided that cavities were a price worth paying for hours of peace.

That particular Friday night we didn't go to the sweet shop, taking the overground to London instead. A taxi to Regent Street, Hamleys. My mother folded my chariot, wheeling it. My father lifted me up as we passed through the heavy glass doors. Everything was colour and noise. Running children, harassed-looking parents. The whirr of tiny trains. The lift pinged us to the fifth floor, but I was too happy, too excited to be frightened by the forest of strangers' legs.

'We have to be quick, son. The show starts in forty-five minutes.'

Hamleys would have been enough for me. I didn't know that the evening was a celebration. My parents had finally received the educational physiologist's report, my statement. A local primary was willing to try me out in September. I was leaving Charlton Park. The headmaster had advised my parents against the move. It was not just the fact that I might not manage it. I'd have to find a new physio. Children could be very cruel. What would they think? What would I? He reminded them I was special, it was a risk. As they stood to leave, the headmaster assured them that there would always be a place for me at Charlton Park, should the experiment fail. I didn't understand that the photograph, the overstuffed toy-shop, the show were my reward. That my games with Mr Gardner would open new doors.

I chose a Lego castle, with horses, a working drawbridge. Primary-coloured plastic battlements. My mother wheeled my pushchair down the street, weaving it along the fast pavement, Friday crowds, the huge Hamleys bag looped over the handle. I don't remember much about *Underneath the Arches*. A lamp post, a mizzle of dry ice that made my mother cough from the velvet circle. When the singing, trench-coated actors removed their hats, the widest smile, the brightest, belonged to Christopher Timothy. I crushed my mother's hand, disbelieving, wondering if he could see me in the dark.

5

Hopscotch

The morning I started at Brindishe Primary, our cat, George, gave me a good-luck gift. I was eating my cornflakes, hair brushed, nervous, when he jumped into my father's empty chair and on to the table. I was about to put my hand out to greet him, when I saw his lopsided smile and a tail, like a thicker whisker, poking from his jaws. I flinched back, staring. George let the mouse go. It dropped into my bowl, the sugared milk; its neat pink fists still clenched, defensive. But the animal was already dead. Even though the bowl was a favourite, part of a set, a present from Peg that everything tasted better from, Mum knew I wouldn't use it again. She threw it in the bin, along with the unfortunate mouse.

When we had received the Spastics Society report, the Local Education Authority's approval, I had assumed I'd be joining Luke and Emily at Ennersdale. The school was so close. We had talked about it all summer. But Ennersdale was a tall, sooty Edwardian building, and the headmaster wasn't keen. There were too many stairs, too many faster children. Brindishe Primary was an ugly new-build, not much older than I was. A single, prefabricated storey, and only ten minutes away.

George's gift made us late. The playground had already emptied when we arrived. Mrs Turner dismissed my mother's breathless apology with a smile. 'Oh, I think we can allow it, on the first day. No problem.'

No problem. I had visited the school, a try-out afternoon,

the previous term, but had forgotten Mrs Turner was an American. She sounded like my Aunt Vicky, her voice full of summer. Vacations, 747s, silver-foil Hershey's Kisses. The teacher's voice, her ready smile, was the only thing that wasn't new.

'Have a good day, Peach.' My mother ducked a kiss to the top of my head, and left.

A boy turned, smirking, at my private name made public. He had a squint, dark hair, shaved holiday-short, even though it was September. Mrs Turner indicated a chair at the front of the class and I sat, stowing my sticks underneath. Suddenly wanting to disappear. The classroom looked like Charlton Park, its dull, wipe-clean functionality brightened with pupils' paintings. Dripping grins, macaroni collages. Primary-coloured families lined in front of primary-coloured houses. I thought of Mark, his helpers kneeling next to his wheels. When the paintings dried, they black-markered my friend's name at the top. Smiling, pretending that their efforts were his.

A voice called out, 'What's wrong with you?'

The voice, the boy, had red hair. A gappy smile. He gripped his desk, pushing off, tipping his chair on to its back legs. There was no malice in his question, only a round-cheeked, freckled curiosity.

Mrs Turner looked up, the sweetness in her tone sharpening. 'That's enough, Simon. Sit properly, please.'

My cheeks burned. I heard the boy thump down, stung.

'My granny has one of those. She walks a bit like you, but she's *old*. Are you a spastic?'

There was an uneasy ripple round the classroom, a few swallowed giggles. I didn't turn. Mrs Turner looked at me, her eyes wide with apology. 'Simon, that's enough. I'm sure Emmett will tell you if he wants to.'

But of course Simon was right. At home I was just Emmett, needed no explanation. I didn't recognize myself in the words the doctors used at my six-monthly assessments at Guy's. I smiled at their pen-clicking, professional kindness, agreed to them taking my trousers off, the painful measuring of my flexed angles. I sat on high couches, or in cubicles whose curtains never quite met. They knelt, helping me on with my socks. Looked forward to seeing me in six months. I hated the appointments, their specialist attention. I smiled through it because of the McDonald's we always got on the way home. A quarter pounder, large fries, the sweet-sucking effort of a chocolate shake. The three of us didn't talk much until we'd eaten the last greasy chip. Dad would always stop the car before we got to our door, throwing the wrappers, the evidence, into a neighbour's bin. McDonald's wasn't real food, Mum said. It was a treat I got at no other time, and so I came to associate it with hospitals, bad news. The word 'disabled', the sharply medical 'spastic', still stuck in my throat. Looking round the classroom, I didn't see myself reflected in the frank stares.

Mrs Turner's smile clicked back on, over my head. 'Now, Emmett's come to join us this term. I wonder if any of you would like to show him around?'

There was a loud, shuffling silence. Mrs Turner waited, an auctioneer with a difficult lot. A girl raised her hand from further along the front row. She had a thick plait and a thin, cautious smile. 'Please, miss. Me, miss.'

Mrs Turner's smile stretched, as if she was trying to attract more bids. The girl asked again. After another moment, Mrs Turner nodded. 'All right, Joanna, thank you. I'm sure you'll be the best of friends by the end of the day.'

I wasn't sure of anything, just grateful to be claimed.

I followed Joanna into assembly. The hall was a large, windowless space with a wooden climbing frame bolted back to one wall, ropes looped lazily over the crossbeam. I hoped I wouldn't be asked to climb them. The rest of my class folded themselves on to the floor, sitting in cross-legged, obedient lines.

Joanna put her hand up again, told Mrs Turner I couldn't sit on the floor, didn't have a chair. My teacher gave me hers, running back to the classroom for another. All through the singing, 'He's Got the Whole World in His Hands', then 'All Things Bright and Beautiful', I noticed Joanna's fingers, tight round my chair-leg. She held it until our songs ended, as if she might be told off for not keeping me secure. As if I might blow away. I was relieved I knew the words, that the songs were ones I'd sung at Charlton. Everything else was different. I thought of Mark, and raised my voice.

The bell rang for first break. Before everybody could go outside, there was milk. I hated milk, only drank it to please Peg, unless it was mixed Hershey's, and even then, I preferred the sweet syrup straight from the can. The crate of bottles had been on Mrs Turner's desk since registration. She went down the rows, counting, slapping down blue straws. She watched me drink. The milk was warm, thickly cheesy, another new thing. Mrs Thatcher, the milk-snatcher, had ended free primary-school half-pints. Brindishe had obviously decided to buy its own. Drinking it, I would gladly have given the Prime Minister mine.

The playground was a steep-sided concrete pen behind a tall wire fence. There were white-painted goals at either end, fading into the tarmac. Children ran, screaming. They bounced off the high walls, ricocheting, bright as ball bearings. Play at Charlton needed assistance, any joys much more muted.

'You sit over there,' Joanna instructed, directing me to a bench.

She propped my sticks, neatly, within my reach, like Luke did. I noticed she was wearing a black sweatshirt, a quilted, sad-eyed panda stitched on to the front. It looked serious, sombre in all the noisy colour.

'You don't remember me, do you? I met you last term. I told my mum that, well, if you ended up coming here, I'd look after you.'

I didn't remember Joanna, but hoped my answering smile would cover the lie. My new friend took a piece of chalk from her pocket. I watched her walk backwards, bending to draw a quick red line at her feet. Counting off numbers under her breath. When the grid was finished, Joanna paused. 'You can play too, if you'd like?'

I had seen Emily's games of hopscotch from the front garden wall, watched her precise jumps, her swift, white-socked turns, and wondered how.

Joanna ran to a weedy flower bed next to the railings, crouching to select a stone. Coming back, she offered it to me. 'You can throw, and I'll jump to where it lands.'

It was a kind compromise, the first of many Joanna would make, but I shook my head. If I couldn't really play, then I'd rather just watch. She shrugged, threw. The stone skittered on to six, and she jumped after it, counting.

I saw Simon playing on his own in a far corner, tight against the fence. His finger was cocked, as if it was lethal, and he rolled down the wall, a spy in pursuit of an enemy. James Bond, Jim's favourite on a drizzling Sunday afternoon. Then his arms were sudden wings. Simon was flying; he ran in a wide loop around the goals, a fighter pilot spitting rapid-fire rounds. I almost saw the bullets thudding into concrete, his delight so loud that I could share it. He turned, coming in to land, aiming his guns at Joanna, who carried on jumping, oblivious to Simon's game.

He squeaked to a halt near my bench, grinning at me before throwing himself on the tarmac, crash-landing. He lay there a moment, his head on one side, playing dead. Then, death no fun, he jumped up again, slapping the dust off his jeans. I noticed he was wearing a Buck Rogers T-shirt. It was too big for his thin shoulders, hung almost to his knees. Luke had one just like it, and I had begged for my own. As we didn't have a TV, my mother didn't know who the Captain was, and said no. Simon's toes were scuffed, like mine, rubber soles starting to come away from the leather. He hurled himself at the bench. 'I didn't mean to upset you. This morning, I mean.'

'It's all right,' I answered, just glad that Simon had chosen to crash next to me.

When I visited Peg earlier that summer, she had taken me to the cinema, a deserted matinee of *Pinocchio* at Jesmond Picture House. She bought everything I asked for, popcorn and Maltesers, a bath of fizzy orange, but despite vibrating with E numbers, sugar, I was quiet on the bus back. I was thinking about the Blue Fairy. I knew my grandma would offer me anything she could. I loved her more than anyone, but I also understood that the only thing I wanted then was to give my body the slip. For the shimmering, silken-voiced Blue Fairy to turn me into a real boy.

I knew Peg would shush me, unwrap a toffee to sugar the truth. Tell me that anything was possible, I just had to be good. She would have another word with Him Upstairs. So I kept my mouth shut, looked out of the window. It was the first time I had felt alone, lonely, with my grandmother so close.

I thought Simon was the realest boy I'd ever seen. He reached into his pocket, handing me a sweet, a Fruit Salad. Chewing his own, he smiled and said, 'I give all my friends nicknames. Joanna is Dunlop, because she wears boys' trainers; she's always playing football with the boys. I thought of Tiny Tim for you, because of that film, the one that's on at Christmas, but that wouldn't work, because it isn't always Christmas . . .'

Simon thought a moment, threading his arm through the cuff of one of my crutches. He lifted it, firing desultorily. Maybe all boys played at killing?

'Got it!' he grinned. 'How about Crutch-face?'

I was pleased the name meant we were friends, but hoped it wouldn't stick. After that, I swapped all my morning half-pints for Simon's penny chews.

The library at Brindishe was a wide corridor joining two sides of the school. It had heavy, hushing doors. They were closed at the end of every day, while we sat at Mrs Turner's feet listening to the next chapter of *The Witches* or *James and the Giant Peach*. Unless being read a story, Joanna had no patience, couldn't sit still. She hated the playground's whispering corners, its cat's cradles and sharp-slapping rhymes. If she couldn't play football, she couldn't be bothered.

Sometimes, Joanna would ask me to fall, gently. After the teacher had scooped me up, wiped my forced tears, Joanna would walk me to the library, her grey eyes round with pretended concern.

One afternoon, my lie bit me back. Going to the library, I caught my foot on the threshold, splitting my head on the metal door jamb. Joanna smiled a moment, thinking I was faking, that we'd laugh. I did not feel pain until the shock of blood. It was darker than other wounds. Too much, and too quick for a plaster. Viscous. It ran down my face, thick drops hanging from my eyebrows. I remember thinking that it looked like it ought to taste sweet. I heard Joanna's trainers, squeaking fast. Her shouts for Mrs Howard. The pain pulsed in my head, and I was sure I was going to die, was sure I was going to run dry. Tight with panic, I turned my head. A small but spreading stain on the carpet. I would be in trouble. The carpet was a dirty brown; if I was lucky, it wouldn't show. I threw up.

Mrs Howard was the headteacher. The next minute she was smiling over me, asking me how many blurred fingers I could see. She carried me to her car. I could hear Joanna behind her, running with my sticks. Mrs Howard laid me on the back seat. I started to cry, realizing I had made a bloody mess of her pale upholstery. There was an air freshener, a traffic light, hanging from the rear-view mirror. A sweet, synthetic freshness. The motion of the car, the scent, made me throw up again.

'I'm sorry, so sorry,' I kept saying, my snotty remorse mixing with vomit.

The head turned, smiling kindly. 'Don't worry, it's my husband's car. You're far more important.'

In Accident and Emergency, the doctor closed the curtains. I could hear voices, adult voices. The beep of machines. I would need stitches, quite a few. There were two cuts; I must have bounced, hit again. It was lucky the longest was on my scalp. I heard the doctor joke, from under the paper sheet, that it wouldn't show until I went bald. The idea of being old enough to be bald, ancient, was absurd. I laughed, was told to keep still. Mrs Howard talked soft nothings at me. Squeezed my hand with each pulling stitch. When Dad burst round the curtain, he thanked Mrs Howard, then burst into tears.

On the way home, I wouldn't stop worrying the stitches, pinching at the cat-gut ends. Dad took his hand from the wheel, slapping mine away.

He grinned, relieved. 'There's nothing for it, Em. We'll have to get you a crash helmet.'

Because I was now in the mainstream, I had occasional physio sessions at Lewisham Hospital. I hated going. The spit-smelling blue mats, the briskly cheerful sadism of just one more stretch. I rarely had the same physio twice, and though they all smiled, coaxed, we weren't friends. I was a job. I had refused a crash helmet, more scared of playground laughter than more stitches, so my mother insisted that I learn to fall.

The physio told me her name was Fiona: Fi. She had short,

no-nonsense hair and a short, no-nonsense manner. Kneeling at the edge of the mat, she told me to show her how I would fall normally.

'I just do . . . just land,' I answered, thinking of the way the ground lurched up to wind me. 'There isn't really time to plan it.'

I hoped Fi would laugh, that she'd understand the absurdity of a lesson in falling. Falling was an inevitability, nothing that could be taught. 'Just show me.' Fi smiled stiffly.

I stood up, letting my sticks fall. Thwacking down on to the blue. I heard my mother wince, then stifle a laugh, at the parping rubber.

'Now, watch me.' Fi unlaced her neat white trainers. She stood at the edge of the mat, flexing neat white-socked toes. She straightened, as if about to dive from a high board into still water, then raised her arms, pressing her palms together, before executing a perfect, Olympic-gymnastic forward roll. At school Joanna's rolls were beautiful, flawless, the proof in the badges sewn to her gym leotard. I envied the badges, her composed, fluid grace. I smiled from the mat. 'Now you try. Tuck your head in, try to turn,' barked Fi.

I fell again. After the third attempt, I still looked like a bag of washing thrown in a screaming fight from a fourth-floor window. I fell again and again, trying to land wide of my sticks. When the hour was up, Fi smiled at my mother, saying, 'I'm not sure we can teach him much. He doesn't really have the coordination to protect himself; he just needs to remember to put his hands out. They should break his fall.'

'But that's just instinct, isn't it?' my mother answered.

'For most people, yes.'

My mother smiled back tightly, helped me on with my shoes.

Unusually, my mother kept all the school reports, class photographs, from my time at Brindishe, yellowing proof that our efforts were worth it, that she and Dad had been right to push so hard. Mrs Turner's first report states:

> *Emmett is a happy, usually cheerful child, cooperative and friendly both with adults and other children. He can display great imagination and sensitivity. There is a tendency for Emmett to give up too quickly when faced with initial difficulties, or problems in a specific task. He must strive to overcome this, but is otherwise a pleasure to have in the class . . . He prefers to mix with girls rather than boys . . .*

The shortest in my class of eighteen, I was always in the front row of the yearly photo. In the first one, my crutches have been whisked out of shot by the photographer. We are stiffly arranged in front of the only bit of green, a gentle hill. Joanna stands behind me, arms rigid at her sides. I can tell there has been a fight that morning. Her mother would prefer her in ribbons, a dress. But Joanna has won, proud in her favourite England shirt. We are all different, and we are all the same. To-order, say-sausages smiles. The future only hinted at in delicate, unfinished faces. Sitting, I look just like everybody else.

I didn't understand we were relatively poor, didn't think of money at all, until I was invited to Joanna's for tea. All the houses on my street looked the same. There was enough food, and more laughter. My father would come back with fish and chips every Friday. We would eat them from the paper, licking ketchup from our fingers. Afterwards, they'd roll back the rug and I'd watch my parents dance, slow to Joni Mitchell, or stamping hot and fast to the exuberant rhythms of *Zaire Choc!* Mum would sway, loose with a glass too many, her smile stained purple. 'Dance with us, Peach. Come on, who's here to see you? Who cares?'

My parents' records lived in a wooden filing cabinet. I loved looking at them, reading the titles, tiny letters on spines: David Bowie, *Diamond Dogs*; Chilli Willi and the Red Hot Peppers, *Bongos Over Balham*. A tight, tatty rainbow of learnt songs. I'd slide them out of their sleeves, even though it was forbidden. It was amazing to me, seemed a kind of adult magic, all that music wound in the liquorice grooves. Watching the dance, I itched to join them. I never did, just tapped along with the beat, but I felt rich all the same.

Joanna lived in a tall, tight-lipped house on a leafy street five minutes from mine. It was a short walk from my scuffed red door to her shining black one, but it might as well have been the moon. Her mother, Madeline, was always kind. When she saw how difficult it was going to be, she didn't insist I took off my shoes. She defrosted pizza, fed us Fanta, before disappearing upstairs. After we'd finished, we went to Joanna's room. It was neat, airless. I remember the curtains matched the wallpaper, which matched the bedclothes. Just sitting on the bed, I felt I spoilt it. Joanna had a pair of ballet shoes, pink ribbons hanging from the back of her door. When I asked to see them Joanna stared, as if I was mad.

'I only go to please my mum. She says, promises, I can give it up soon.' Joanna looked pained, as if that day couldn't come fast enough.

There was a shelf of dolls above her pillow, glazed expressions on porcelain faces. They looked stiff, as uncomfortable as Joanna would be in velvet. I wanted one. Wanted to sleep, watched over by these stern, frilled toys.

'I get one every year, for my birthday,' she explained. 'But they're too valuable to play with, so I just look at them. They can't do anything anyway.'

Nothing in my loud, messy house was off limits. Too valuable for play. Even the lacquered Chinese egg on the mantelpiece was a lucky junk-shop find. When it was time to go home,

Joanna zipped a doll in my schoolbag. A Barbie she'd given a home-haircut, had never wanted in the first place.

My father got a place to study for an MSc at Cranfield Business School. This meant he disappeared every weekend. I missed him, missed the fish and chips. He came home exhausted, just in time to leave again for Young Lewisham on Monday. When I asked my mother why he had to go, she stamped up the stairs. 'Ask your dad, Peach. Apparently, we need more . . .'

Returning late the following Sunday, Dad was too exhausted for questions.

To celebrate his change in direction, he bought himself a racing bike. A Cosworth 300. It was too precious to be chained to railings outside. I loved squeezing past the sleek, mint-metallic frame every morning. It looked fast, even propped against the radiator. The low curve of its handles, like butting ram's horns. My mother was less keen. When she found out the bike cost almost as many pounds as its name – a huge bite from their shared savings, yet another after his course fees – she kicked it.

The following week, my father gets me a bike. A blue-framed Raleigh Budgie, its chrome handlebars a confident grin. He kneels on the kerb, screwing toe clips to the pedals, training wheels to the back. The finishing touch is a Mickey Mouse bell. Testing it, the lever is stiff under my thumb, but the ring is bright.

Dad smiles. 'Now everyone can hear you coming.'

My father lifts me into the saddle, bending to put my feet in the clips, fix them to the bike.

My mother is still standing in the front garden, arms crossed. She is smiling, but it doesn't convince. 'It's a nice idea, Charlie. But how's he going to fall off?'

My father isn't listening. He has taken hold of the

73

handlebars and is leading me between the parked cars into the empty road. 'I had a bike when I was Em's age, so did you. We can't protect him from everything, spoil all his fun. It'll be fine.'

He smooths my hair, moving behind me. I feel his grip on the saddle, a gentle shove. 'There now. Follow the pedals, push. Keep going. I've got you, I won't let go.'

I waver up the road, between the ribbons of parked cars. Then suddenly I'm doing it. I look at my feet, the scuffed, orthopaedic boots. The air feels different: faster, brighter under my wheels. The freedom is impossible, but it's happening. A great, green rushing that fills my lungs, powers my feet. I feel my father let go. He lied, but I don't care. His voice is behind me, moving further away. Everything else is still.

'That's it, that's it. Head up, now, watch where you're going. Keep the wheel straight . . .'

I look up, and I'm almost at the parade, the zebra, the sweet shop. The sun-faded, square-jawed smiles taped in the window of the gents' hairdresser next door. They always feel like a greeting. I love the shop, its red-striped cylinder, like a stick of seaside rock. Dennis always waves from the door, even though he never gets his hands on my hair; my mother cuts it in the garden.

Suddenly I can go anywhere, do anything. I'll go to Joanna's, show her. It is the furthest away from myself I have ever been. My mother's panic breaks the spell. 'Careful, Peach, it's a main road. Try and turn around. Come back now.'

I turn the wheel sharply, mounting the kerb, freedom dashed on the neighbour's pebble-dashing. I bounce off the wall, going down with the bike, wheels spinning. I am trapped under, and over, the wheels. Tangled in the spokes. My mother's sandals slap fast up the street. She undoes my straps, throwing the Budgie aside as if it weighs nothing, pulling me up. She sits me on the wall, breathing hard. I am worried the neighbours will see. The hubris stings more sharply than any injury. My mother takes a hand, putting my torn knuckles in her mouth. She spits grit from the wounds into the gutter. There is a moment before pain; I do not realize I am hurt until I see the blood on the pavement.

The next day I got back on the Budgie, riding it to school. I still have a ridged scar on my left hand, a silver feather below my knuckle. A permanent reminder of my first ride. I never had the balance to lose my training wheels, still fell more often than Luke, but scabbed knees were a small price to pay for such ordinary freedom.

6
Baci

When she felt I had settled at school, my mother went back to university. Ever since my diagnosis she had wanted to retrain as a doctor. Her A level results weren't quite good enough for medical school, but she had been accepted on a microbiology degree course at Queen Mary College, where my father had gone. There was a mountain of reading, a whole new language to learn. Dad worked late all the time now. My mother decided we needed help.

Mum put an advert in *The Lady*, but nobody answered, and in the end we got a gentleman. She found Davide via an agency in Air Street. The owner had tried to put her off. Davide was eighteen, barely more than a boy himself. In her considerable experience, things always went easier with girls.

He arrived for the interview late. Davide shrugged off his jacket, an aviator's sheepskin. I remember the tiny badge, a gold aeroplane, that had landed on his collar. He looked around the room, lacing his large hands together in an effort to keep still, a toe tapping out a nervous Morse code into the carpet. He had dark, carefully greased curls over amused brown eyes. A mouth that tried hard not to smile. Before my mother came back in with the tea, I decided that I liked him, that I wanted him to stay.

Davide jumped up, helping her with the tray, the plate of chocolate biscuits bought for the interview, our only matching cups. I hoped this effort meant that my mother had already made up her mind.

'So, why don't you tell me why you're in London? Why you want to study English?' She used a crisp, older tone I'd not heard before. A smile I hadn't seen.

He sat forward, smiling too. 'I want . . . I want very much to be a pilot. To fly, maybe one day, if my English improves, with the American air force.'

He made a whooshing movement with his palm, a plane slicing the air. Flashed her what she would come to call his 'shit-eating grin'. 'My English is already good enough for the visitors in my place – I'm from Rimini, it's close by the sea, very touristic – but it's not good enough for my flying examinations. I start at a language school next week. A very good school, near to the Leicester Square, the West End.'

Maybe it was because she liked the cloudy height of his ambition, or maybe it was because he talked about America with an enthusiasm that meant he'd never been there, only seen her country in the movies. Or maybe, like me, she just liked his smile. Whatever the reason, Davide got the job.

He arrived the following weekend, with a single bag, a poster tube tucked under his arm. My mother gave him his first week's money in cash, fanned under the spare key. As soon as she came down from showing him the room, I went up.

'Hey, let him settle in, Peach. He'll be down when he's ready.'

But I wasn't listening. I pushed past, up the stairs. The door was open, and Davide was kneeling on the narrow bed, sticking photographs to the wall. Without turning round he said, 'Come in, come on.'

He smiled over his shoulder, his tongue between his teeth. I remember thinking how big they were, square and unusually white. Normally I crawled when there were no strangers in the house – it was faster – but now I handed myself along the wall, wondering what I must look like to him. I dropped down on his bed, the new sheets that Mum had bought the day before. Davide pointed to a couple in a photo. They squinted happily into the lens, laughing at a joke. 'My mother, my father,' he said.

He indicated another picture. 'And this is my girl, Sara. I wanted her to come in London with me, to have an . . . how you say? . . . to have an adventure, before we become married. But she didn't want to leave home. She says that she is never going to leave Italy, so why does she need to learn English?'

Even behind sunglasses, I thought Sara looked cross. She pushed her blonde hair off her forehead, looking away from Davide, beyond the frame. She seemed unhappy to be photo-graphed, unhappy he was leaving.

Davide unrolled the last picture, throwing the tube on the floor. He knelt up, smoothing the image on to the wall. Not happy, he repositioned it higher, leaning back to appraise it, before fixing the bottom corners. It was a large poster of an ascendant sharp-nosed Concorde, captured mid-air, its super-sonic flight stilled.

The room decorated, now his, he flopped down. Davide gave a happy bounce. He seemed pleased with this modest place, until three days ago my father's office. Our quiet street was only twenty minutes by train from his classes, the louder noise of London. He looked at me. 'Your mother, she told me about your legs. She told me I don't have to treat you any dif-ferent from the other children. Told me it would be good for you to have a brother . . . that you don't have one. So, what do you say?'

'Yes!' I smiled.

Davide put his hand over mine. The knuckles were large, with fine, dark hairs. The hand covered mine entirely. He laughed suddenly, at the difference, removing it. Pulling me into his shoulder. He smelt clean, citrus-sharp. He pointed at himself, then at me. 'I hope you and me are going to be friends?'

*

78

Three days a week my mother fought across London, from south to east, before nine a.m. My father had left Young Lewisham, had a new job at a bank in Bishopsgate. Dad always left for the City at first light. 'Sparrow's fart,' he'd smile. So Davide and I had the place to ourselves. If we overslept, he would burst into my room, laughing. He would turn on the taps before running downstairs to put some bread in the toaster. Five out of ten times, we would forget, remembering only when smoke drifted up the stairs. I loved winding him up, kneeling on the floor as the minutes ticked round, playing with last night's discarded Lego, pretending I'd lost a sock. When it came to curses, Davide's English needed no improving. 'Shit! Fuck! You not helping me this morning, I get in trouble with your dad. *Che cazzo.*'

He would pretend to cuff me, lifting me up to the top bunk to force my shoes on to my feet, tie the laces in tripping loops. He would carry me downstairs on his hip, parking me on the bottom step while he threw the blackened toast out the window to the birds, grabbed two Jordans Cereal Bars, one for me, one for him. If we were really late, my feet didn't touch the floor. Davide charged with me, all the way to the silent playground.

For the first month he lived with us, Davide went to every class. He sat at the kitchen table, eating dinner with us. He washed the dishes, played slow, frowning games of chess with my dad. Davide would have laboured conversations with my mother as they stood side by side at the sink, her smiling encouragement.

My mother thought it would be good practice if he read to me. She dug out the books I'd outgrown: *Not Now, Bernard* and *The Enormous Crocodile*. Davide would lie on the floor, close to my bunk, the book open above him, sounding out the words. Often, I never really heard what he said. I was lulled by his nearness, the soft cadences running together, until he dropped the book, slept. I would watch him in the nightlight, his ankles crossed, head to one side, slack-mouthed, snoring on the carpet. Sometimes, when I woke up for school, Davide would still be there.

Then he discovered nightclubs. He would go dancing every evening at the Hippodrome. Bedtime stories were raced through while the bath ran. He would leave the door ajar, perfumed steam filling the hall. I would wait just outside the door, talking through the gap. His legs were too long for the tight enamel, and he spilled happily over the sides. Sometimes I would sit on the toilet and he would splash me. I would pretend to be loudly upset. Would pretend not to look at his broad shoulders, the fan of slicked, dark hair that rose to his neck. He seemed to own his body in a way I didn't. I thought the difference was simply adulthood, and that I'd get there one day.

After his bath Davide would thump down the stairs in his favourite silver shirt, Armani jeans, running on a cloud of Fabergé and expectation. I wanted to go too. Instead, I sat with my parents, played disappointed games of Connect 4 with Dad, not really caring who won.

He would often come in as we were having breakfast. Smiling, sheepish, round the door. My father would have already left for work, and my mother was too charmed by Davide to do anything but feign annoyance, undermining her momentary sternness by smiling, pouring him a coffee. Sometimes he would change his clothes, appearing a moment later in white shorts, his tight, polished dancing shoes swapped for slapping pool sliders. More often than not he would drop me off in his tired silk shirt.

I loved that shirt. It seemed to me a symbol of everything adult that was to come, a future so much more exciting than times tables, bedtime stories. And of course, Davide would take me, when I was older. I began to think that Davide would always be there.

I looked for his grin at four o'clock. I loved the shock he caused at the school gates, towering over the other parents with a slouchy ease. He would ask me questions about my day on the short walk home, pretending to be interested in my answers. He would make me bowls of pasta in red sauce. Fry slices of ham in flour, dipped in egg, that he said was his favourite, that his own mother made for him. He was amazed I'd never had it before.

One morning, a morning my mother had already left for university, we really overslept. The clock over my desk ticked just past ten. I scooted out of my bunk in a panic, crawling along to Davide, pulling myself up on the door handle. His dark curls were just visible under the lump of duvet. He was snoring, unconscious. I tugged at his shoulder. 'Davide! Hey, Davide . . . school.' He turned, his eyes unfocused, face still blurred with sleep. 'Come on,' I urged.

Davide flipped on to his back, throwing the covers wide, reaching for his watch. 'Shit . . . shit . . . shit.'

He balled his fists into his eyes, laughing. He was still wearing the silk shirt; it was open, stained. Davide swung his legs over the bed. He smelt of spilled beer, cigarette smoke, the exertion of dancing. Sour-sweet. His brown eyes widened under sleep-mussed curls. 'It's too late. Do you really want to go to school today?'

Until he asked me the question, there was no possible alternative. School was what you did. Dad went to his office, Mum went to university and I went to school, as predictable, as automatic, as breath.

I leant into him, looking at the floor, the kicked-off Adidas sliders that made me think of the beach, that were his lazy rhythm. 'What do you mean? Of course I have to go.'

He smiled, swallowing a laugh. 'I have an idea. But you have to promise me –' Davide sat back, suddenly serious '– you have to promise me you won't tell your mum, OK? Or we won't go.'

'OK,' I agreed, my answer small, thrilled.

We took a taxi from Charing Cross to Regent Street, Hamleys. Where else would a nine-year-old boy, a boy on the run, with birthday money to spend, want to be? We stopped short of the store, because Davide wanted to walk. He hoisted me on to his shoulders, my crutches in one hand, even though the weekday pavement was still. I bounced along happy, my hands in his hair. He ducked me inside when we got to the wide glass doors. The shop was quiet, the demonstrators standing in bored corners, with no one to make the hours faster, no one to entertain. For once, the whirr and click of train sets was louder than the children who usually swarmed greedily all over the shop. Davide made enough noise for ten. We had gunfights in the rainbow aisles. He ricocheted between the walls of toys, bullets flying, falling on the floor in a smiling agony, before jumping up again, hiding to ambush me.

He bought an Airfix Concorde, which once he had glued it together was too large to fly on his windowsill. He tried to buy me one, but I insisted on riding to the next floor, buying a Play-Doh set I'd seen on TV. The Mop Top Hair Shop. You filled hollow plastic figures with the dough, sat them in the hairdresser's seat, and a huge blue screw forced the paste through holes in their smiling heads, making the hair grow.

As we stood in line to pay, Davide was unconvinced. 'Why don't you let me get you the plane? You don't have to spend your money. Keep it . . . it's disgusting, this thing. Not a toy for a boy. It's a toy for girls.' He smiled, teasing, tickling the back of my neck. 'Are you a little girl? Are you?'

For Mum, there was no such thing as boys' toys. Toys were

either fun, or they weren't. When Joanna had given me her unloved Barbie, my mother had bought me a Sindy. Seeing it, Luke had laughed, throwing her across my room. He told me I must secretly be a girl, if the doll was what I'd wanted. After that, I still loved her tiny plastic heels, Sindy's look of permanent, painted surprise, but only played with her when I was alone.

'No!' I spat at Davide. 'Of course not!'

We ate burgers for lunch, at a deserted tourist restaurant in the Strand. Even though it was empty, we stood obediently behind the sign that ordered us to PLEASE WAIT TO BE SEATED. When the waitress saw us and came over, she raised her eyebrows. 'Two?' she said, looking behind Davide for a non-existent lunchtime rush.

Davide folded himself into the booth, sliding my crutches under his feet. His knees were tight against the wipe-clean, plastic-gingham cloth. I looked at him while he looked at the laminated menu, decided what to have. I would have been happy to stay there, to never go home. I ate my sundae, its bitter chemical cherry, thin chocolate sauce, until the last rattling scrape. When she brought the bill, the waitress smiled at Davide, then at me. 'Somebody enjoyed that, didn't they? Is he your son, is he?'

It was the sugared, disinterested tone I was already used to. A way to ignore my disability. An answer wasn't really required. Davide grinned at her short-sightedness, the impossibility of him having a son, of his child being me, my age. He counted out the notes, careful. 'He . . . he's my little brother.'

That night Davide went dancing as usual. I heard him singing in the bath, running down the stairs, slamming the door just in time to catch the nine o'clock train. I lay awake, trying to keep my eyes open until I heard his key in the door.

I hid the Play-Doh, the girls' toy, in the drawer under Davide's bed. I only played with it once. I enjoyed the day, the shared secret, more than anything I could buy.

My mother bought a pair of morello cherry trees, planting their slender trunks in a bright patch near the kitchen window. On the mornings she didn't have lectures, got me to school herself, I often saw her checking their spreading growth. She planned to make jam when they started to fruit.

As soon as the cherries appeared, Davide and I massacred them while my mother was upstairs, at her books. It started innocently. Davide sent one cherry over the fence into Luke's garden, its shine split by my father's ping-pong bat. I tried to copy, but my aim was bad, and I missed more cherries than I burst. We were shouting, keeping score. By the time my mother came down to see what all the noise was, the fence was stained, peppered with cherry-bullets, dark explosions of juice. Seeing our vandalism, she didn't speak. Her mouth too tight, too angry to shout. Her face instantly sharp, pale. Because I was nervous, because I suddenly realized what I'd done, I started to laugh. Davide laughed too, hysterical. He rolled helplessly on the sticky, cherry-bombed grass. When we looked up, my mother had gone inside.

Davide left the next morning. I refused to go to school, sitting on the edge of his bed. I watched him roll the poster, the Concorde, back into its tube, peel his parents' smiles off the wall. It was just a room again, not his. I burst into loud, snotty sobs, soaking the front of Davide's T-shirt. 'Where are you going to go?' I managed finally.

'I don't know yet. I'll talk to the agency – maybe they find me a new family. If not, I go back home.'

He handed me a photo. One my mother had taken soon after Davide arrived. I hadn't realized he had kept it. He was smiling into the camera. The same shit-eating grin. The same striped pool sliders, brown toes. I was sitting on his lap. Looking at him rather than the camera's lens. Laughing.

That Christmas, and the Christmas after that, until we moved, Davide sent my mother a box of chocolates. Baci Perugina, their tight silver foil hiding love messages. Sweet words, waxed paper, wrapped round bitter chocolates. In the card that came with the second box, he wrote that he had given up on dreams of flying. Davide had settled by the sea, in Rimini, married Sara.

7
The Junior Skylark

When my mother was eighteen months old, still an only child, her parents took her swimming in Lake George. She splashed happily, loved the water so much that every time Hilary tried to lift her out, dry her off, Fran screamed. She was in the crowded shallows for well over an hour. They put her to bed, and my mother slept for three days. She had caught hypothermia. Fran recovered, but after that she was always too hot, ascribing it to her early swimming lesson. She kept our windows open even when it was raining sideways, even after my father had lost his Cosworth to burglars. He had grown up in overheated rooms, and teased Fran, calling her Nanook of the North.

Her habit changed when Luke started the violin. Every Wednesday at four sharp, I would watch his teacher, Malcolm, come up the path. That was the signal for my mother to run round, slamming our windows against the noise. Malcolm would stand a moment before ringing the bell, rummage for a smile in his corduroy pocket. His own violin case was battered, the corners rubbed grey, stuck all over with airport tags. It was a loved, hardworking companion. Caroline had given Malcolm the job because he sang in their congregation, never seemed to have much money. But after nearly a year of Wednesdays, Luke's Junior Skylark was still pristine. He never practised, had to be dragged to a music stand, so his noise was just that. It never got any sweeter.

Because Luke played, of course I wanted lessons too.

Alongside the Creedence Clearwater Revival records, Mum had a small selection of classical discs. Real music, she said. My mother would close her eyes, listening to Beethoven, the 'Kreutzer' Sonata. I wanted to learn to play it for her, was sure I could do better than my friend, so asked for a violin. Dad laughed, dropping the pink serrated edge of his *Financial Times*. Seeing I was serious, he folded the paper. 'But, son, I don't think you could play. Your hands – you just don't have the dexterity. Think how long Luke's been playing, it's still bloody awful . . . murder.'

'But he doesn't practise. I'll practise all the time, every day, I promise.' I was so sure that all I would have to do was clamp the Skylark under my chin and the notes would come.

A few days later, I bumped down to breakfast to see a violin sitting in my seat. 'It's Luke's, Peach. I had a word with Caroline. She's given up on him, told me you could have it. Don't forget to thank her the next time you're there.'

Dad didn't look happy. He picked up his briefcase, put down his tea. 'You realize this is bloody mad? It's ridiculous to get his hopes up like this . . . stupid. I'll see you both tonight.' He pushed past us, slamming the door.

I loved the violin. The sticky, lacquered toffee-apple shine of it. The smell of the amber rosin in its felt compartment. To begin with, I kept my promise, doing my mountains and valleys, bowing exercises, every day. Malcolm smiled encouragingly, but it never worked. The violin never sat comfortably under my chin. I had expected it to agree with me, but instead we argued. The sounds were no music, only a sharp, obdurate whining. Every week, Malcolm played, grinning. He would wait, watch as I tried to copy his phrases. But as time went by, his smile became fixed. When I still couldn't master 'Twinkle, Twinkle, Little Star' after two months, he'd had enough, telling my mother, 'He just can't. He'll never have the fine motor skills, the lightness of touch that make a violinist. It isn't his fault, and continuing with lessons . . . well, it might make him feel as though it is. I can't keep taking your money, wasting Emmett's time, mine.'

The Skylark wasn't like my Budgie. There were no adjustments I could make to my uncooperative hands, tone-deaf fingers. I watched Malcolm drain his cup, press up the last crumbs of cake, stinging with my failure. I wanted the teacher to go. Wanted never to have met him. When he left, Mum clicked the violin back into its case. She put the instrument on top of my wardrobe, where I tried not to see it.

A few weeks later my mother said, 'How about singing? Joanna goes . . . There's a group every Saturday. No God songs or churchy stuff, it's much more modern. You don't need your hands to sing. Might be fun, what do you think?'

Privately, I thought I'd make a terrible singer. I had enough trouble with pavements, never mind 'Walking in the Air', but I agreed.

Even from three hundred miles away, despite a bad line, my grandmother's disapproval was clear. 'You don't mean beautiful, Em. Boys aren't beautiful. Handsome, if they're lucky, but not often. And even then, it's not something you should notice. You certainly don't talk about it . . . it isn't nice. Tell your mother I was asking after her.'

There was a brusque click. Peg had put the phone down, without sending me her weekly love.

I didn't understand. Peg closed her ears to her son's cheerful swearing, but her mouth puckered when I repeated any playground profanities, expecting a laugh. It was vulgar, not right coming from a nine-year-old. But as far as I knew, 'beautiful' wasn't a dirty word, forbidden. I replaced the phone, sitting on the bottom step a long time.

But Ben was beautiful. It was just a fact. Like the sky, or school. As obvious to me as the fact that I wasn't.

We were late. Because it was Saturday my mother had circled the music school, a quietly imposing Victorian building, for fifteen minutes before we found a space. Scales and strings competed loudly as we looked for the right room. It was on the top floor. By the time I sweated round the last bend, I could hear the class had started. Joanna's hesitant, sweet note under more confident voices. She smiled up from her music. Even though the semicircle was half-empty, one hand saved the seat next to her.

A man stood in front of the bright windows. He was wearing a black shirt, tucked in too tightly over the beginnings of a belly, faded black jeans. It was a shock that the choirmaster was young, that his hair was dyed the same flat black as his clothes.

'Emmett, hi. Welcome . . . welcome. Sorry about the climb: we'll change it for next week. Can you get on to the floor? We do warm-ups on the floor. It opens up your diaphragm, your voice. I'm Mr Williams.'

Mr Williams smiled, blue eyes disappearing in amused lines. I didn't know I had a diaphragm, or a voice. I wasn't sure I wanted to open either of them. It sounded medical. But I dropped my sticks, got on to the floor.

'Good-o,' grinned Mr Williams. 'Now, everyone, repeat after me: red lorry, yellow lorry, red lorry, yellow lorry, red lorry yellow lorry, redlorryyellowlorryredlorryyellowlorry . . .'

I lay on my back, looking at the ceiling, feeling hotly stupid. I followed the choirmaster, trying to keep control of my lorries. Trying to prevent a multiple pile-up.

It was Ben who helped me up off the floor. I hadn't noticed him during the warm-up. Now he took the seat next to me, ignoring Joanna. I noticed his neatness first. Polished toes, even though it was a Saturday. I hadn't even brushed mine, but his fair hair was parted, arrow-straight. Ridged with comb-tracks, crisped with hairspray. Close to, the boy had a sharp, chemical sweetness. He seemed a different species, altogether alien. His large, long-lashed eyes were quick with some private joke. Even though he was slight, I was sure this boy was older.

Smiling, I was suddenly conscious of my cheap trainers, their babyish Velcro. I wondered why he had chosen to sit next to me. He smiled back, his teeth as neat as the rest of him, straight and white. He took my hand, shaking it. His confidence reminded me of one of my father's new friends. The City-striped men, new names for me to learn. He had a Casio Calculator watch. A ring. A thick, dull-gold band that looked too large for his thin fingers. Both seemed like markers of adulthood, the sophisticated space between us.

'I'm Ben,' the boy said.

Ben's eyes were blue, sharp. Not at all like my undecided, murky brown. I felt like I was glowing, suddenly. Like one of the Ready Brek kids. I looked at my own hands, the bitten nails, perpetually healing grazes. I was sure that he would notice, move away.

'That's Emmett, he's my friend, goes to my school,' said Joanna, rescuing me, as she always did.

'Hello.'

Unlike Luke, Joanna – almost anybody I'd met outside a hospital who didn't need to – Ben did not ask why I walked the way I did. At the end of class he shouldered his bag, disappearing before the rest of us had put away our music.

That night, I pushed aside my fish and chips, half-eaten. I wasn't hungry; my mouth was full of the lesson, this boy.

'I'm pleased you had a good time, Peach, but enough now. Let someone else get a word in, hey?'

I stopped, stared at my cold chips.

★

The following Saturday Ben was already waiting for me at the bottom of the stairs. He leant against the peeling paint. Taller than I remembered, brighter than his scuffed surroundings. He reached for my bag without being asked, held the door while I ducked under his arm. I started to count the days from Saturday to Saturday.

After I'd been singing a month, we agreed to go to the cinema. The following Saturday, my father picked us up after class, dropping us outside the local fleapit ABC. Most people had deserted it for the novelty of air-conditioned, surround-sound comfort, the newly refurbished Odeon in Bromley.

'You'll want some folding,' Dad smiled, slipping two £10 notes into my top pocket, honking as he pulled away.

Ben bought me a popcorn, juggling with the two huge cartons of sweet as he held open the door to Screen One. He walked right down to the front row, throwing himself at a sagging seat. 'You get to see the picture first, this way,' he grinned.

I don't remember much about the film. It was something about space travel, could have been *Space Camp* which I'd already seen, or *Flight of the Navigator*. Something loudly perilous, but still a PG. An adventure safe enough for the children we still were. The memory which is much clearer is of my friend's nearness, his laughter, in the dark. The feeling of his arm against mine on the fraying plush. I remember wanting to hold his hand, but knowing I couldn't. I thought of Simon. He would call me a poof. A bender. I already knew that wanting to made me odd, odder even than my four-legged shadow. I didn't really know what the break-time shouts of 'bender' meant. Every day, someone new got singled out. I just knew I didn't want that kind of jeering attention. That the word was a spitting shorthand for everything I didn't want to be. I saw a year of films next to Ben, in the front row of the ABC, without seeing a thing.

Near the end of the first term, I was invited to Ben's house. In all the hours I had thought about my new friend, imagined his home, I had never pictured a snake. The reptile wasn't caged. It hung, glaring freely at me from a stand in the window. The snake's languid appraisal, the sudden, startling fact of it, gave the ordinary kitchen an awful note. It inched higher, tail tightening around the perch, a slow marble eye still fixed on me. Not able to look away, I thought of the Animal Man, a keeper from London Zoo who had visited school assembly when I was eight. He had wound an albino python around my neck, laughing when I flinched. I had hated its muscular curve, the weight of it. The orange-eyed, impassive stare. He had passed it along to braver hands, but for weeks afterwards, I wouldn't get into bed until my mother had checked it for snakes.

Now, I couldn't move. Ben's mother, Sarah, pulled out a kitchen chair. 'Help him, Ben, don't just stand there growing moss.'

Ignoring her, Ben said, 'I should have warned you we live in a zoo.'

I hadn't noticed on the short drive from the lesson, but Sarah was almost as exotic as her pet. Her eyes were Ben's, but her hair was dyed, blonder. Pinned up over a large, laughing mouth. Her smile was painted the same red as her long nails. She sat, kicking off her shoes. Her toenails were immaculately red too. Like her son, she seemed altogether alien. I was sure Sarah was older than my mother, but so different I couldn't guess at a number.

Ben went to the fridge, coming back with two Cokes, sliding me one over the glass tabletop. He cracked his, taking greedy gulps. The snake looped around its perch, unhurried, insinuating. Sarah saw me stiffen. The brown-mottled diamond on its flat head flicked up. It regarded me steadily, tasting the air with a quick tongue. It was beautiful, and terrible. I wanted to leave, to get out. For my father to appear with a bogus emergency.

'That's Freddy,' Sarah said, nodding towards the snake. 'It's a carpet python. Ben's father gave it to me as a wedding gift, though God knows where he bought it. I think it was a present for him, really. Silly sod, we couldn't have anything ordinary. We thought she was a boy at first, but we got that wrong, so Freddy is actually short for Frederica. I've grown to love her, but I might have preferred a cat. Rich, Richard, Ben's dad, well, he didn't realize how long pythons can live – twenty, thirty years sometimes. She'll probably outlive us all. And Ben doesn't want her. I often think she'll outlive the marriage.'

No adult outside my family had ever spoken to me like this. So openly, as if I was one too.

Sarah stood, going to her snake, stroking its head indulgently, as though a python in your kitchen was perfectly everyday. A tail-thumping, delighted dog. Freddy drew back. 'Lovely, aren't you, girl.' Sarah smiled at me. 'It's nice to have you here, Emmett. Nice for Ben to have a new friend. You're always welcome.'

I thanked her, but wasn't sure Freddy was as keen to see me.

Ben picked up my sticks. I followed him to his room. He shut the door, throwing himself down on the single, tightly made bed. Patting the space next to him. There was a large portable TV at the foot-end, resting on a video machine. I noticed the paired lines of shoes under it. More shoes than I had ever owned, ever seen. One whole wall was a tank of tropical fish. They zigzagged and schooled, flashing under the UV lamp. Going nowhere. Ben ignored them, kicking off his shoes, bent to pair them with the rest. The other wall was floor-to-ceiling toys. Robots, Action Men. Boys' toys. The kind of brash, breakable amusements I was only allowed on my birthday.

Everything was new. Shiny. So unlike my own room. I looked, but couldn't see any books. A framed, soft-focus image of Michael Jackson stared down from over Ben's pillow, surrounded by lesser images, torn out of pop magazines.

Ben saw me looking. 'Do you like him too? He's just the best, the best . . . the best there is. Imagine being able to dance like that. To sing like that.'

I understood that my answer was important. That it was a test, a passport to more afternoons, so I lied. 'The best,' I said.

Ben scooted forward, reaching for a remote control on the windowsill, switching on the TV. Michael Jackson glittered from the screen. Ben turned up the volume, the opening bass-thump of 'Billie Jean'. He stared as Michael slid, liquid as mercury, over the stage. The singer's silver-sequinned socks flashed, getting the audience to their feet. I thought they were absurd, but found myself trying to follow the beat. Even the overfed record executives clapped along, but perhaps they were only thinking of the money this man on the moon would make them. Ben was silent, transfixed. At the end of the song, he wound the tape back and his hero glittered, spinning in reverse.

We watched again, my friend drumming the beat on his *Transformers* duvet. Ben was watching Michael, and I was watching Ben. At the end of the song he reached for his Walkman. 'Come closer, idiot. You can't hear it from over there.' He stretched the earphones' silver wire round our two heads, pressing the orange sponge to my ear. We listened to 'Thriller' twice, didn't hear Sarah's knock.

'Your dad's here, Em, time to go.'

My father stood, fixed, in the kitchen doorway. When he saw me he looked relieved, put his untouched coffee on the counter. Freddy had moved from her stand, was climbing a gilt-framed mirror on the opposite wall. Dad was white-faced, terrified. He never came in for coffee again, just honked his arrival from the kerb.

I spent most weekends with Ben after that. In his house, or mine. His room, or mine. I only saw Joanna at rehearsals or at school. I felt bad, but not bad enough to phone. Saturday singing was supposed to make my world larger, louder, but instead it shrank to one face, one song. I saved up, buying all of Michael Jackson's albums from Our Price.

The first afternoon he'd picked me up from choir, Ben's father had told me to call him Rich. Not Richard, or Mr Stone, Rich would do just fine. He leant over me, clicking my belt, flipping down the passenger-side visor against the sun. His car was beetle-black. Sporty, and low to the ground. Richard pulled out sunglasses to match. It was difficult for me to get into. I was sure that my crutches would scratch the waxed shine, that I wouldn't be asked again. Mr Stone was always kind, but despite his friendliness, I never felt entirely comfortable. I never did learn to call him Rich.

One afternoon Sarah wasn't there. 'Ben, get some pizzas, OK? We'll be back late. Try not to burn the house down while we're gone. I'll drive Emmett home tomorrow. Have fun, both of you.'

Mr Stone pulled some notes from his wallet, then clicked down the hall, slamming the front door. Ben went to the window, watching until his father's car had disappeared. It was the first time they'd left us. The first time we'd been alone in the house. I felt excited, but also scared, complicit in an unexpected lie. My parents assumed we were being supervised, would have insisted on Ben staying with us if they'd known.

If his parents' house was neat, careful, their garden wasn't. I don't think I ever saw them use it. A balding lawn, ringed by bare earth, a few sparse pampas stems. A small chest of drawers standing against the back fence completed the impression of a neglected room. Ben gulped his Coke, burping, wiping his mouth with the back of his hand. 'Come on, let's build a campfire.'

'But we're not going to sleep out there, are we?'

He pushed his chair back from the table, suddenly animated, twitchy with freedom. 'Come on. Don't be a baby all your life.'

I followed. I always followed.

Ben must have been planning it, because the drawers were already filled with newspaper. There was a can of Swan lighter fluid on the top. He opened each drawer, soaking them. For some reason I thought of Peg. The chest was old, unfashionable, with tarnished drop handles, the kind of thing she would care for, preserve. He poured the rest of the can over the faded top, reaching into his jeans for a lighter. It was silver, not the disposable plastic corner-shop kind. He flicked it open with a practised movement. Turning, to make sure I was watching, he knelt to light the paper in the bottom drawer. The next, then the next. Before long, the whole thing had caught. It was a still, weatherless day, and it took no time for a thick column of smoke to rise, choking the neighbouring gardens.

I took a step back, watching my friend. The flames burned higher. Hot, even from a safer distance. I imagined the back fence catching light. The fire spreading to more colourful, prized gardens, scorching everything. I saw fire engines, the police. My father's shouting alarm. I would never be allowed to come again.

Ben didn't look at me, didn't seem to see me; just stood, hands in pockets, watching the flames.

'Put it out! Put it out! It stinks, really stinks.' I hoped I sounded calm. Hoped my smile was big enough to cover my panic. The varnish had blistered black, beyond even Peg's effort. This was another boys' game I didn't understand. Ben seemed mesmerized by the fire, fixed.

I remembered what his father had said about burning down the house, feeling sure that there would be sirens. 'Put it out. Please, Ben.' I hated the sound of my voice, the fact I wasn't brave.

'Don't be such a baby. It's meant to be fun.'

'What will your mum say? When she sees?'

Ben smiled, but it didn't reach his eyes, there was no joy in it. 'They probably won't even notice.'

It was only when I went inside, when his audience had left, that Ben put the fire out. I watched from the window, thinking how strange it was that his garden had a hose, but no flowers. When it was embers, Ben peed on it to finish the job.

In all the times I'd stayed, I'd never seen Ben's parents' bedroom. It felt like trespassing, a transgression almost as serious as the fire. The bed sat in a wide, white-curtained bay window. A huge chrome frame, like the prow of a ship. It didn't look restful, more like a bed from a Hollywood set. Ben threw himself down on it, unlacing his trainers. There were tall vases of artificial roses on each bedside table, a red-lacquered Chinese cabinet. The place had the immaculate impermanence of a showroom, rather than the comfortable mess of a home. I felt uneasy, as if the bed suggested a life I wasn't sure I aspired to. Ben threw his jeans at me, laughing. They smelt, we both did, of the bonfire.

'Come on, slowcoach.' He grinned.

Joanna wouldn't ever have called me that. I missed her suddenly. Ben's socks arced, one by one, over his head, into the fireplace. Soon, he stood in just his pants. They were red. The kind my mother bought for me, children's multipacks, age 10–12. He pulled them down, stepping neatly out. Seemed utterly unconscious of his nakedness.

I knew I shouldn't look. Shouldn't want to. I took off my shoes, my jeans. My legs were thinner, paler than his.

The ensuite bathroom had gold taps, a deep tub. Ben locked the door, even though we were alone. He bent to turn both taps on full. I wondered if Sarah would notice the half-empty bottle of Badedas Indulgent Bath Gelee.

I sat on the edge of the bath, pulled my T-shirt up over my head, throwing it in a corner. My chest, next to Ben's, looked disappointing, breakable as twigs.

The mirror above the basin fogged with green-scented steam. I was glad. Didn't want to see myself. The room smelt sharply clean, of icy Alpine forests I'd never seen. The fact the door was locked, that we'd waited until Ben's parents were gone, meant we were doing something wrong.

Ben slid into the water, the tap-end. 'You're the guest. It wouldn't be fair to give you the taps.' He sat there, bubbles up to his chin. He tilted his head back, then spat. It found its mark, sliding down my chest. I started to laugh, felt suddenly weightless. We sat in the cooling bath until our fingers pruned.

The Saturdays Ben stayed, Mum would evict my bears from the top bunk. He would ignore the ladder, climbing the frame instead. Grinning over the edge. She'd click off the light, and I'd listen as her feet receded, *Moondance* starting again, low, through the floor. We went to different schools, had different friends, only saw each other at weekends. From Monday to Friday, there were night terrors. Monsters under the bed, behind every door. I still slept with a nightlight. When Ben was near, I forgot to be scared.

I'd push my fingers into the tight gap between the slats and his mattress, listening to him talk about when we were older. When we had saved up enough money to fly to California, Neverland. Of course we were really going. When you're ten, the future is only another game. Another whispered sleepover plan. Only as far away as breakfast.

In Ben's room, the day of the fire, I watched him dry his hair, throw our towels in a corner. He tilted his desk-chair under the door handle, gently, as though his parents might still hear us. He turned on the TV, before switching off the light. In the blue beam, he looked softer, blurred. I felt something more than happiness.

He bent to pull on his pyjama trousers. 'Budge over.'

Downstairs, I heard the sound of a key missing its lock. Tipsy, overbalancing laughter. Sarah's voice. Loud shushing, her heels on the stairs. 'Stop it! You'll wake the boys.'

The next morning Mr Stone stayed in bed. Sarah drove me home. Her dented Mini was easier to sit in, as friendly as she was. I thought she was the kindest woman outside my tight family, as open as her husband was shut. My T-shirt smelt smoky, sour. I realized I hadn't brushed my teeth. I was sure she had noticed my smell, the charred chest of drawers in her garden, but she chose not to mention our game. Pulling up to my house, she reached behind her for my crutches. 'You know, I was older when I had Ben. They told me I couldn't, shouldn't, have any more. You're a good boy, a good influence . . . It's like having a brother, I suppose, for both of you.'

Her mouth pressed into a sudden, thin line. She kissed me, before jumping out to open the passenger door.

That Christmas, our choir gave a concert at a local church. Mr Williams thought I was ready for a solo, a whole song of my own. Joanna was singing 'Finlandia' and he had chosen 'Tomorrow' from *Bugsy Malone* for me. When my mother heard the lyrics, she exploded. 'But you can't, Em. You just can't sing that. Is he joking . . . taking the piss? Have you heard this, Charlie?'

Reading the lyrics, she blew out her cheeks. I loved the song; it was about a man, Fizzy, who worked as a handyman; a man that nobody noticed, who secretly longed to dance. 'But you *can't* dance, Peach, everybody will know that. I don't want them to laugh – or, worse, pity you. You'll just have to tell Mr Williams you won't sing it.'

But I did. I learnt the song backwards. I sang it on the way to school, and on the way home again. I sang it at the table, in the bath.

The night of the concert, St Michael's was lined with parents wearing slightly dutiful smiles. The pews were banked with artificial holly. Sarah beamed from the front row. My mother ignored her, frowning from the fourth. Joanna's mother Madeline was there, sleek in a fur coat. Mr Williams bursting with pride in a too-tight black tie. In November he had sent a bossy note home with each of us, insisting on shiny shoes. Long black skirts and white blouses for the girls. White dress shirts and black bow ties for the three boys. My mother had laughed, saying we were children, just kids. Not silver-servers. It wasn't the Albert Hall. The rest of us looked cobbled together, awkward. Ben was immaculate, starched. I thought he looked beautiful, before remembering that that word couldn't apply to my friend. Mr Williams whispered, 'Now try to enjoy yourselves. And if you get lost, can't remember your words, just improvise, like we practised, until you find your way back. Whatever you do, don't just stop. It'll go like a rocket.'

I saw my dad waving at Madeline; my mother jostling, already bored. My mind went blank. I didn't remember any words, my own name. Not just the lyrics to my song, but any song. I wasn't even sure I knew how to sing. I'd timed it. 'Tomorrow' was four minutes, just four. I felt Ben's smile. He ducked out of line, straightened my tie, tried to smooth my stubborn cowlick. I liked this tiny intimacy. Liked being claimed in front of all our parents. 'Hey, scruff-bag. That's better,' he smiled. And suddenly it was.

We did make it to the Albert Hall. The following summer Sarah took us to the Proms. It was a hot August evening. Still too boiling, she decided, for the Tube. We took a taxi from Charing Cross, but the treat was a mistake. The traffic was bad-tempered, honking, all the way to Kensington Gore. As we stalled, Sarah looked at her watch, started to sing, 'We're late for a date, late for a date . . . late for a date at the Albert's Gate . . .'

I don't remember much about the music, just sitting too high in the pillared gallery. The itch of velvet and gold. I didn't dare look over the edge. Hoped that Ben hadn't noticed my fear. As the lights went down he reached for my hand. It was just a moment, while Sarah fussed with the tickets, but I was so happy that night, so sure of being in the right place, I would have applauded silence.

Later that summer my father got a new job and we bought a new home in Ladywell. A large Edwardian place on a wide crescent, wrapped around a graffitied park. It was another blue, boiling day when my parents got the keys. The previous owners had bred dogs, and the smell of ammonia, ancient puppy pee, stung our eyes as soon as my father opened the door.

They spent two days ripping up carpets, soaping floorboards. Sniping at each other, while I tried to blend into the new surroundings. I hated the high-ceilinged change. George made his feelings clear as soon as I undid his carrier, disappearing over the back fence. The cat stayed away for two nights. Our furniture had fitted the old house so well, but it was somehow reduced by these grander surroundings. I suddenly noticed the rings from hot breakfast mugs, the frayed rugs, chipped willow pattern.

The first thing my mother unpacked was her gardening tools. The garden was huge, and she couldn't wait to make a start. In one overgrown corner we discovered a well, the date the house was finished – 1914 – carved on its base. Deep black water, a long fall, covered by a metal grille, but it didn't stop lines of orange-bellied slugs. There was a cracked stone birdbath, and close to the fence, under a pear tree, my mother accidentally disturbed a graveyard of barely buried skeletons: pug puppies that hadn't survived to be sold.

The thing I liked most about the house was the fact it was closer to Ben's. But I also blamed our new home. It was the reason for my parents' longer days. I heard my father now, his fast feet on the stairs, running for the 8.15 to Cannon Street, much more than I saw him. Loud voices over another night working late, forgetting to phone. They were followed by silent days. Thick, hurt silences, which our new rooms weren't quite big enough to contain.

The records were unpacked, but there was less music. Less dancing.

A few weeks after I turned eleven, my father dropped me at Ben's house. Ben must have heard me, but didn't look up as I came in. He was sat at his desk, busy cutting the heads off matches. The pink unstruck heads were too small to see, but I heard them, a light rain on the wood. I watched, but Ben still didn't look up, just started gluing the decapitated lengths together, forming walls. He picked up a match, then another, pressing the glued edges hard. I didn't understand. Surely there were easier, better things to build with? I sat, waiting. Feeling suddenly invisible, insubstantial. He put the Stanley blade down, looking at me. I saw he had saved a candle from my birthday cake, a dinner at Pizza Express with my parents, just the four of us. It was on the windowsill.

'You'd better go home. I'm busy, not like you. Just go away. Go home.'

I didn't know what I was, but went downstairs, sure Ben would smile after me, tell me he was joking. I waited on the stairs. When he didn't follow, I asked Mr Stone to take me back. His polished car pulled up to my door, Ben's father smiled, reached for my belt, pressing the red catch. 'I think you'd better leave it for a while, eh? Take care.'

The next weekend, I didn't feel like singing. When Joanna phoned, I didn't speak to her. Every time the phone went, for months afterwards, I jumped, expecting Ben's voice.

I saw my friend again – I had never quite stopped thinking of him as one – eight years later. Standing in front of the departure boards at London Bridge, I felt a hand on my shoulder. The face I remembered was still just visible under sharper features, hastily shaved stubble. He was with a girl, pretty, shorter than him. Her arm through his, claiming him casually. She was wearing a blue-flowered cotton dress, a bag from the Whistlestop looped over her wrist. He didn't introduce her, and we didn't ask each other's names. I noticed the gold foil, bottles of wine, and wondered if they were headed to a party. I remember being ashamed of my uniform, my summer-job polo shirt.

'I'll bell you, yeah,' he grinned, turning towards the platforms. Suddenly the same smile. Looking over his shoulder, he shouted, 'You on the same number?'

I realized I still remembered his, even though I'd crossed it out, lost the book.

I shouted back that I was. Watching them go, being absorbed into the impatient rush hour, I knew it didn't matter, that he wouldn't call.

8
Chasing Bells

It was an unspoken tradition at Brindishe that in your last term before leaving, before sliding down the snake of secondary school, beginning all over again, you wore your new uniform in the playground.

Joanna hated hers. In September she was starting at a local independent girls' school. She sat beside me on the bench, looked both younger and older, a child playing dressing-up in her sensible navy blue. Pinching, polished lace-ups. I was in my usual Velcro trainers. It was July, and I still had nowhere to go in the autumn. She tugged at the hem of her new skirt. I would have been happy to wear it myself if it meant that I could stay with her. If it meant I had a place.

The local comprehensive had refused me without an interview. There were over a thousand boys, and as many steps. The closest independent school turned me down flat, because I couldn't play cricket. They thought that having a pupil who was no good with a bat might undermine their proud sporting traditions. My body was non-traditional, so I wasn't even permitted to sit the entrance exam.

My father wrote to another local independent school. They wrote back saying that though they'd never had a pupil like me in their hundred-year history, and the places were allocated for the Michaelmas term, they'd like to see some examples of my work. I can't remember a word of the story I wrote for the headmaster, but he must have liked it, because they agreed to let me start in September.

We drove to Harrods to buy my new blazer. I'd never been there before. It was a still, grey August afternoon, but inside everything was glitter. The air was thickly sweet, smelt expensive. I felt my father hook a finger into my belt while we waited for the lift. He didn't want to lose me, he joked, in all that money.

A sales assistant appeared, soundlessly, almost as soon as the lift doors opened. He gave us a professional smile, taking a tape measure from his neck. 'Which school?' he asked.

The Schools Department seemed to stretch for green-carpeted miles. There were polished mahogany shelves stacked with bright caps. Hats intended for equally polished boys. Apparently, I belonged there now. The sales assistant didn't need to write down my measurements, probably didn't even need his tape measure. He disappeared, coming back, almost before he'd gone, with an armful of clothes. My new blazer had shiny brass buttons, a silk-embroidered crest on the breast pocket. The saint whose name the school had taken, his arms spread in welcome. I watched the assistant fold everything into bags. As my father handed over his card, the man smiled again. 'You won't need the cricket pads, will you?'

'Well, obviously we don't,' my father snapped, snatching up his receipt.

In the car, Dad fiddled with the radio, searching for *Saturday Sports Report.* 'I've never been so happy to spend a hundred pounds on a blazer. And that arsehole's right, Em, at least you won't need the sports kit.'

The traffic was sluggish as we inched down Knightsbridge towards Constitution Hill. I looked out of the window at the blue haze over stalled cars, happy. I had a place, an expensive belonging, but wanted so much to need the cricket pads. My father had a good job now. He wouldn't have minded the extra expense if it meant freezing on a touchline. Having a son who could chase after a muddy ball.

A silver Mercedes fumed next to us. The driver fanned herself irritably, thought about using her horn, before realizing there was nowhere to go. I watched my dad bite at his thumbnail, peeling it off. It annoyed me that his thumbs were always bloody, that he could never let them heal. When the acceptance letter had finally landed on the mat, he had sung his relief for days. 'We're all on the up, Em,' he grinned.

Mr Collins was my new form master. A nervously smiling man, the goldfish of Christian Fellowship shining discreetly on his lapel. Shortly before term started he came to see us. My mother had bought a cake, something we never normally had. She had put on lipstick, a bright dress. My father was at the kitchen counter, brewing tea. He'd come home early for the meeting, but was still a stranger in his work pinstripes. Mr Collins smiled broadly, as though we were friends. 'I want Emmett to feel comfortable, to feel fully a part of the school community. As well as being his form master, I'll be taking him for French, so we'll be seeing a lot of each other. I'm quite new there myself, actually. Not an old boy, like a lot of the other masters, so we'll be learning together.'

Taking a bite of cake, Mr Collins explained that he knew Patricia, Pat, my first physio. She was retired now, played a lot of golf, but they still sang together in church every Sunday. I thought of the grins she had drawn on my knees, the smiles fading in the bath. She had told him all about me, all about my condition. He finished his cake, glancing at his watch.

'It's good of you to make the time,' Dad said. It was a brisk, businesslike tone that was as new as his suits.

Mr Collins reached for his jacket, shaking my father's hand. The shoulders were thick with dandruff. I don't know why this made me recognize his own unease, feel sorry for the teacher.

'I'm sure we'll make a great success of it, won't we, Emmett?'

'Yes, sir,' I answered, liking him.

'There's no need for that quite yet. You've still got a week or two of freedom.' He squeezed my shoulder, following my father out.

Mum started stacking the plates. 'Shame he's a God-squadder. Otherwise he seems quite nice.'

The school looked more like a minor cathedral rather than a holding pen for unruly, privileged boys. When it was built, in 1888, the area around it had been sleepy, semi-rural. It had spread out prosperously over green fields it still owned. By the time I got there, a hundred years later, urban expansion had almost swallowed the place whole. Rising above newer, shabbier buildings, it looked to me like an elderly, disapproving relative, ambivalent at having lived so long.

It's the noises I remember most. Lesson bells. Feet running on stone. Sports bags chucked like overhead missiles in the fast corridors. Shouts silenced by barking masters.

It was an atmosphere I didn't recognize. Along with compulsory Latin, there was another language to learn. I missed Joanna, missed girls.

I'd lost my name the first morning I put on my new blue tie. Now I was just de Monterey. As well as a form master, I had a house master, Mr Lawrence, a round, red-faced man who was always in a hurry. He was probably only fifteen years older than his pupils, but seemed, like the Victorian Gothic building, to be ancient.

From the first moment he saw me, Mr Lawrence decided that I made the place untidy. There were much more complicated, double-barrelled names on the register, but from the start of term he chose me a new one: Dermot-or-whatever-your-bloody-name-is. A long name for a short boy.

The Lord's Prayer was printed in the front of my gold-leafed hymnal. I lost the book years ago, but still can't lose the prayer. I heard it every morning in chapel. The headmaster made us bow our heads, repeat it after him. The captains of the four houses would sit behind the masters in the choir stalls. I envied them their maroon blazers, bound with baby blue. Envied their straight-backed swagger, immaculate confidence.

I bowed my head just enough so that it looked like I was praying, but really I was looking at the captains. Every morning, as we filed out, I told myself that I stared because they were beautifully ordinary. Because I wanted, more than anything, to be like them. Left and right of the chapel doors were two tall glass cases filled with sporting silverware. I always stopped there, not because the tarnished cups were beautiful, but because I wanted to win one. I hated having to watch the house matches, hated the way Mr Lawrence, seeing me sat on the wall, never lost an opportunity to ask me where my kit was, why I wasn't wearing it. I hated the way I pretended to laugh.

Mounted above the cases were gilded lists of old boys turned soldiers, killed in the Great War and the Second World War. Above them, in a case so small you might ignore it in your hurry to class, was a white-hooked cane. The masters weren't able to beat us any more; still, the threat was preserved for posterity.

I was sure the only master who was truly devout was Mr Collins. The rest of them were simply following the rules. I kept silent, didn't believe in a God who could kick my legs out from underneath me.

★

By the end of the second week, I was still getting hopelessly lost, would arrive for French or Latin untucked and breathless. Take my seat at the front of the class, getting my books out as quietly as I could. One morning Mr Collins said, 'I'm sorry, de Monterey, this isn't a good start is it? It's my fault, we need a system to look after you better.'

There was a ripple of laughter from the desks behind. Mr Collins ignored it, writing my surname on the blackboard, underlining it as if I were homework. 'We need a rota so that de Monterey always has somebody with him.'

He smiled amiably, slapping the chalk dust from his palms. Unlike at Brindishe, twenty-two hands went up immediately. Most of my classmates were kind, but I knew it had more to do with the fact that I always missed the first ten minutes of a 45-minute lesson. Over the week, that would add up to hours of missed teaching, and a good deed into the bargain.

The next day the rota was pinned above Mr Collins's desk in the form room. It was a solution, but it made me feel like a problem.

My first real friend at school was a boy called Abbott, Tom. We were opposites. He was already nearly six foot tall to my five-foot-nothing. A smiling redhead with an easy, freckled confidence. He was always breaking his bones on the pitch, was quick to tell me he'd been on crutches, knew a bit about what it was like. Because he was an Abbott, and first in the form alphabet, he was also the first of my helpers. One afternoon, taking longer than we both needed to climb the stairs to the physics lab, Tom asked, 'So this thing you've got . . . with your legs, is it permanent?'

I liked that he'd asked me. Nobody there had asked why they needed to help me until then. It was good manners, easier not to pry. But collective tact made me feel like both the most visible pupil at the school and the most invisible. Still I didn't know how to answer, so I made a joke. 'I didn't do it skiing, if that's what you're asking?'

Tom coloured, jumpy with the possibility of having caused offence.

'Yes, it's permanent,' I said.

'I'm so sorry,' he said. I knew he meant it.

'We'd better hurry up, we're really taking the piss,' Tom smiled, shouldering both our bags.

Even with the rota, chasing between the bells left me exhausted. Often, I would fall asleep, only to be jerked awake by another bell. I was embarrassed to be found out by the sleepy-silver skein of saliva on my sleeve. I would sleep all weekend. Emptying the fridge as soon as it was filled. Fuelling myself to run after the bullying bells of a new week. My weight dropped as fast as my grades; my parents started to worry.

They met with the headmaster. He was glad to see them, worried too. I was a bright boy, but if I didn't pay more attention I wouldn't get good GCSE passes, passes he knew I was capable of. If that happened, he couldn't recommend me for the sixth form. My parents suggested that they might adapt the timetable so that I could have most of my lessons on the ground floor. There was no precedent for the request, so the head smilingly refused.

I was being helped to biology by a double-barrelled Jonathan. He was the only eleven-year-old I knew who carried a briefcase. Who kept a tin of Kiwi polish in it, so as not to lose house points for scuffed toes. Jonathan liked me less than he liked learning, and the feeling was mutual.

I felt Jonathan looking at his watch, felt his irritation, and caught my foot on a top step, falling to the bottom. I felt hot embarrassment before I felt the pain.

Jonathan helped me to my feet, got my crutches. 'Are you all right?' he asked, terse.

I wasn't. I had landed across my sticks, winding myself. Tearing my palm on the worn aluminium adjusters.

He walked me to the matron's office. She took my temperature, even though I was bleeding, not feverish. There was blood on my crutch handles, the tails of my shirt. Despite the evidence, she bustled crossly, as if I was faking a headache to be excused double maths.

'I can only give you one,' she said, coming back with a paracetamol, a plastic cup of weak orange squash.

The school secretary had rung home, but there was no answer. If she'd asked me I could have told her that both my parents were at work. I lay on the high, narrow bed, closed my eyes, listened to the traffic. My mother arrived just before four, the concern on her face masked by bright make-up, her own boxy-shouldered corporate uniform.

'Come on, Peach-face,' she smiled. 'Let's get chips on the way home.'

A few weeks later we were sitting in the waiting room of the Newcomen Centre again; Dr Baird was still my consultant. She smiled round the door. I liked the way she always spoke to me first. Always used my name. Her voice was warm, gently amused. I liked the fact that her office was always the same chaos of files, photographs. She pulled out a chair for me, taking my sticks. I could feel my father's smile, nervous, on the back of my neck.

'Well, Emmett, you look smart today. Couldn't wangle a whole day off, no? How are things going at school?'

'He falls a lot. Sleeps a lot. Eats a lot . . . but can't put on weight.' My dad offered his own neat summary before I could open my mouth.

'I'm sure I wish I had the last problem,' Dr Baird laughed.

'Well, Emmett is growing, but he's also shrinking. I saw on the walk here that his legs are forcing him into a tight crouch. His hamstrings are much too tight, and they're drawing him down. It takes an enormous amount of energy to walk like that all day, too much. Which is why his weight won't stick.'

Dr Baird looked at me. 'Emmett, it's all right at the moment, because you haven't gained your adult height, adult body mass, but when you do, it's likely that your tight muscles will pull you off your feet. It might be time to try the Baclofen, just to see if it helps you walk, to buy you a bit more time.'

Baclofen is a muscle-relaxant derived from botulinum toxin. The drug had been suggested before, at previous assessments, but my parents had always refused it after seeing its effect on my classmates at Charlton Park.

I remember Dr Baird's kind eyes, unblinking behind power-ful lenses. It had never occurred to me that I would need pills, that eventually I might not walk. I couldn't answer.

'But that drug turns bright kids into floppy dolls,' Mum snapped.

Dr Baird leant back in her chair, suddenly serious. 'If we don't act soon, Emmett's likely to be in a wheelchair, and while it's not the worst thing, I can't see how he'd manage in his cur-rent school. As you know, any treatment options we're able to offer at Guy's are limited. You've already rejected most of them, but I wonder if you'd consider America? If it's not too far?'

Again, before I could take it in, before I could answer, my father spoke. 'It's not a problem, we can go anywhere.'

Dr Baird stood, reached for a book on the crowded shelf behind her desk, handing it to Dad. 'You might be interested in this.'

The Identification and Treatment of Gait Problems in Cerebral Palsy by Dr James R. Gage, MD.

I sat in the back of the car, silent on the way home. We drove straight past the golden arches. Pulling up to the lights at the junction of St Thomas Street, I watched the busy pavement. A woman pushing a double buggy, a blond-haired brother and sister. Two white-coated doctors, a businessman clicking briskly towards London Bridge. I didn't envy him his money, the boast of a gold watch that looked like it would take him straight to the bottom. I envied him his fast walk, the fact it never crossed his mind. I would have been any one of those people if I had had the choice.

Just before I had started at Brindishe I had been cast for a new pair of splints. They were sweaty plastic tubes that kept my disobedient feet from turning in, kept me in line. I hated them, hated needing them. Luke went barefoot all summer, but my splints were the reason I seldom wore shorts, even in a hundred degrees, even in my own garden. I hated them, but loved the smiling orthotist. His striped shirtsleeves, always rolled above the elbow, arms flecked with plaster. When he had cut the casts off, scrubbed my legs with a green paper towel, he went to a cupboard in the corner, coming back with a large white box. I recognized the three navy lines on the lid: Adidas.

'We got these in just yesterday; they're a new thing. I know you hate your boots. These are fashion shoes, but made for special kids. Made to go over your splints.'

He folded back the tissue paper. They were beautiful, looked like they could run fast. Snow-white leather, with pale suede toes. Three electric-blue stripes on each side. A tiny logo, tooled in gold. I saw my mother's worry, the money we didn't have, which would need to be found.

'It's very kind, but we couldn't—'

'Emmett would be helping me out . . . testing them. It's a present, my pleasure. Really.'

'What do you say, Peach?'

I'd worn them on my first day. I wouldn't wear anything else, so they were in holes by the end of my second week. But Simon had still noticed their bulbous difference, saying, 'I didn't even think they made special shoes like that . . . I mean, for spastics.'

Along with my Adidas, the orthotist had given me the idea that I could be moulded, fixed. Dr Baird seemed to think it was possible, a plane ride away.

As we turned right on to Southwark Street, I noticed a woman pushing a child in a wheelchair. A boy about my age, but, like Mark, he was strapped in, didn't look left or right. The handles were looped with shopping, groceries. We were the same, him and I. Our difference made us conspicuous, but also invisible. The woman looked tired, straight ahead, not stopping for anyone. I twisted in my seat as she passed down the pavement, scattering the lunch-break crowds who pretended not to see either of them.

9
Moon Landings

The steward had an expensive, engineered smile, framed by a clipped blond moustache. As we started our descent over Bradley International Airport he spoke into the public address system. 'Onboard today we have a little boy by the name of Emmett. Emmett is from London, England, and is coming to have surgery at Newington Children's Hospital. And we sure wish him all the best.'

I felt crumpled passengers, who had not noticed me before, hadn't cared, turn to look. Over my shoulder a cameraman bent to catch my reaction to this kindness. I was sure the good wishes were genuine but the public announcement was for the lens. The steward twisted sideways, squeezing past the camera, squeezing my arm. I noticed the flashy, blue-faceted class ring – Class of 1977 – on his little finger.

'Sir, I'm sorry but you'll have to stop now. You have to strap in for landing.'

The sudden noise, the buzz of attention, meant I had allowed myself to forget the surgery, the reason for it. Looking out of the window at the white raft of cloud, I didn't want to land. The captain had turned on the seatbelt sign, and I wondered if I could ask him to turn the plane, if we had enough fuel left to go back.

We waited as people unfolded themselves, reaching for overhead bags. Forced flight-swollen feet into tight shoes. Passing my seat a woman reached across my mother, grabbing my shoulder. She was older than Peg, white-haired, but elegant like her. A generation that still thought air travel glamorous, dressed well to fly.

'Good luck, Emmett. Where's that name from? Unusual. Anyway, I'll be thinking of you. You'll be in my prayers tonight.'

The stranger seemed confident that her prayers wouldn't go unheard, in her personal hotline to the Almighty. Her face crinkled kindly. I was about to acknowledge her, when my mother cut in. 'Thank you,' she smiled, not thankful at all. 'It's good of you, but I don't think we need trouble God. He's done quite enough already.'

After the consultation with Dr Baird, things had moved almost too fast. We had gone back to Guy's the following week. In a windowless room, the hospital's basement, my gait was recorded. I was still just light enough, my centre of gravity still low enough, to be able to walk short distances without my crutches. I swayed knock-kneed, up and back, up and back. Arms splayed like a tightrope walker, guided by the camera's steadier red light. It was all over in less than twenty minutes. If I'd known then how important those minutes would be, I would have made sure I didn't have holes in my socks.

It was after three. Too late to go back to school. Walking to London Bridge Station, we passed McDonald's.

'Come on, Peach. Don't tell your father . . . he's cooking tonight. You can pretend to be hungry later, can't you?'

'Of course.'

The tables were crowded. White-coated doctors who'd worked over lunch. Grey-faced, worried families. Not hungry, just looking for a place to absorb bad news, wait until visiting hours. We got our food, the only free space nearest the window. Mum looked tired, sallow, in the noise, neon brightness.

She smiled, reaching to steal a chip. Wiping the ketchup from her fingers.

'They're mine,' I said, pretending to be outraged. Enjoying it.

'Don't sulk, you'd finished. Anyway, everyone knows that theft makes even cold chips taste good.'

Balling her napkin on to our tray, Mum said, 'What do you think, Em? If you got picked, would you do it?'

She looked past me, out the window. 'Do you remember your friend Sol at Charlton? You went to his birthday? He was always having surgery. That awful Dr Henry . . . Poor Sol only had to heal, and Dr Henry was suggesting more. Cutting him up, hamstring lengthening, every few months. He wanted to do the same to you, thought we were being stubborn because we said no. All I asked him was to explain his reasons, to tell us what to expect from the operations. But he wouldn't, or couldn't. So we sacked him.'

She took a sip of her milkshake. 'I think he was quite surprised. I just explained that I wouldn't allow him to carve up my child on a hunch. You know, if you don't want to do it, that would be all right too – we'll understand. We don't know whether this will work either. And a wheelchair, well, you'd still be you. It isn't up to us. It isn't your dad and I who'll have to do it.'

'If I have to go in a wheelchair, I'll have to change schools. And I've only just got there, I like it. I don't want to be in a wheelchair . . . I don't even want to be on crutches. But probably, I won't get picked.'

Turning away from her, I said, 'If I do get picked, I'm definitely going.'

One Small Step was a charity named after Neil Armstrong's giant leap on the moon. Its aim was to raise a million pounds in order to build a Gait Laboratory at Guy's to help children with cerebral palsy walk. It was the first of its kind in the UK. A week later, the phone rang. Of the six tapes, six children Dr Gage had seen, I was the best candidate for surgery. The charity would help, if I would help them raise the money, lend them my smile. They wouldn't have to send me the 238,855 miles to the moon, just the 3,360 miles from London to Newington, Connecticut. If we worked together to keep the story in the papers, it might only take a year, maybe two, and I'd get a new walk in return.

I said yes. The following week I was back in the same room I'd been recorded in, to meet Dr Gage, who had flown over from the US to meet his chosen candidate, the journalists who were going to cover the story.

The length of Fleet Street, news crews, were crammed awkwardly up the walls. My mother reached for my hand.

'Christ, Charlie, I wasn't expecting all this.' Mum smiled, automatic. It was a look I hadn't seen before, didn't recognize.

My father reddened. I felt him grip the back of my chair.

A tall, neat man came forward. He held out a hand, bending to my height. 'I'm Jim . . . Dr Gage. It's good to meet you.'

'I'm Emmett,' I said unnecessarily, forgetting that the doctor had already seen my walk, seen me in my underwear.

Dr Gage had kind eyes behind serious lenses. In an unassuming suit, he didn't look much like the wizard I needed. I thought of the moment Dorothy finds out the great and powerful Oz is simply a carnival showman. A suitcase full of tricks.

My wizard smiled shyly. 'I wasn't expecting all this. I think we'll be able to get you a good result, Emmett. The tapes looked promising.'

He took off his glasses, wiping them. Even though it was the first time I'd met him, the doctor gave me a look I'd seen before. All doctors, however kind, had the same expression. It was as if he was trying to see through me to my bones. As if I was both a person and a set of equations. A complex problem to solve. After a long moment, he patted my shoulder. Got stiffly to his feet. Before going to find my father, he said, 'I guess the next time I see you, we'll be operating. Have a safe trip. We'll do the best we can for you.'

All I could do was smile.

I noticed a woman across the room. She was wearing sharp-toed cowboy boots, three loops at the ankle. A gilded bullet shining in each. She came over, kneeling on the carpet, smiling warmly. 'They're great, aren't they? I got them on holiday in Nashville, oh, years ago now. I couldn't really afford them at the time, but haven't really taken them off since. I must be the only Jewish princess in North London who loves country music. My mother just hates them. She blames the boots for the fact I'm not married yet. I'm Nina, I'm a TV producer. I'll be making the film about you and your family.'

I thought the boots were the ugliest things I'd ever seen, but already liked Nina's breathless candour, so just agreed. She bent to pull a cartridge from its loop, dropping it into my palm. The blunt end of the shiny casing was edged in tiny diamonds.

For the two days before I was admitted to hospital, we lived with the journalists in an anonymous business hotel that over-looked the I-91 highway in Hartford. It was a cloudless July day when we arrived. A screen mounted on the wall informed us it was currently seventy-eight degrees, with zero chance of rain, but the reception desk was ready for Christmas, banked with red poinsettias. I saw my mother reach to test a leaf, dismissing them as plastic.

A man stepped out from behind the flowers. He pointed to the gold MANAGER on his chest, smiling. 'Welcome, welcome, I hope you have a pleasant stay with us. And if I can do anything at all to make you more comfortable, be sure to let me know.'

Seeing the ponytailed cameraman, heaps of sound equipment, he smiled again, saying, 'Wait . . . should I know who any of you are?'

It was a joke, well meant, but my father was tired from travelling all day, smiling on demand. 'We're not on holiday,' he snapped. 'My son's the reason for the cameras. He's here for surgery. It isn't a good time.' Dad snatched up the keys.

The manager's own smile froze, but didn't disappear. He pretended he hadn't heard.

My mother stood by the window of our shared room, a hand under the greyed nets, looking for a latch.

'Leave it, Fran. Can't you just leave it? There's air conditioning.' Dad was sprawled, eyes closed, on the flowered coverlet, the furthest of the twin beds. He was still wearing his shoes. Mum was trying to open the window, knocking uselessly on the glass. 'For God's sake, give it a rest, will you?'

'Piss off, Charlie. Can't you take your shoes off? I'll have to sleep there too. I'm going to find some air.'

I saw her remember the reason why the three of us were in that airless, ugly room. With an effort, she swallowed the argument. Smiling too brightly, she said, 'Come on, Peach. I think I saw a pool somewhere around. Let's go for a swim, shall we? After tomorrow it'll be a long time before you'll be able to do it again.'

'Why don't you remind him?' snapped Dad.

'It's not as if any of us can forget, is it?' my mother shot back.

I didn't want a swim, but I did want to get out of the room.

The pool was empty behind a high chain-link fence. There were loud red signs at intervals, stating that THIS POOL IS

ONLY FOR PATRONS OF THE RAMADA INN. But we were the only ones. Over the fence cars zoomed past on their way to somewhere better.

I didn't feel frightened, just a flat sadness. Before my father changed jobs, we couldn't afford the airfare often. But shoe-boxes full of Hershey's at Easter, Christmas gifts that arrived either too early or too late, Sunday off-peak calls, meant America usually felt like home. But then, we were usually on vacation. Surrounded by the noise of family.

Watching my mother peel off her T-shirt, pull at the straps of her old bathing suit, I wanted to go home. She was comfort. Iodine on scraped knees. Kisses that made everything better. I loved being in bed listening to the rain on the roof. I felt safe knowing she was downstairs or just across the landing. She tested the water with a toe, dropped in. The pool wasn't really long enough for lengths. One kick sent her almost to the other side. I'd never thought myself alone when she or Dad were there. Seeing her frustrated turns, I understood now that I was. It was the first time I felt they might be better off without me, without the effort of my care. Mum turned again, taking a breath. I felt trapped, sealed behind glass.

I reached for the ladder, dropping my sticks. Sat stiffly, pushing my legs over the side. The concrete was still hot, storing the last of the sun. My mother stretched for the edge. The pool was shallow enough to stand. She dipped her face in the water, smoothing the hair out of her eyes.

'It's lovely, so cool. Aren't you coming in, Peach?'

'I don't want a swim, Mum. I want to go home.'

I hadn't meant to admit it.

'I want to go home too, Em. But we're here now. We've got to do this.'

She turned again, kicking off the tiles, swimming away.

★

121

I used to love *Star Trek*. Before we bought a TV, I would go to Luke's to watch it. Or lie on my stomach at Jim and Peg's, much too close to the screen, completely absorbed by Captain James T. Kirk, the adventures of the starship *Enterprise*. Maybe it was because I fell, couldn't trust the pavement not to floor me, that I dreamt of being beamed aboard. Or perhaps I was beginning to understand that I was earthbound in quite a different way to my family. I used to imagine my own zero-gravity possibilities. A parallel dimension where my legs wouldn't weigh me down.

Hospitals, like airports, are countries in themselves, and Newington Children's Hospital was like every hospital I'd ever been in. A long red-brick building. Miles of brightly lit linoleum. Bland flower prints. We were filmed arriving, three times, and I shook Dr Gage's hand another three.

'You found us all right?' he asked, as though we were new neighbours, had travelled no distance.

The Gait Lab was another long, windowless basement. A bank of monitors at one end, a camera on a tripod. The other wall was filled by a picture of the moon. Its silver-cratered curve, seen from the Earth. Soft toys sat on the floor in front of it, looking like an advance party of lunar explorers. The white, wipe-clean floor was divided by a blue line of tiles, a runway of pressure sensors. Seeing me looking at the moon, Dr Gage said, 'It gives the patients something to aim at, so they don't get distracted by the camera. And I thought it'd be neat, as some of the technology we use here to track your muscles was originally developed during the space race.'

I grinned at this. I was going to be a spaceman.

Dr Gage knelt down in front of my chair. 'We're going to record you today, just like in London. I want you to walk along that blue line, you see? We'll be able to get a pattern, a picture of your movement, from that . . . a blueprint for surgery. You'll have to take your clothes off, I'm afraid. Let me know anytime you need a break.'

'He's used to it, aren't you, Em?' My father smiled, awkward at having nothing to do.

The doctor noticed my necklace, a thin silver chain. A birthday present from Sarah that she pretended Ben had bought me. I hadn't stopped wearing it since. He said, 'You'll have to take that off too, I'm afraid. It'll distort the images, show up on camera.'

A woman came forward. Her eyes were hidden behind enthusiastic blonde curls. She gave me a pink-frosted smile. 'I'm Lorrie,' she said.

Lorrie told me she was one of Dr Gage's assistants, a physiotherapist. Before I had a chance to answer, she'd knelt behind my chair, taken off my necklace. 'Who's Mom?' she asked, coiling it into her palm. 'I'll give this to her.'

'I'm Mom,' my mother said, her accent twanging back.

'Oh, you're an American?' asked Lorrie.

I knew I was the reason for all this fuss, but felt suddenly absent, boneless. I watched my mother zip the necklace into her bag. 'I promise I won't lose it, Peach.'

I hid behind a smile after that. Feeling like a body, not a person. Separated from myself by the line of blue sensors, the tiles on the floor. Understanding that I was just something to be studied, taken apart. A disabled person in a room full of able-bodied doctors, who understood me via a textbook, a medical model. Only a problem they hoped to fix.

I had chosen to be there. I wanted their help, the benefit of their brisk-smiling expertise. But I also didn't. That day I learnt to think of my body as something distinct from myself. Something stitched together, shameful. A thing I carried unwillingly. It took me years – sometimes it's still difficult – to be grateful to my hands for holding me up. To recognize my reflection as me.

My mother helped me off with my clothes, on with the specially bought shorts we'd almost left behind at the hotel. The doctor rolled them right up. I was stuck all over with silver markers, my arms and legs studded with balls of reflective tape. A battery pack, wires that measured the electrical impulses in my muscles, was hung round my neck. The metal was cold.

Dr Gage stood behind the monitors, watching my data. I walked barefoot, flat-footed, up and back, up and back, trying to tune out everything but the image of the moon, the jerky slap of my feet.

At my first break, Lorrie brought over a toy. A pink plush, battery-operated pig. She turned it on, and we watched it oink over the tiles. Every few steps it stopped, its tail juddering, excited, then flipped, landing on its trotters. Lorrie laughed at its stiff, snorting progress, dropping it in my lap. You could feel the pig's metal beneath the thin padding, the skeleton underneath.

I must have walked to the moon and back a hundred times that day. My toes caught painfully underneath me. I kept expecting to fall without my sticks, but didn't. When the doctors had what they needed, I had to do it again for the BBC cameras.

I was conscious of being nearly-naked in a room full of dressed strangers. Conscious of the performance. I was an English child in America, hoping for a space-age miracle, who was also pretending to be an English child in America, hoping for a space-age miracle.

'Would you like to see your data?' smiled Dr Gage.

A glowing stick-man, line of tiny green dots, slouched bent-kneed across the monitor. I didn't recognize myself in the computer-generated pattern, but hoped it would be enough.

'Gait analysis used to be a research tool, not a diagnostic one. You'd have two children who presented the same way . . . and you'd do identical procedures and get drastically different results: one would be better, one child might be much worse.

This allows us to take the guesswork out. We can get an accurate blueprint of your walk, which means we can tailor what needs to be corrected, the surgery, to you.'

I didn't want this kind man to explain it to me. I didn't want science, was only interested in miracles. I was going to be corrected, made bionic.

'I'll come by and see you tomorrow morning. You won't really see me, probably won't remember, but I promise to take good care of you. We'll do our best for you, Emmett. You did well today. Of course you can't eat now, but try to have a nice evening.'

'Thank you,' I said.

Before the day ended there was another interview to do. A local media station, WFSB Eyewitness News. The interviewer was glossy, her voice soft with concern. A cooing, saccharine tone I imagined she used both for children and the elderly. She knelt down in front of my chair, reaching to steady herself. She was wearing a square-shouldered silk jacket. My monitors and wires had been removed, but I was still in my shorts. Her professional polish, bright padding, made me ashamed of my nakedness. Too aware of the anxious spot, the first one I'd ever had, brewing on the bridge of my nose.

To close the interview, tie a bow on it, for the mildly interested people eating dinner round their sets, the reporter asked me if I had a girlfriend. I understood. It was a way to reassure viewers that, while I might be disabled, I was still a normal boy. Sexualizing me was a way to sugar my difficult difference. I couldn't tell her about Ben, say that the nearest thing I'd ever had to a girlfriend was a boy. My best friend. So I just laughed. Told the camera I was much too young yet.

The reporter stood, smoothing her skirt, already elsewhere. 'Did you get it all, Greg? Are you sure you've got everything you need? Great.'

She took my hand, absently. Her fingernails were long and immaculately red, sharp. 'Good luck, young man. You'll be in my prayers.'

Like the stranger on the plane, the journalist seemed confident of God's undivided attention.

My memories of the next week are confused. I'm never sure which are mine and which I've seen on TV. While I was in surgery, my father was filmed calling his parents from a hospital payphone. Telling them I still wasn't out, that it was taking longer than anybody had anticipated. He was red-eyed, bitten-nailed. To the end of her life, Peg was sure that they had spoken, insisted she wouldn't forget the worry in his voice. Except he hadn't called his mother until the next morning. Until I was safely in the recovery room. My father's worry was real, but the call was staged for the BBC.

In the end, redesigning my walk took eight hours, two teams of surgeons. One for each leg. The cameras were there, but I wasn't. I was kept under heavy sedation for almost a week. Before the pain, I remember a song. Richard Marx's 'Right Here Waiting' coming from a radio on the nurses' station. That song had been everywhere the previous summer. My mother had bought it for me in Our Price. She had grown tired of the double-denimed, stadium-filling angst long before I did. I wedged myself in the dust next to the stacking system, rewinding the tape. The singer made love sound painful, and painfully exciting. Finally, Mum had had enough, stormed down the stairs.

'Tell me it wasn't me. I've never liked this sappy-crappy MOR bullshit—'

Now I felt her hand, cool on my forehead. 'Hello, Peach-face, welcome back. At least this bloody song is good for something.'

In a chemistry lesson at school, we had been allowed to heat some granules of magnesium over a Bunsen flame. The chalky-grey pellets flared in the beaker. A sudden, searing, nauseous brightness. We were given safety goggles, told not to look directly at it. The pain felt like that. I was trapped inside it, felt like I lived in its eye.

It was there in the Get Well cards, gently deflating silver balloons, tangling with beeping machines. The new soft toys. A brown mouse, a butterfly stitched to its pink nose, that my parents had bought me while I was under.

The pain was there every time I tried to move, and every time I didn't. The journalists had crept in to say goodbye while I was out, before flying back to London to file their stories. They had left behind a mountain of goodwill from the hospital gift shop. Every surface that wasn't machines was toys, cards. Brightly stitched grins of encouragement. The whole circus, all the reporters, the cameramen, had become sudden friends. I realized I missed them. Our family had shrunk, contracted to three again.

A nurse wheeled in a TV, but Fred Flintstone's roars for Wilma made my broken legs spasm, sending jagged bolts of pain from my teeth to my bandaged toes. The TV was switched off, wheeled out again. I felt like I'd been removed too, somehow. Like I occupied the smallest corner of my body. The anti-spasmodics made me constipated. When a night nurse slipped a plastic bedpan under my hips, I cried with embarrassment, the regression of it. Seeing my immobilized legs when she pulled back the sheet, I cried again. They were tightly bound in what, ironically, looked like cricket pads. The white Velcro straps were heavily soiled, rusty with blood. We shared a bed, but my legs didn't look like they belonged to me any more.

Time sped up with pain, and slowed with drugs. Hours not

measured out in coffee spoons, but with plastic pill pots. I was hooked up to a self-administering morphine pump, but the beeping limit only blurred the afternoons. The busy pain-management specialist stood at the end of my bed. I couldn't have any more, no. He was sorry.

My parents had moved from the Ramada Inn into hospital accommodation, smiling at me in the widening gaps between consciousness and unconsciousness. My mother couldn't stand stillness for long, and was always marching round the block, to the cafeteria. Coming back with more mountains of things. Gifts I didn't need. One afternoon, I heard them talking outside my door.

'Christ, Charlie. He looks like he's been run over. I don't see how he's going to get up again.'

'Dr Gage knows what he's doing,' Dad said, but he didn't sound sure.

Looking at my tented feet, it seemed impossible.

Because American healthcare is so expensive, every Tylenol itemized, I was discharged on day nine. My mother was packing my parents' things, my father was signing me out, when Dr Gage smiled shyly round the door, knocking after the fact. Standing, as there was nowhere left to sit. 'That's quite the menagerie you've got there, Emmett.'

The doctor reached for a small brown bear. A gift I hadn't noticed before. He put it down again. I felt embarrassed, suddenly too old for toys.

'Good luck. Dr Neville in London will keep me updated, and we'll keep in touch. He'll send me some tapes when you're back on your feet.'

It seemed absurd that I ever would be. I had too many questions, but I didn't know how to ask them. So I just smiled and thanked him.

He looked out of the window at bleached grass, sun

bouncing off parked cars. 'You know, Emmett, the hard part really is now . . . the next few months. You have to be serious about the exercises; my work is nothing without yours. People prefer to talk about miracles. Why wouldn't they? Me too – miracles are easier. But actually miracles are usually sweat and tears. They take work.'

We went back to the Ramada for one night. Seeing me again, the manager didn't smile, pretended he hadn't. My parents parked me by the pool.

I still couldn't sit up past forty-five degrees, or in a normal car. My father rented a huge wheelchair, more like a wheeled stretcher, and a brown Dodge van. My parents made me as comfortable as they could on the back seat, buffering me with hired hospital pillows. I swallowed my screams when they moved me. Tried to pretend every mile of the long drive to my Uncle Charlie's in Pleasant Valley, Poughkeepsie wasn't agony.

Looking out the window at the passing cars, I saw a sporty blond couple in a sporty red convertible. They pulled ahead, sunglasses on, hair whipping round broad grins. They looked so free, so happy. Shiny with delight. They were singing along to the radio, a song I couldn't hear.

My father flew back to London. The bills wouldn't stop just because I had. The other Charlie was my mother's youngest brother, my favourite uncle. As my chair was too wide for his narrow house, he made me a bed in the den. Every morning, before he went to work, he would take my order, kneeling by my wheels, a pad in his hand, towel over his wrist. 'Hey, I ain't got all day, you know. Got plenty other customers besides youse.'

It was his best indignant Noo Yawk, and I laughed until pain stopped me. He would come back with pounds of chocolate, gummy worms. Piles of the latest Blockbuster blockbusters. I didn't care what we watched, as long as my uncle was there. We watched one tape, then the next, undiscerning, automatic as breath. When I couldn't sleep, woke up clenched and crying, my Aunt Marti had an idea. She put a tape recorder in the open kitchen window, recording the crickets singing in grass outside. Their nightly concerts, my aunt's kindness, lulled me when Tylenol and codeine couldn't.

I was finally able to sit up past forty-five degrees, and we flew back to London. Because I still needed to lie almost flat, we were given seats in First Class. It was a night flight. My mother handed me some painkillers. I woke to the sound of her knife rattling a pot of jam. 'Morning, Peach-fuzz. Look, real jam. Fortnum's, I think. Real china too.'

As we began our descent over a raining Slough, a steward knelt, fastened my seatbelt. 'Good morning, sir,' he smiled.

It was the same smile as the steward's on the flight from London. The same expensively engineered teeth. I hadn't brushed mine, and his immaculate courtesy made me remember my boxer shorts. They were the only things that would fit over my immobilizers. I knew I lowered the tone, spoiled the gilt-edged illusion for the whole cabin.

As if reading my mind, he tucked my blanket back in. 'It's a shame you missed it. When I fly, on my own vacation time, the airline will only spring for Business, never First. I've only worked First, never flown it. It's a real treat.'

I thanked him. Told him that if I was ever lucky enough to fly First again, I hoped I would be wearing trousers.

10

I Got Rhythm

Peg had made a cake to welcome me back home. It was the cake she always made – the only one, Dad said unkindly, she could make. A Victoria sponge, baked with Stork, not butter, sandwiched with a frugal layer of jam. It was the cake that marked every smiling arrival, its stale remains tinfoiled for every relieved departure. It sat on the table next to a tall stack of newspapers and a jug of irises, my mother's favourites.

'It all looks lovely, Peg, thank you,' she smiled, too brightly, as if she was a guest.

Grandpa Jim had wheeled me to the table. I no longer fitted under it so he kicked the chairs out of the way, parked me alongside. He hung on my handles, still puffing slightly from the effort of bringing me inside. When my parents had bought the house, the three shallow steps were no problem; I hadn't even considered them. Now they were a two-man operation.

Peg couldn't meet my eye, didn't sit. She hovered, worrying at the thin gold bands on her fingers. 'It was just something to do. While we were all waiting, you know. I wanted it to be nice for Em.'

Jim said, 'Your gran's been up with the birds. She's been baking all morning, all kinds.'

He put a hand on my shoulder. Its work-calloused weight was comforting. 'I tried to tell her it wasn't exactly a party. She wanted to get balloons 'n' all. But I told her you probably wouldn't be up to celebrating.'

131

Normally Peg sang all day long. Snatches of MGM musicals, Glenn Miller. The big-band numbers she and my grandfather had danced to, fallen in love to. Now she was silent. She still couldn't meet my eye. Wasn't at all sure that this beached, bony child was her Em. Neither was I. There is no time in hospitals. When you're in pain there is only the gap between one pill and the next. I'd filled them thinking about Peg, about home. They were the same thing to me. When my parents went to the family accommodation to sleep, I'd watch the thin blade of light under my door. Listen to the nurses' whispered conversations, urgent-squeaking shoes. When I couldn't sleep I would think of my grandma. I tried to remember what her hands felt like in mine, the weight of my feet on hers. I tried to picture her kitchen, the balding plush of her slippers. Our laughing, marionette waltzes.

Still standing, she smoothed her apron. Peg had a tea towel on her shoulder, like an epaulette. She folded it unnecessarily, keeping her hands busy. 'Don't force yourself, Em. It's probably revolting. Daft, really.'

Peg always did this. Disowning her many kindnesses in case they turned to disaster. I smiled up at her. 'It looks delicious, Peggy. Thank you.'

Pleased, she cut a large slice, pushing the plate over the table. Peg didn't cut one for herself. She never ate any of the cakes she made. She didn't have the stomach for it. When my father was fifteen, Peg and Jim had sold up, moving to Australia. They got cheap passage, were part of the Ten Pound Poms scheme, an immigration incentive. Peg's brother Nicholl had fallen in love with a girl from Queensland, was already living there. His letters to his older sister were filled with sunshine and space. He wrote that they'd always be welcome. Could stay with him and Jean until they found their feet. It was so much better than rainy terraces, grey Newcastle.

But my grandparents had barely put their cases down before Peg became seriously ill. An ulcer in her stomach had burst. She started haemorrhaging. A priest was called to administer the last rites. The surgeons saved her, but Peg lost most of her stomach. The four of them, Marie only seven, flew back to England as soon as the doctors declared Peg fit. It might have been only ten pounds each to go, but it cost them hundreds to return. Nicholl enclosed an ebonized boomerang with his next letter. She displayed it proudly, but Peg had lost her appetite for adventure, never went back. Afterwards, she still cooked for her family, but she seldom sat down with us. Her pleasure was in seeing us eat.

I'd glimpsed her scar once, accidentally, one half-term, when Peg had taken me swimming. It was ridged, hadn't silvered. The thin band cut her almost in half. I pictured a magician's assistant, her Saturday-night smile sent one way, legs the other.

Because she'd been so ill herself, I hoped Peg would understand that all my prescriptions – the two-hourly green pills, anti-spasmodics; the four-hourly Tylenol and codeine – made sugar bitter. The twice-daily iron pills made everything taste of tin.

'The girls at church are asking after you, wearing out their knees. They've given me cards for you, so many came while you were away. I've put them all upstairs.'

At sixty-eight Peg was the youngest of the stout-heeled girls in her congregation. The rest of them were lavender-rinsed, shampooed and set. They would never have admitted it, but they preferred bad news to good. Enjoyed swapping their sufferings almost as much as the sermon. Every time I went to Mass with Peg she would show me off. Her neighbours would whisper over my head, when they thought Peg wasn't listening, that it was such a shame. They filled my pockets with useful coins, useless medals. Gold, spray-painted blessings. I always left jingling.

'Tell them thank you,' I said.

Peg was still standing. She smiled tightly, knotting her fingers. 'I've got some jam tarts, pet, if that would be easier? You look like you could do with one. My Emmett always used to have space for a jam tart.'

Dad had started on the stack of newspapers, reading the interviews about us I didn't want to see. I read a headline: THE BRAVEST BOY IN THE WORLD. Underneath, there was a photo of me, standing between my parents, smiling. The boy felt like a stranger. Dad pushed aside the paper. Peg trusted the *Daily Mail* almost as much as the Holy See. If they had decided that 'brave' was the word for me, then she wouldn't allow me to argue.

'For Christ's sakes, Mam, they've only been here five minutes. Give him a chance, can't you. He's not dead, he's right there.'

Dad pointed at the proof, but I felt like Peg was right to use the past tense. 'Be good for Mam,' he said, bending to kiss me.

When he had worked for Young Lewisham my father had smelt of soap, the occasional weekend slap of Old Spice. Now he worked in the City, Dad smelt expensive, splashing himself liberally with Eau Sauvage. I loved the scent, but also associated it with the change in our fortunes, the fact we hardly saw him in the week.

'We'll be champion, won't we, Em?' Peg said brightly.

My father slammed the door behind him. I listened to the smart click of his heels receding, shocked by a sudden dislike. Normally I was thrilled to see Peg, but I realized I would have been happier to see her pick up her bag, go home.

What nobody had told me was that, a few weeks before we went to America, Dad had lost his job. He had moved from the

Bank of Nova Scotia when I started at Brindishe, and was working for another bank in Moorgate. His expected bonus was denied. My father had depended on that money. One Small Step had agreed to pay for my treatment, but Dad had agreed to cover my hospital costs. He took the bank to court, and lost. I never knew whether Jim and Peg had any idea that he was meeting with headhunters rather than going to work. My father never let his smile slip in front of me. He still smelt like success, so I had no clue.

Even though we'd been in the new house for over a year, most of our pictures were still stacked against the walls. My mother had only hung one. A large lithograph of a Matisse cut-out, *La Tristesse du Roi*. The print had been a present from my father not long after they had left the squat, had walls of their own. Living around it, I had never really seen it. Now I stared at it for hours. The picture was a window into a world I wanted to join. I convinced myself I could almost hear the music. The slap and spin of the bass, smoky late-night laughter. The colours seemed anything but sad. Sharp and vivid, so much louder than my quiet, drugged days.

To start with, I liked looking at the Matisse. It seemed to promise so much. But as the weeks passed me by, I tried not to notice it. The scene began to make me feel trapped, tight in my skin. Pressed against the walls. It felt impossible, ridiculous, that I'd ever be part of the noise again.

The five of us lived the same day for three months. My parents went to work, and I watched the grass grow. But Peg's songs came back. I would hear her singing from upstairs, cheerful snatches of 'The Flat Foot Floogie', our favourite Slim and Slam, or 'A Couple of Swells' from *Easter Parade*, glad to be useful again.

Washing my hair in the garden one sunny morning, Peg

lathered Johnson's Baby Shampoo, raking the suds with her nails. I think she enjoyed my new dependence on her. Made a game of the babyish regression. The invalid-sweet tea she brought me on the hour meant she was always running in with the pee bottle. Before flushing it down the toilet she would examine the pale liquid, a tea towel over her wrist like a wine waiter at a five-star hotel. She would wink, declaring it a very fine vintage. Not to worry, it wasn't anything she hadn't seen before. She didn't mind. But I minded. I hated the game but needed her help, had no choice but to play along. Now, kneeling on the patio, Peg filled another bowl, rinsing again. Drying my hair, she said, 'I don't know why you had to mess on, truly I don't. You could walk, Em . . . I saw it that day, on the way back from church, and now you can't. Just look at you – you've really sliced yourself up. I'm sorry, Em, but I can't see how it's going to work. It's been ages . . . you're so ill still.'

She went on, towelling roughly. 'You had such lovely hair when you were a baby. Lovely, long blond curls. The first time your mother attacked it, it was never the same. Grew back just an ordinary brown.'

I snapped, pushing her off. The months of waiting, simmering, suddenly boiling over. 'I'm not ill, Peggy. It would have gone dark anyway. That's just what happens. I'm not going to be in this forever. And without the operation, I would have been— At least this way I've got a choice. You always told me I could do anything. But you're wrong. You didn't mean to, but it's a lie. I can't do everything. All I ever wanted was to be ordinary, like everybody else . . . you, and Dad . . . and I'm just not. I'm lonely, even with you.'

My legs were still in their blood-rusted immobilizers. They were stained with months of use, the metal bones working their way out of frayed channels. I hated them. Hated my new legs, the fact that other people could read my story on a nodding commuter train, turn the page and leave it behind on the seat. My legs and I had never been friends, were acquaintances at best. Now we weren't even on speaking terms. I hit them, hard, watching Peg's face crumple. The pain flared, jumping. I suddenly wanted to smash them.

'Don't! Don't do that, pet. Please, you'll hurt yourself.' Peg flushed, her eyes large behind smeared lenses. She turned away. 'Don't, now. What do I know? Your dad wouldn't have let you do it if he didn't think it was for the best. Ignore me, I'm just a silly old woman. I'm sure you're right, Em.'

She offered me a careful smile, as unconvinced as I was.

In the afternoons Peg would finally let herself sit. Jim would disappear upstairs to sleep off his lunch, and Peg would draw the curtains. She would pull up a chair next to my wheels, smiling. 'It's better than the pictures, this, isn't it, Em?'

I would smile back, agree. I would try not to think of Ben, our Saturdays at the ABC, the musty almost-darkness. It wasn't better than that, but I was grateful for the game. We watched all of Peg's favourites again. *Mrs. Miniver, Top Hat.* Everything starring Ava Gardner, who Peg declared the most beautiful woman ever born. Movies were better, realer to my grandma than anything else. Deities she didn't fear, could actually see.

One afternoon, after we had watched *Gone with the Wind,* she told me about the first time she'd seen it. Just sixteen, Peg went with her younger sister Olive to the Odeon in Newcastle. They had sat in the third tier, the nosebleed seats, for 1/6. A flask of cold tea between them, sandwiches from home. They had gone again the next Saturday, had argued all the way back to Walker over who would be the first to get to Hollywood. Who would be the first to marry Clark Gable.

The following day we watched *An American in Paris.* I was silent until the credits rolled. It wasn't just that he was beautiful, wasn't just Gene Kelly's smooth Technicolor swagger that moved me. His smile was the smile of a man on the street. He wasn't a polished black-and-white god like Astaire, something chilly and unreachable. If I couldn't dance like that, then I might at least meet a man who could. A man who would smile at me like that. Peg tapped her foot, reaching for her forgotten tea. She grimaced slightly, putting it down again. I thought of Ben, and wondered what he was doing. As if reading my thoughts, Peg asked, 'Whatever happened to that nice boy you were so friendly with? I was half-expecting to see him, that he'd visit.'

I looked at my hands. 'He's still nice, Peg. I expect he's on holiday with his parents . . . busy. We go to different schools, and I'm not singing any more, so . . .' I let the word stretch, to cover what I couldn't say.

'Well, it's probably for the best. You should mix with more than one at your age . . . it isn't healthy. Is that lovely Joanna still your girlfriend?'

For Ben I had been a way station. A stop on the road to a shiny normality. I tried to picture him older, with a girlfriend, but couldn't. He was suddenly the only person I wanted to see. Our Saturdays were just that. He had grown up. Grown away from me. I knew I needed to do the same. Peg smiled, stood. She kicked out her slippered feet, stretching the tea towel in both hands, as if it were a stripper's glove:

> 'I got rhythm
> I got music
> I got my gal
> Who could ask for anything more?'

I watched her, stinging. Love was for Gene Kelly and Leslie Caron. Love was for Jim and Peg, Mum and Dad. I would have to get used to never being able to dance, now I was too big to balance on my grandma's toes. I would have to get used to being alone.

'Sit down, Peg, please. Please.'

She stopped, her smile clicking off like a light, unsure of what she'd done. Peg sat down again. We were silent a long time. Then she said, 'You know, I always wanted to be a dancer. I was quite good-looking when I was a girl, if you can believe that. I had red hair, like Maureen O'Hara. Good legs. Beautiful hands too. I wanted it so much I could taste it. But I had to help my mother. I sometimes think God stamped "worker" on my foot the minute the cord was cut . . . I couldn't afford to dream. I got a place at the local grammar, but my mother worried about finding the money for the uniform. There was always too much to do. Your Grandpa Jim was a good dancer, light on his feet for a big man. So I married him instead. It hasn't been bad, not at all. But what I'm trying to say is . . . most things don't turn out the way you hope they will. I just don't want you to be disappointed, Em, that's all.'

In late August I was invited to a gala screening of *My Left Foot*. The film was being shown at the Curzon Mayfair, a benefit for One Small Step. When Mike, the chief executive of the charity, rang to tell my parents, he had expected them to be delighted. But my dad was worried. I was able to sit up, but still had casts on my feet, was still in a wheelchair. The screen had no lift, so surely it was impossible? After ten minutes Mike rang back. It was important that I was there; they'd just have to manage it, would have to carry me and my wheelchair up the stairs.

Peg clapped her hands when I told her. A real premiere, in front of a real princess. That night I couldn't sleep, kept imagining being dropped, my new legs shattering to shards. Having to smile for the cameras while gathering up the bits.

His old job meant my father had a new set of evening

clothes. My mother went to Harrods to buy a dress. Dad had rung round all the hire shops in London, but the weekend before the screening I still had nothing. At four that Saturday, we drove up to Moss Bros. in Covent Garden. The store was brightly lit, crowded. The brass and mahogany trying to suggest an expensive, bespoke atmosphere. An exclusive, button-backed clubbiness, even though all the suits were off-the-peg. After so many weeks at home I felt brittle, thin-skinned. The shop was deafening. Looking at the rows of suits, loud silk ties, I wanted to disappear, was aware of the shoppers looking past me. Widening their paths so as not to see me. My worn blanket, fibreglass casts were nothing to aspire to. A woman with blonde hair, discreet gold earrings, flashed me a discreet, apologetic smile. She picked up her bags, straightening. There were suddenly worse things than work on Monday.

A man stepped from behind the counter. He was pink-faced, with a pink tie. A tape measure round his neck. The sales assistant ignored me, talking to my father. 'Are you the gentleman I spoke to on the phone? He looks like a thirty-two short, and the smallest tux we carry is a thirty-six regular, but I'll have a look for you. When do you need it by?'

I saw my dad deciding not to tell the stranger that I was right there. That he should talk to me instead. He just smiled. 'Tomorrow night.'

The man went off on soundless feet. He ducked behind a baize curtain at the back of the shop, returning minutes later with an armful of black jackets. This time he smiled straight at me. I saw he was young, handsome, perhaps only a few years older. 'I've brought you some of the smallest. You're going to be sitting down, right, so bigger is probably better anyway. If the trousers won't fit over your casts, we can alter them, open the side seams. If we find one that fits, you can come in and pick it up tomorrow morning.'

At the till, my father thanked him again, his voice tight. When he handed over his card the man lowered his voice, told us it wasn't necessary. It was his pleasure, he said, absolutely.

There was a china dish of silk knots, cufflinks, next to the register. The man came round the counter, kneeling to tuck the tiny bar-bells into my pocket. It was kind, but I didn't have any shirts that needed links. He stood, straightening his arrow creases. I saw him decide I was ill. That the suit might be the first, the last black tie I ever wore. He held the door open, helped my father with my wheels. 'Have a good time tomorrow, OK?'

'OK,' I agreed, returning his smile.

My mother had to cut the trousers further to get them over my casts. Moss Bros. wouldn't accept them back now. Before my operation the plaster technician had asked me what colour I had chosen. I told him I'd never had a choice before, that the NHS only did one colour. The technician had grinned, incredulous. This was America – didn't I know I could have anything I wanted? Waiting in the receiving line at the Curzon Mayfair, I felt like Christmas in August, regretted my one red foot, the other green.

'All right, Peach?' my mother whispered.

'Yes, Mum,' I answered, not looking.

When I was at Charlton Park we had all been given a silver-plated spoon to commemorate the wedding of Prince Charles and Lady Diana. I'd loved the gift. The satin-lined box, dual portraits of the couple stamped on the metal. Mum had scoffed, called them bloody parasites, throwing it into the sink. But we had still watched the ceremony at a neighbour's. The adults had got drunk on supermarket champagne, toasting the coming revolution. The kids had sat under the table, felt-tipping their parents' shins. Watching the royal coach arrive on the kitchen portable, I was round-eyed with the spectacle. Amazed that all the golden adulation, thousands of flag-waving subjects, could fit on to the tiny screen. I wanted to be a subject too. Wanted to be in the noise, squashed tight against the barrier. Nothing that made people light up like that could be as bad as my mother said. When Diana started up the stairs, smiling shyly from under yards of crumpled silk, the weight of the fairy tale, I turned to my friend Grace, telling her that I was going to be a princess one day. She laughed sharply. 'Silly! Everybody knows boys can't be princesses, only girls. I'm going to be one, but you can't.'

'Awful dress,' spat my mother, over our heads.

'Who cares what they wear?' said Dad. 'They're bloody idiots. Haven't got a brain cell between them.'

He drained his glass. Smiling, red-faced, round the room.

When we got home I had hidden the spoon right at the back of the cutlery drawer, forgotten it. Now we were going to meet a real princess. I glanced at my mother, stiff in green silk, new gold, and hoped she would smile. The woman next to me had roses to give. I was holding two programmes. On the front was a photograph of Daniel Day-Lewis as Christy Brown. The back cover was a picture of me, the moon rising over my shoulder, nearly naked in the Gait Lab. The real Daniel Day-Lewis stood against the opposite wall. Tall, and more than beautiful. An alien visiting from a different atmosphere.

He gave me a diffident smile, but didn't speak, come over. I was suddenly angry. A wheelchair was just a prop to him. He had been able to walk away, to leave it behind, as soon as the director yelled, 'Cut.' He had no real idea what Christy's life had been, or mine was now. A performance, however well-intentioned, Oscar-winning, was just that. Playing, dressing up. Looking at him, I didn't envy his starry privilege, Hollywood money. I just wanted to be able to leave my chair behind as easily. To walk up the stairs, hands in pockets. I wanted the opportunity to be somebody else.

There was a sudden white-blindness of cameras. Shouts from outside. Then there she was. Princess Alexandra knelt down, smiling kindly. I handed her the programmes, shook the offered hand. Her hair was swept up, complicated with diamonds. 'But have you got one?' she asked.

'Not yet,' I answered.

'Well, I think you'd better have mine, then.' The princess gestured to her husband, standing behind her. He looked too hot, but resigned, in his evening suit. 'We can share.'

'But I think I'm supposed to give both to you.'

'That's all right,' she smiled. 'You've given it to me already. I'll have his.'

'She can do as she likes, always does,' he muttered, laughing.

Before moving up the line, the princess said, 'We've both read about you in the papers . . . I think you're very brave. Does it still hurt?'

'Not really. Not any more,' I lied.

Later, I watched the film again. I don't remember much about the screening, except the sweating effort of getting my wheelchair up the narrow stairs. Men I didn't know telling me they wouldn't drop me, their faces shining. I held my breath, shut my eyes, knowing that every step up was another back down.

II

The Muscular System

A month after the screening of *My Left Foot* I finally saw my new legs. I went back to Guy's Outpatients to get the stitches out. Dr Neville was already waiting for us in reception. We followed him down a brightly lit corridor, my father pushing my chair. Pulling a curtain round the narrow couch, the doctor smiled. 'I'll be as gentle as I can, but it'll probably feel quite uncomfortable. You'll want a good bath afterwards. If you lie back, we'll get the casts off first. Then we'll see . . .'

There wasn't really room for four. My parents stood awkwardly just inside the curtain. I looked at the ceiling, the tiny fissures in the plaster, to avoid their smiles. We had smiled for the cameras together, we had gone to America together, but this felt private. That morning, singing round the kitchen, Peg had asked, 'It sort of feels like Christmas, doesn't it, Em? Are you excited, pet?'

I had agreed that I was.

Dr Neville knelt, plugging something in, a saw. He switched it on. The low whine made me flinch. The doctor smiled again. In the yellow buzzing overhead light he looked older, his face thinner than when I'd last seen him on the morning of my operation. He had hovered at the side of the hospital bed, wished me luck, though he was sure I wouldn't need it. A kind man, he had already flown back to England by the time I was brought round.

'This can't cut you, Emmett. It'll get hot, but that's all. Look,

I'll show you.' He pressed the buzzing silver blade to his palm. For a second I still expected blood, but there was none. Dr Neville snapped on a pair of gloves from a dispenser on the wall.

'See, Em, it's perfectly safe,' said Dad.

'Magic,' the doctor agreed.

Over his shoulder I noticed a poster, THE MUSCULAR SYSTEM. It showed a flayed man, his direct blue stare made alarming by his profound nakedness, the raw, red striations. He raised his thumb as though hailing a taxi, as though he had slept through his alarm, left his skin hanging on a hallway hook in the rush. He looked a monster without it. It was a shock to realize that under my thin skin I must look like him too.

'Good job, Emmett, good job,' smiled Dad, a nervous, nasal imitation of the 24-hour cheer of the Newington nurses.

'Oh, stop it, Charlie!' my mother snapped.

The saw carried on buzzing, didn't hurt. I didn't want to look. Didn't know how I was supposed to feel. Dr Neville prised the casts off. 'D'you want to keep them, Emmett?' he said. 'Some patients like to.'

'Yes, yes please,' said my father.

'No,' I said.

'They'll be pretty revolting by now,' said my mother.

'If you could just sit up for me, swing your legs over the side, I'll help you get your trousers off.'

I did as I was told. My feet felt light, like they weren't anything to do with me. Barely tethered, impatient to float.

For some reason I thought of John. Apart from Tom, John was my best friend at school. Slight and bookish, he always had a note from his mother excusing him from games because of a year-round cold. He wore Metallica T-shirts under his regulation white cotton, his hair always nudging insolently at his collar. John was forever losing house points for the state of his shoes, but didn't care. He had drawn an anarchist's 'A' on to his schoolbag even though he lived in leafy affluence, a commuter-belt mansion in Bromley.

On my last day in class, he had given me a card. A sad-eyed bear, holding a blue balloon. GET WELL SOON it said. Until I saw the card, I had no idea I was ill. Inside, under his name, John had drawn a sketch of my crutches, with one snapped in half. He had written, 'You won't be needing these any more.'

I'd packed the card in my carry-on. Half-watching the inflight movie, I had read the message again. The film was an unfunny police comedy, and instead of laughing, I found myself crying at 35,000 feet. My mother gave me a tissue, but didn't ask why I needed it. She already understood how much I wanted John's drawing to be prophetic, a miracle.

'If you could just pop your trousers off for me . . .'

'I'll help you, son.' Dad pulled down my grey jogging bottoms. The only trousers that would fit over the casts, the only trousers soft enough.

I felt boneless, absently acquiescent. Dr Neville started to peel off the dressings. I dared myself to look. The sutures were nylon, bright blue zigzags on my knees, my thighs, my ankles. There was blood, dark, where each stitch met the next, as if they were struggling to contain it. I ran my finger along an incision just where my knees bent. It felt sharp, tender. I tried to remember what my legs had looked like, to picture the bones under my skin. The pins and metal plates that held me together, held me up. I didn't know how to feel. They were a stranger's legs, not mine. My father looked horrified, but was trying to disown it with a grin. I thought I looked like an accident, an unplanned emergency. A fingers-crossed stitching-together.

'Looks good, Em. Really good.' Dad grinned, gave me a more doubtful thumbs-up.

'It looks as though they've healed nicely,' said the medic. 'How does it feel?'

'Great,' I said. 'Thank you, doctor.'

The day he had taped me, Dr Neville had asked me to call him Brian, just Brian. I tried, but to me doctors, however kind they were, had too much power for casualness, so it never stuck.

'It'll look a lot better, Peach, when you've had a wash, got all the blood off.'

My mother kept a framed photo on her side of my parents' bed. A black-and-white picture of Luke, Emily and me. We must've been about five, the three of us naked in the garden on a blue-sweltering afternoon. Mum had turned the hose on to cool us down. Emily was snapped mid-scream. Luke stood, too young yet for shame, smiling at his sister. I had my back to the camera, grinning over my shoulder. Perhaps she kept it because, sat down, I looked like any other child.

Eyeing my legs – the new scars, red, angry, above my knees – I saw it wouldn't ever be possible to fool myself again.

Dr Neville had me lie on my side while he cut the stitches on my hips. I closed my eyes, counted to a hundred, then started again. He worked quickly, but I still winced at every snip and pull. I felt like I was being undone, that I might spill. Turning on to my front so he could finish, I felt fragile as stunt-glass.

'All done.' Dr Neville leant over me, smiling cautiously. 'They've really done a good job, very neat. They'll fade nicely. You probably won't even notice in a couple of months.'

I smiled back, hoping it was wide enough. What he wanted. Over his shoulder I saw the pile of stitches. Dried blood on a green paper towel. I watched my father make a careful package of the towel, put it in a suit pocket.

When we got home, Dad carried me straight upstairs.

'There now, that's better,' said Peg. She was kneeling on the bathroom tiles, one arm in the water, testing the temperature with her elbow, as if I was a baby. Her glasses momentarily blind with steam.

My mother hovered in the doorway. 'Try not to be quite so feeble, Em. You can run your own bath.' She looked at Peg. 'He'll have to get used to doing things for himself again.'

I took off my trousers, looking at the opposite wall – the striped seam in the wallpaper, just starting to loosen – and unbuttoned my shirt. Peg tugged at a sleeve, still wanting to help. I covered my sudden nakedness with a hand, wanting them both to go.

'Don't be daft, pet. It's nothing I haven't seen a million times. Boys and their toys . . . Such idiots, aren't they, Fran?'

My mother didn't answer. Instead, she lifted my legs, lowering them gently into the water. It was too hot, but I didn't care. 'We'll leave you, Em,' she smiled, pushing Peg out in front of her, closing the door.

The water felt good, the heat numbing my legs. I shut my eyes. Because I was so filthy, had been washing with a bowl and flannel for months, the tall bubbles dissolved almost instantly. Daring myself to look, it seemed like there wasn't an inch of skin that hadn't been touched. Tender filaments at my knees. Deep, still-bruised channels on my hips. Tight pink zippers ran up my ankles; I felt them pulling at the backs of my knees. I thought of all the hands I'd passed through. All the doctors, all the surgeons. Two teams, eight hours. All the appointments, waiting rooms. All the smiles.

Looking at my floating legs, I thought of school, swimming lessons. Swimming was the only sport I was required to join. First period every Wednesday. I hated the changing room's slippery tiles, the risk of falling. The sour smell of forgotten trunks, Daktarin foot powder. I hated having to get undressed. The loud, towel-flicking confidence of my classmates. But I loved Tom. Even though we were the same age he might have been a different species. He was the captain of the First XV, and whenever our house was playing I would watch from the wall. Changing, he always took the peg next to mine, but I was always careful to keep my eyes fixed to the floor. Careful not to look too long at his broad-shouldered grin, in case he found me out. Tom always waited for me, carried my bag whether rostered to or not.

In the first term of the second year, my classmates had to enlist in the Combined Cadet Force. Thursday afternoons were now for playing soldiers. A few boys were conscientious objectors, preferring to help the local elderly with their lawns, shopping. But most were eager to learn to shoot. When it came to me, Mr Lawrence smiled. On Thursdays he was a major as well as a master. He told me: as I couldn't walk, how could I be expected to aim a gun? Of course, Tom decided to join the army. Everybody knew the navy was full of poofs.

I didn't mind sitting out my friends' war games, thought twelve-year-old soldiers ridiculous. If I'd had the choice I would have mowed lawns. I hated mud. The greasy, shit-smelling camouflage sticks they painted their faces with. But those manoeuvres were another reminder of just how different I was. A difficult fit for the school's clipped, masculine atmosphere. I kept expecting to be bullied, but never was. It wouldn't have been fair play, not sporting, to pick on the cripple.

If you were unlucky enough that your birthday fell on a schoolday, you'd be stripped, your trousers run round the rugby pitch. When you joined the school from outside, you had your tie cut. If you'd come from the prep school there could be other, more serious losses. Smaller boys were hoisted on to shoulders of bigger ones and 'posted' against the iron railings behind the physics lab. My friend Sam was posted so hard that he had to have a testicle removed. His mother removed him from the school soon after that. The boys responsible were sorry. It was only a joke. They were suspended, but allowed to stay.

None of these rituals applied to me. I had joined from a state school, so of course I was glad to keep both balls. Glad to be exempt. Pleased with my new friends. But part of me wanted to be included in the louder, rowdier risks. Most boys were kind, helpful, because it was expected of them. I sat quietly. Pretended to read. I knew I wasn't prized, because I couldn't shoot, couldn't run. I understood the school didn't really know what to do with me. On Thursdays, while Tom played at killing, I sat in the house library. Kept safe, carefully apart.

Tom was neither bullied nor a bully. He fitted in everywhere. I envied him his cheerful belonging, his smiling sense that the world was his. Legs that carried him wherever he wanted to go. The silver cups he won so easily. I always wanted to know what his muddy exhilaration felt like. Even though Dr Gage had spoken of improvement, not miracles, I hadn't wanted to listen. I spent the hours in hospital hoping I might still be able to grab that freedom for myself.

Tom had written me letters while I was away. Four, each two sides of blue Basildon Bond. He had a careful hand, told me careful, dull news of school. I was moved by them, kept them for years, long after I'd thrown out the yellowing newspapers. Even after Tom had let slip that they were an unofficial home-work assignment. A kind suggestion of Mr Collin's that nobody else had followed.

Sat in the cooling bathwater, thick with shed skin, brown-floating clots of dried blood, I cried. Looking at the awful soup, I tried to swallow the sound, worrying that Peg was still out-side, that she might hear. I didn't want to be comforted. Finally understood that I was no miracle. I might learn to walk again, but I'd always be balancing on my hands.

12

New Shoes

I went back to school at the end of October. The night before, I watched my father polishing his shoes. He sat cross-legged on the hall tiles, his brushes, tight tins of Kiwi Parade Gloss Black, spread on newspaper. I loved to watch him, loved the weekend ritual. The tar-sweet smell of the polish, busy rhythm of his brush. Dad had never taught me how to do it, because my shoes never lasted long enough to need shining. We still bought them in bulk from the discount shop on the high street. All the stock permanently on sale, the windows full of handwritten neon stars. White wire bins of mismatched carpet slippers on the pavement outside. My father took such good care of his office Oxfords that they hardly ever needed replacing. When they were finally beyond repair, new ones came from Jermyn Street. Privately, I hoped that my new legs would mean new shoes, that I'd be able to make them last.

He put down the shoe he'd been buffing. 'You'll want to look smart tomorrow, Em, so shall I give yours a polish?'

I hadn't worn shoes in months. 'I don't know where they are,' I lied.

Dad wiped his fingers on an old T-shirt. A souvenir of an inter-bank triathlon. When it had become too scruffy, even for sleep, it had been saved for polishing. He pushed past me up the stairs, coming back down a moment later, a shoe in each hand.

'Christ, Emmett! Why didn't you tell me these were

knackered? They're useless, totally fucked. You can't wear them, you'll fall.'

He put a finger through one of the holes, wiggling it, incredulous, before letting both shoes drop. Dad looked at his watch. It was a Sunday. Peg was at evening Mass, but everything apart from St Saviour's would be shut.

'You'll just have to borrow some of mine . . . double your socks. It's a big day tomorrow. We can't have the *Daily Mail* saying you look like a hobo.' He softened again, a hand in my hair.

'I'm sorry,' I said.

I didn't want to think about how big the day was. For months of quiet days, I'd looked forward to the noise. Now it was only hours away, it felt safer to stay in bed. To watch *Top Hat* with Peg for the hundredth time, eat KitKats.

I was awake before the alarm, watching for the day to edge under the blinds. Because the school building had changed less than I hoped I had, the crowded flights of stairs were still impossible. So while I healed, my teachers had agreed to carry me. I lay in the dark, worrying that they'd drop me. Worrying that their kindness would make me even more conspicuous.

I had the uniform, knew all the words to the school song, but I still didn't fit, couldn't conform. Privately I felt I was going backwards, felt like an infant. Anxious that my reversal would mean pity. That my friends – most hadn't seen me for months – would walk away, finally bored of the difference between us. The Friday games I still had to sit out. No thirteen-year-old wants to be carried by their teacher. But at least I wouldn't have to worry about chasing bells.

The clock-radio glowed five. Just before six, there was a soft knock at the door. A softer smile round it. I clicked on the bedside light. Peg came in. She was wearing Jim's dressing gown, one of his leather-elbowed cardigans over it. The pockets hung past her knees. It made her look like a child playing at adulthood, rummaging through the dressing-up box. She held a mug of tea in both hands. Without her glasses, her eyes looked smaller, tentative. 'Morning, pet, I thought you might need this. Are you awake?'

'No, I'm dreaming,' I smiled.

Peg smiled back, careful. There were steel grips in her night-time curls. She sat on the very edge of my bed, avoiding my legs, balancing the tea on sharp knees.

'How'd you sleep, Peggy?'

'Oh, champion, just champion, Em. Beautifully.'

Peg looked past me to the window, putting the mug on the floor beside her. She shook her head, swallowing a quiet laugh. 'Why do we do that, Em . . . lie like that? I didn't sleep a wink. Your grandpa was snoring as soon as I turned out the light; he could sleep on a bed of nails, that man. He was really sawing logs last night – I'm surprised you didn't hear him, I was worried he'd wake the whole house. And of course I was worried about you. D'you not think it's too soon, pet?'

I did. Learning to walk for a second time had been so much harder than the first. Dr Gage had been right to warn me that miracles were actually sweat. The moment my stitches were out my father had bought me a bike, but these new wheels were much less fun, less freeing, than my Budgie had been. He had set up the exercise bike next to the French doors, so that I'd have a view of the trees. The green illusion of speed. Adjusting the saddle, he had smiled, saying, 'This way it'll almost be like you're cycling through the country.'

I pretended absorption in the television, bit my tongue. I hated the new bike before I'd sat on it, and it shocked me how much I thought I hated my father then. I understand now that what I really hated was the fact he had a new racer in the hall. A silver-framed, ten-speed Cosworth. Legs that could carry him as far and as fast as he wanted. The only silver frame I was wheeling was my Rollator. An adult version of the one I'd first needed at Charlton Park. Practising on it, I felt both one hundred, and one.

I was supposed to cycle a mile a day, but didn't. It was a fight to get me to do a few yards. I watched the red numbers tick grudgingly upwards, scowling at the unchanging view. Most evenings ended in screaming matches, tears. The only power I felt I had was to refuse. My father would redden, ball his fists. 'I just don't understand it, Em, after all your effort . . . after ours. It wasn't just you, you know, who chose this. I don't understand why you'd want to chuck it all away.'

'That's right,' I'd snap. 'You don't . . . You can't . . .'

I would stare past him into the garden. Dad would give up. Retreating to the top of the house, his office. Slamming the door. And the next day we would start again.

As well as the stationary bike, there was daily physiotherapy with an easy-smiling Scottish woman called Jane. Jane had come with us to America to learn how to handle my new legs directly from the surgeon who had built them. Every Monday morning, Wednesday afternoon, Peg would wheel me the short distance to the hospital for a walking lesson. The Physiotherapy Department was in a separate annexe. A squat, concrete building with a single line of steel-framed windows, hard against the flat roof. An ugly, prosaic place that didn't look like it had witnessed many miracles.

Peg made sure we were always early, but however eager she was, Jane was always earlier. She was patient, with a firm, no-nonsense manner that matched her no-nonsense haircut.

Jane spent hours, months on me, gladly, but I hated every minute, hated having to need her. She would pull me out of my chair, guiding my hands to the parallel bars. There was a mirror at one end. I always preferred walking away from my reflection rather than towards it. I walked stiffly up and back, ten or twenty times, while Jane pressed for just one more. Peg grinned encouragement, telling me I looked like a dancer at the barre. A suggestion so absurd it was as close as my grandma ever came to cruelty. I bit my tongue.

It was Jane's goal that I should walk into school on my crutches. It would make for a better photo, she said. A better story. But my hands had softened without the daily effort of holding me up. And I still didn't trust my legs. We were still strangers.

One day, wheeling home from a lesson, Peg turned me right rather than left. I knew where she was headed without having to ask. It was a sunny, late-August afternoon, the market on the high street busy. People weaved between the stalls, stale cardboard rubbish, green AstroTurf. Dusty gluts of strawberries. The traders with their three-for-a-pound smiles. The church was quiet after the noise of the street. Peg pushed me between the deserted pews. I watched her bend before the altar, rummage in her bag for an offering, the price of a candle. Giving it to me. Sitting down, I couldn't reach the slot. Peg took the coin, lit the candle. I remember asking the God I didn't believe in, not even for Peg, to help me.

The Lord knew I couldn't dance without her, but I only wanted to walk. On the way out, a woman was coming in. She held the door for us, was wearing a blue sundress, her free hand full of shopping. She followed us back out, balancing the bag between sandalled feet, tanned toes. The woman had a smiling gap between her front teeth. 'Are you the boy in the papers?'

Peg nodded proudly that I was, before I'd decided to admit it.

The stranger knelt, reaching for my hand. 'What a shame it didn't work, but I'll pray for you. What's your name again?'

'Don't trouble,' Peg said crisply, wheeling me away.

On the first day back, it had rained overnight, was still trying. The pavement slick. I was suddenly glad of my frame in the boot. As we turned into the school drive, my mother straightened. 'Christ, Charlie, look at all this.'

The railings were tight with jostling, black-blazered boys, the drive double-parked with outside-broadcast vans. ITV and ITN, the BBC. Even Newsroom South East had got up early. For a moment I thought journalists had come because a famous old boy had agreed to give a speech, plant a tree. When I saw John's smile from the top of the front steps, I remembered and felt sick. The headmaster stood next to him. He had had his hair cut for the cameras, was wearing his graduation gown. My borrowed shoes, even with two pairs of socks, felt loose. I imagined catching my foot, landing hard.

'Shit,' said Dad under his breath.

Mum wiped the condensation from the inside of the car window, as if trying to clear everybody away. I was sat next to her on the back seat, grateful for her other hand. 'Shall we keep driving, Peach-face? Just keep going?'

I looked at her. She was wearing a new suit. Her hair was new too. Discreetly, expensively blonde. There was a brooch pinned to her lapel. A gold leaf, turning as it fell. A single large sapphire, imitation dew on the stem. It was so different from her usual cheerful paste, the plastic junk-shop beads, protest badges.

Just before we went to America my mother had got a new job. Now she caught, or more often missed, the 8.30 to Charing Cross every day. The role was something vague in sales. All she would tell me about it was that the other people seemed nice. A million miles from anything she'd planned, but her microbiology degree meant either testing soil samples in the Fens or spending six months of every twelve on a remote research station, Signy Island in the Antarctic. The rest of the crew were all men. She would have to fly over eight thousand miles for under twelve thousand pounds. My father and I would have to stay behind in London. It would be freezing, too cold even for her.

Fran declined, the degree certificate disappearing from her bedroom wall.

A month after starting the new job she got the gold leaf as a reward for exceeding her targets. A gift, but also a shiny incentive. A month after that, my mother folded her easel into the cupboard under the stairs. I missed her paintings, missed the quick midnight-charcoal sketches I used to find on my pillow. Now the only thing she painted was her face; it was a corporate requirement. I squeezed her hand, trying to remember her out-at-the-knee men's 501s, rubber-band ponytail. The casual slap of her sandals. My name, Peach, was the only thing I recognized about the three of us. I hated the name now, felt I'd outgrown it. Usually I brushed off her affection, embarrassed. But looking at the crowd, so many strangers, I was glad.

'Please,' I answered.

My father unclipped his belt, turning to smile at me. 'You know we can't, son. We can't keep everybody waiting.'

'We can do what we bloody like. They're all waiting for Emmett anyway,' my mother hissed.

Dad's tie was too tight under a pinkly shaved chin. He only used to have one, a Christmas present from his father; Jim was never seen without one, even when digging his garden. Now Dad had racks of bright silk. Polka dots, stripes, spares and pocket squares, for every day of the week. I missed the father who went to work in jeans. Who always had time. Looking at him, the change felt like my fault.

'You've got toast in your teeth, Charlie.' Mum smiled, not kind.

'Thanks,' he said, not thankful, scraping at a front tooth with a fingernail.

Dad lifted my Rollator from the boot, wheeling it round to the passenger door. The moment he did, the cameras started clicking. If I wasn't quite the miracle the journalists expected, they were all too polite to say anything.

'I've got you, son. Can you just give the lad some space please, give us some room? I'll just get him settled, and then you can have your pictures, OK.'

I made my way stiffly to the bottom of the steps. The head-master, realizing he couldn't shake mine, put a proprietorial hand on my shoulder. He shook my father's as though they regularly played golf, but I was sure he had had to ask the school secretary Dad's name. He ignored my mother, except when the cameras were rolling. We arrived four times, for four different crews. Smiling to order, until the smiles started to slip down our chins. I followed the shouted instructions, grateful to see Nina, her quick thumbs-up in the noise. After what felt like hours, Dad wheeled me round the side entrance to the chapel, for interviews.

The reporter from ITN was more used to war zones than schoolboys. Keeping his cool while the bombs were dropping. David had come with us to America, flown home before I woke up. He left behind an autographed picture of the female anchor on *News at Ten*, a ceiling full of balloons. When he wasn't on camera he had a soft voice, a diffident manner. A genuine smile that meant I never felt like a job.

'Thanks for the picture,' I said. 'The balloons.'

'Oh, that's quite all right, Emmett, you're welcome. Nobody wants my face, Fiona is much more popular.'

Towards the end of the interview, David said, 'You must be so glad to be back. Has it all been worth it?'

It was the first time anybody had asked the question. At that moment I didn't think it had. My legs still felt like nothing to do with me. I felt like I was walking backwards.

'Yes, yes of course, I'm very happy. Everyone has been very kind.' I smiled through too many teeth.

What I didn't say, what I couldn't say, what wasn't appropriate to a teatime bulletin, was that I felt like a stranger in all the ways I had once felt familiar. That I didn't recognize the crowded smile in the news. That home no longer felt like one, and that everyone's kindness meant I could never forget myself, could never have a day off from my difference. Even my body wasn't home any more. It now felt like a dilapidated rental. Facing the camera clicks, the ready smiles, I had never felt as alone as I did then.

When we were finished, my father pushed me back to the car. As he lifted my feet into the front seat, a boy came forward. He was older than me, maybe seventeen. Taller than my dad. Square-jawed and square-shouldered. He wore the maroon blazer that meant he was a captain of something. His smile was immediate. So warm I thought I must already know him. Normally, the senior boys ignored my year. They ran to pull me up if I fell, but otherwise I was beneath their notice. Treated with a benign indifference. The stranger squeezed my shoulder, saying, 'It's great to see you back, Emmett. You're very brave. We've been saving all the papers at home. Anyway, I just wanted to wish you luck.'

I heard myself thanking him. He had large green eyes that made me remember Mark, obedient black hair. His top lip was already shadowed blue. He smiled at my parents, a minor noble dispensing largesse, shouldered his sports bag, running for the first bell. I envied him his clean-minded confidence. The precise rhythm of his steps. He was in the sixth form, would soon be out in the wider world. The boy knew my name, but hadn't told me his. I was sure he would leave it behind him when he left. Engraved on a silver trophy or gilded on the honour roll.

'What a nice boy, Em. How kind,' Dad smiled.

'I didn't know you had so many friends, Peach,' said Mum, fastening her seatbelt.

'I don't . . . I don't know who he is.'

When it was just the three of us again, we were quiet. Driving, Dad fiddled with the radio before deciding on silence. I thought of the stranger. How, for everybody else, it was uncomplicated, an easy story. A newspaper read, then forgotten on a train. An example of space-age advances that weren't just for *Tomorrow's World*. Looking out of the window, I wanted to be this boy so much it felt like panic. It was like being trapped in a room that had been locked from the outside. I remembered my mother's short, frustrated turns in the motel pool in Connecticut. If I reached out, I could touch her, but we didn't live in the same atmosphere or navigate it the same way. Since Mark had died, and I had left the daisy-chained safety of Charlton Park, I was the only person I knew who walked like I did.

That evening the five of us sat in front of *News at Ten*. I was the 'And Finally' story that night. John Suchet smiled down the lens, right at me. Happy to be able to send viewers to bed with good news. Watching myself was like when you first hear a recording of your voice. The sound so different from what you imagined. So alien somehow, but apparently yours. The small boy on the screen looked brittle, breakable. The geriatric frame huge, legs stiff, clumsy.

'Turn it off, please. Turn it off.'

Peg looked over. Jim, dozing in a wing chair, woke up. 'But why, pet? I want to see you. I wasn't there, remember?'

'You could have come; I asked you to.'

Jim straightened, adjusting his tie over the well-fed curve of his belly. 'You look smashing, son, just champion. You're a brave boy. We're just proud, that's all.'

The word was kindly meant, but made me bristle. Looking at my grandpa's smile, I remembered holiday afternoons playing Submarines, a favourite game. We would sit in his greenhouse, between the tomato plants, bags of compost. His prized, prizewinning fuchsias. Jim would close the glass door, tapping the thermometer. We would watch the mercury rise, laughing. Pretending that we were trapped, saving our air. Pretending that the murky, cobwebbed panes were portholes under green sea. I loved him best in our submarine. One afternoon, Jim was quieter than usual, less eager to pretend. He said, 'I was never in a submarine, Em, but I was on a boat, a big boat, in the war, HMS *Uganda*. Hundreds of men on it . . . hundreds. We were bombed, hit. They detonated underwater. It was my job to go through the ship sealing the hatches, so the ship, the rest of us, didn't sink. They were calling, asking to live . . . to get out. But I had to— I would have been court-martialled. I never got over it. When I close my eyes at night . . . less now, but I still sometimes hear them.'

I knew I was too young for this knowledge. But I also knew that Jim had to tell me, so that he would never have to play Submarines again. I told him he was brave, because I couldn't think of another way to fill the silence, just needed to say something to block out my imaginings. My grandpa's kind lines sharpened. His voice was angry, urgent. 'But I wasn't brave . . . not at all. It was an order, with consequences. Nothing to do with bravery. You just live with what you've done, that's all. Brave is something people say when they want to dismiss you . . . when they'd rather not think about what you've been through.'

My situation had been nothing like as stark as Jim's. Not war, life or death. The consequences were only mine, but I still felt like there hadn't been a choice.

'I'm not brave, Grandpa, not at all.'

'He isn't, Jim,' agreed Mum.

Dad reached for the remote, clicking the television off.

By the end of term, I was finally back on my crutches. My hands gradually calloused again and I started doing full days.

Jim and Peg took the train back to Newcastle. I missed my grandma's songs. The school decided to give me an award. I was a middling student, and would never win anything for my Latin or French, so the headmaster invented one. 'To Emmett de Monterey for Perseverance in Adversity'. Privately, I thought Mr Collins deserved one for carrying me up the stairs. We all, even I, stood to sing:

> *And did those feet in ancient time*
> *Walk upon England's mountains green . . .*

I was the last prize. The headmaster stepped off the stage, bending to shake my hand. Mr Collins hadn't been able to find the Maigret books I'd asked for in time, so the head handed me a hardback of the school's centenary history, tied with a bright ribbon. Jumping back on to the stage, he smiled round all the politely bored parents. It travelled right to the back rows, bouncing off the discreet silver reflectors. The kneeling cameramen. The prize-giving was being filmed for the evening news. From the row behind, I heard a woman's voice. She whispered, loudly, to her son, telling him how lucky I was. All this attention. All this fuss. I didn't turn round. As he settled himself back behind the lectern, the headmaster beamed. 'If you hurry home, you'll all catch yourselves on *News at Ten*.'

The following weekend, my father, John and I drove to Soho to see a rough cut of the documentary. My afternoon matinees with Peg meant that the film company's office was a shock. I had imagined chrome-plated glamour. Polished conference tables, long enough to have a different postcode at either end. Instead, Nina grinned up from chaos. Yellowing piles of newspaper, bitten polystyrene cups. Shelves of VHS tapes touching the low ceiling.

Nina pulled out a chair, one of only two. My father and John stood, awkward. Sensing my hesitation, she smiled. 'Didn't I tell you television was all glitz? Are you ready? Charlie?'

My father nodded, and Nina pressed Play. The thing I remember most was the noise. The silver whine of drills, blunt metal hammers. I saw myself, eyes taped shut, my body opened, red, slick with blood. Remembered pain shooting up my legs. I saw Dr Gage, his face covered in a surgical mask, bending over somebody I'd never seen before, didn't recognize. Watching, I remembered the filming. Our house filled with lights, tripping cables, people. John had been filmed too. We went to the park, sat on the swings. Something we had never done. The director suggested we make flapjacks. Again, something we had never done. He explained: the scene would show viewers how normal I was. A normal boy who spent normal Saturdays with his normal friends doing normal things like baking. My mother had laughed at the idea, saying that most thirteen-year-old boys didn't even know how to switch an oven on, never mind bake cakes. She made them, not us. John, in his weekend Metallica T-shirt and oven gloves, was filmed lifting the flapjacks out of the oven looking at them as though they might go off in his face.

I felt his hand on my shoulder. 'Bloody hell, Em.'

I looked over at my father. He was gnawing his thumb, stiff, white as paper. 'It's like a mechanic's bench,' he said quietly. 'I think we'll stop there.'

Dad hugged me tightly. Nina hugged me, her eyes filming. I felt numb, absent.

'I know it's shocking, Emmett, but we hope we've made a good programme. I think you'll be proud of it . . . proud of yourself, when you see the finished thing. You did well, and we want the viewers to know that . . . to see that. I hope you're pleased?'

On the way home, a red light at Oxford Circus, I opened the passenger door and was violently sick.

On the last Friday of term I went to my first school dance. I hadn't wanted to go, still didn't trust my legs, but John insisted. 'I made a prat of myself on the BBC for you. You owe me, it's the least you can do.'

The whitewashed bricks of the gym were hung with streamers. Bright paper rainbows didn't quite disguise the institutional drabness, the tang of long-forgotten socks. A sixth-former loitered behind some decks. Girls from our sister school stood stiffly by the doors, as if they had come into the wrong room and weren't sure how to leave. Like reluctant royals, despatched to open a car park. The boys clumped at one end, as far from the visitors as possible, the scratched parquet a steep canyon of embarrassment. The music got louder as the room filled, people chose sides. Beats International, 'Dub Be Good to Me'. You couldn't escape the song that term. Slouchy dub; a loose, lazy rap; a New York voice bragging about being a boy from the big bad city.

John sat next to me, a cup of orange squash between his knees. He had been to the prep school, so the only girls he knew were older, loftier cousins. John saw them rarely, when they came home from university, at Easter and Christmas. They liked him, he was sure, but these sophisticated strangers might as well have been aliens. He tapped his foot, looking everywhere but at the crowded floor. I felt too young for the dance, thought we all were. Watching my classmates, their thin arms in baggy T-shirts, their fresh haircuts, I wanted to be anywhere else. They still ignored the girls, making laughing, larky shapes for each other instead. I knew we were not boys from the big bad city. Most of my schoolfriends lived in

Chislehurst or Sevenoaks, sleeping behind high gates, watched by 24-hour security cameras.

The music changed again, the plaintive, platinum longing of Sinéad O'Connor singing 'Nothing Compares 2 U'. I closed my eyes. When I was a child I thought that if I couldn't see people, they couldn't see me. I thought of Joanna, of Ben, wondered how he was spending his Friday night. I thought that, if I could have danced, I would have asked him. It was just a phase. I would grow out of wanting to, of missing him.

When I opened my eyes again, a few couples were slow-dancing. Arms looped loosely around necks. I noticed Tom, taller than his partner, taller than everyone. He was only a month older than me, but looking at him, it suddenly felt like years. I glanced at my watch, willing the hands round. Teachers from both schools began patrolling the margins as more couples formed. Mr Collins was darting in. Pulling apart the one couple who had dared a kiss. A girl was standing next to John, shy, in a silver dress. She gave him a small, cherry-glossed smile. There was glitter round her eyes. She looked as uncomfortable as I was. As if she couldn't quite live up to the bedroom-mirror version of herself, her own expectations. Finally, braver than my friend, she asked John to dance.

'No, thanks. I mean, thanks, but it's not really my thing . . . I prefer metal. You don't . . . you can't really dance to metal.'

'Why are you here, then?' the girl mouthed over the music.

'My friend wanted to come. I've got to look after him. He can't dance.'

She looked at me for the first time. I saw her take in my sticks, propped beside me on an empty chair. Turning back to John, she said, 'Why's he here, then, if he can't dance?'

Her question hadn't been addressed to me, but in any case I didn't have an answer.

13

Countdown to Air

Jim and Peg were one of the first couples in their street to buy a TV. They got it in 1953, when my grandma was pregnant with Dad, throwing a party for the Coronation. Neighbours from both sides squeezing round the set, plates of cold chicken on their laps, to watch the black-and-white beginning of the new Elizabethan era.

My father was a lonely, only child for the first eight years of his life. His parents were too busy to pay him much attention, so he read, watched TV instead. He would sit cross-legged on the rug, much too close, believing that the people he saw on the screen could see him too. So he brushed his hair, sat up straighter for *The Lone Ranger*, *Muffin the Mule*.

I was nine, nearly ten, when we first got a TV. My mother was worried we'd get square eyes, wouldn't talk to each other, but I wanted to be like my friends. I couldn't skip, but I wanted to be able to join playground conversations. Unlike my dad, I understood that the actors couldn't see me, couldn't care less that I hadn't had my bath yet. I also understood that, simply by being on TV, these people were much more important than me, or anything that happened on my quiet, sunny street.

Mum, Nina and I flew to Manchester when it was still dark, raining. We were due to appear on a BBC morning show. The taxi driver passed me my crutches, smiling briskly. He had a mermaid green-inked on to his forearm, her hair just covering improbable, back-aching breasts. I thought she looked cold. I saw my mother notice her too, wondered if he regretted it.

'I watched you last night. You're famous now, aren't you?'

'Not really,' I said, feeling myself colour as I thanked him.

To me, fame was still something earned. A by-product of being good at something. Talented. Michael Jackson was famous. Madonna was famous. Fame was noise. Flash and glitter. I hadn't done anything. Still didn't know if I was good at anything. Privately, I felt like a cause, the current Disease of the Week. All I wanted was to be anonymous. A fleeting face on the pavement. Somebody you passed and didn't notice.

Inside, the set was carefully informal. Leather sofas at right angles to a coffee table. A bowl of apples, not for eating. Pink flowers in front of wobbly, wallpapered flats. A smart imitation of a bachelor-ish apartment. I was sent for make-up, brought back out to meet the presenters, Eamonn and Jane.

The end of the interview had been a phone-in. A man had called, loudly disgusted, angry with me, the programme. He complained that, yet again, the makers had chosen to present being disabled, being in a wheelchair, as a tragedy, the worst of all possible worlds. He had been in a wheelchair since early childhood and had a great life. His disability was not something he wanted to change, but something intrinsic to his sense of who he was. He had embraced a life on wheels. What did I think of that? The stranger's sharpness shocked me. I had tried to explain that the documentary was only my story. I didn't, couldn't, speak for other disabled people, only myself. That I hadn't wanted to be in a wheelchair until I couldn't avoid it. The first time I had acknowledged that wheels were ever a possibility was live on air.

Now, listening to this man, Jane straightened, turning smoothly to Nina, alert to the possibility of conflict, higher ratings. 'But, how do you respond, Nina, do you think you could have presented a slightly different argument?'

'We set out to tell Emmett's story, his family's. Charles and Fran have always been adamant that they wanted the best for their child. And it was Emmett's choice, ultimately, even the filming. It was what he wanted for himself. We tried not to intrude . . . to present something balanced, respectful. And I think we managed it.'

It had been what I wanted. I wanted to be like my friends, only that. To look the world in the eye, like they did.

As we began our descent into Heathrow, the stranger's words were still loud in my ears. I simply hadn't understood that there were those who were disabled who had found a way to embrace it. Who didn't chase miracles, because they didn't need to. What I didn't see until much later, when I was no longer the only person with cerebral palsy I knew, is that there are as many ways to be disabled as there are to be alive. We are as singular as our bodies, despite a shared label, shared diagnosis. Because my operation had been so public, even years after the story had been binned, used for chip paper, other disabled people sometimes stopped me on the street. Strangers who felt the same way as that caller, who told me that I ought to be ashamed. They told me I must hate myself, pandering to the prejudices of an ableist society that was determined to see us only in terms of a problem. A drain on the resources of the busy, fast-walking majority. A majority that would rather not slow for us, see us at all. I wanted something of their anger for myself. Admired it, understood it. But it didn't leave much space for the grief I still felt.

It was dull, cold when we landed in London. A woman in front of us in the taxi queue shivered miserably. The straw hat and bright sarong, which had been so right on a Spanish beach or beside an Italian pool, were suddenly so wrong in an English drizzle. I wasn't aware I was watching her nudge her bags up the line as the cabs peeled off. She must have felt it because she smiled back at me. 'Go ahead, go on.'

I thanked her.

The woman in the straw hat beamed, already warmed by her good deed. 'There's always somebody worse off than you, isn't there?' she nodded to the queue behind her.

14

Another Country

Not long afterwards, I left my school. The teachers couldn't continue to carry me. And when I walked I'd miss half the lesson, fall asleep. The headmaster had already refused to change my timetable so that I might have most of my lessons on the ground floor. Nobody put it bluntly, said it out loud, but the experiment had been a failure.

So I went back into special education. A college for the disabled in a quietly forgettable commuter town, just far enough from London that I'd need to board. The acceptance letter came with a bossy list of new things I'd need. The discreet logo, obscured by the postmark, meant I already knew what was inside. The letter sat by the telephone for days until, finally, Mum opened it.

Reading, she laughed. ' "All laundry is communal. All items must be clearly labelled. Parents are reminded, please do not send delicates." '

At this, my mother hooted. 'Well, that's you out, Peach. You're my most delicate item, so you'd better not go.'

I smiled, hoping she meant it.

The following Saturday, a sticky, soft-grey afternoon in late July, we drove to Peter Jones to buy the list. Normally I liked shopping, but not that day. Neither of us could get excited about polycotton school trousers, five pale blue shirts. Slippers. I was told to bring a dressing gown, but I didn't have one. Weekends at home were untucked; I normally ate breakfast in the T-shirt I had slept in. Peg lived in fear of draughts, disapproved. She had given me a dressing gown for Christmas when I was six. Navy blue wool, with fussy red piping. I wore her present once, before forgetting it on the back of my door. Looking at the shop's long rails of bleached white towelling, I thought they looked like queuing patients. Clients at an expensive, useless spa.

My mother riffled the rail, finding a medium, throwing it over her arm. I did not want her to buy it. I did not want to need it. I did not want to go. Normally we listened to music in the car. We sang along enthusiastically to the CDs we forgot to change, *Moondance* or *Dusty in Memphis*.

That day, we didn't sing, didn't talk. We didn't even turn on the radio. Eventually, stuck behind a belching lorry on the Old Kent Road, Mum said, 'If there was any other choice, you know we'd take it. But you can't keep falling asleep in class. It's just too difficult for you there . . . you'll leave with no qualifications if you stay. You aren't being sent away; we'll still see you every weekend. Try and see it like working away during the week, hey, rather than living there? I never see your dad much in the week either. It's going to be lonely, Peach.'

I was being sent away and we both knew it. I had been falling asleep right under my teachers' noses, jerked awake by bells. Chasing my timetable all over the building. Miracle or not, we both understood I was failing, and that the presented choice was no choice at all. It wasn't just my grades. I wanted to be a boy like Tom, a broad-shouldered, clean-minded captain of the First XV. We both knew that however many miles I sweated on the stationary bike, I was getting nowhere, fast.

Dr Gage had never lied to me. He found the noise, clicking cameras, the bold-type glib optimism of the headlines, utterly baffling. He was a scientist, not God, a magician. He had tried to warn me, to tell me that miracles were nothing of the kind.

I had thanked him. The operation had worked, I wasn't in a wheelchair. But I had preferred to believe what I read in the papers rather than hear what the doctor was trying to tell me.

I didn't want my mother to feel worse than she already did so just smiled, tried to convince her. 'It'll be an adventure,' I said.

Mum didn't speak. When we pulled up at the house, she reached for my crutches and took the shopping off the back seat. She pushed past me, carried the bags up to her room and we both forgot them for the rest of the summer.

After he retired, my Grandpa Francis sold the farm and moved to South Carolina. Until that summer, I had not seen him for almost two years – since he had visited me, recovering at my uncle's in Poughkeepsie. In that time he receded, becoming a voice on the telephone, airmail packages for anniversaries, Christmases. A slightly sulky Sunday obligation. Now he stood behind the arrivals barrier at Greenville-Spartanburg Airport, taller, older than I remembered.

When he saw my mother he broke into a broad grin, raised his arm. It was the same smile. The same feed-store cap, broken-billed, the edges fraying. The same spreading seventies collars, faded plaid. He stepped round the barrier, reaching for Mum's carry-on before kissing her hello. 'I'll take that. Give it here.'

It was the same gesture of bossy tenderness. The same Grandpa. We passed from the fiercely air-conditioned hall into the short-stay lot. Already, at midday, the white August heat felt like a solid wall. We stood a moment, as if trying to figure out how to move against it. Francis still had his ancient Lincoln Continental, a block long. I sat in the back on the short drive from the airport, the vinyl seats sticky, scorching. Grandpa was driving, talking, but I wasn't really listening. I watched the road, already shining with heat. Asphalt emptiness punctuated by well-kept white churches sitting on artificially green lawns. London, the new school, felt sunny weeks away.

It had taken thirteen hours, two flights – one Boeing and then a juddering thirty-seater from Atlanta that I was sure we were going to die in – to get to my grandfather. I thought my mother was dozing behind her sunglasses, when she said, 'I see God still does good business around here, Dad.' She gestured to a tall, tiled steeple. A sign on the clipped grass read: IF WE CONFESS OUR SINS, HE IS FAITHFUL AND JUST, AND WILL FOR-GIVE US.

And I wondered how happy Francis would be to see me if he knew mine.

Grandpa never exceeded a careful fifty-five, even if, as always here, there was no traffic. He waved at the passing graveyard. 'It's still the biggest concern round here, unless you count IBM. It's crazy. You get all these families, rednecks usually, food-stamp poor . . . their kids are running round with bad teeth, empty bellies, but when one of them dies, they'll spend every cent they can borrow on a huge stone memorial. Better to spend money on the living; the dead can't need it.'

'You can't say "redneck", Dad! Please . . .'

'Well, that's what they are. Trailer parks full of Confederate flags.'

My mother dropped it, smiled too brightly. It was the glazed, exhausted expression of someone who already wished we were driving back to the airport.

My step-grandmother Anne – she always insisted on Anne, never Grandma – said, 'Emmett, you're in the usual room . . . Robert E. Lee's bed. Of course, it can't really be his bed. It's like the splinters of the True Cross – if he had slept in all the places he was supposed to in the South, he'd never have got any fighting done.'

173

She beamed, chuckling to herself at her own joke. 'But it's so good to have you both visit.'

Anne was my grandfather's second wife. An energetic Southern Belle, only a few years older than my mother. Tiny, with a pert prettiness that just missed being beautiful. When she had brought an older man to the family home – a man who had lost his country, his name and his money; a foreigner: more than that, a Jewish widower with five shell-shocked, grieving kids – it was a rude awakening for her lacy, social-register mama. Her daughter was always smiling to cover the strangeness of her choice.

Anne was supposed to marry a starched uniform. A Citadel cadet like her sweet brother William. A boy weighted with Roman numerals. A boy ashamed, but not nearly ashamed enough, of the source of all his money, his generations of mannered ease. There were supposed to have been more antebellum columns in Anne's future. A house, a life, just like her mother's.

I did not understand this at fourteen. Did not know that my mother's dislike of her stepmother had little to do with their age difference and everything to do with Anne's sing-song dismissal of the savagery in her family's past. I did not realize, then, that this was part of the reason we didn't fly to see Francis more often.

'It's lovely to see you too, Anne,' I said, meaning it.

I went down the hall to my room, closed the door. I could still hear Anne, the bright, busy notes of her welcome. I sat on the high white bed, listening to the loud grass. Emptying my pockets on to the bedside table. The wallet that Ben gave me, which I still used every day, was falling apart. The popper lost, corners rubbed grey. We used to spend every moment of the long summer together, in my garden or his. My room or his. I didn't need to fly anywhere. Our tight, tiny world was quite big enough.

Anne insisted on taking us out for a first-night dinner. We went to an expensive Chinese restaurant, an exotic place for Greenville. It was all lacquer. Red-and-gold bustle; laughing, noisily prosperous families. My mother was dumb with fatigue. I saw her glance at her watch. It was almost three a.m., London time, and neither of us had any appetite for the celebration. My grandfather didn't notice – all the more for him. He forked up rice as if someone might take it away. When he had finally finished, he reached for my hand, smiling over the candles. 'So, your mum says you're going to a new school in September. I used to board too. You'll probably hate it at first – I did. Cried most nights for weeks. I couldn't get used to the food. I could speak English, but everybody pretended they couldn't understand me.'

He patted my hand, sighing, replete with food and the nearness of his family. The waiters whisked away leftovers to be boxed. I already knew my grandpa would eat them up for days, until the cartons grew fuzzy, blue with mould, and Anne had to wrestle them into the disposal.

'This school might make a man of you, finally,' Grandpa smiled.

That night, beyond tired, I couldn't sleep. I tried to tune out the singing darkness, insistent cricket-calls outside my window. I stared at the ceiling, thinking of Ben, of Tom, of John, and the dance. I was disabled, and didn't want to be. I was probably gay, and didn't want to be.

I watched the light change through white-frilled curtains. The crickets were still singing softly. I heard Anne join in, brewing coffee:

> 'Toreador, don't spit on the floor-a,
> Use the cuspidor-a . . .
> Whaddya think it's for-a?'

I swung my legs over the bed. My scars were still red, stubbornly livid. Brushing my teeth, I examined my face. My skin yellow in the bathroom light. A spot had come up overnight. There was the same nose I hated. The same overcrowded, child's jaw. I still didn't need to shave. I spat, rinsing out the basin, wondering what General Robert E. Lee would think about sharing his bed with an English boy, a queer? I listed the playground insults in my head. Bender, poof, pansy, nancy, bum-boy, queer. I hoped it was just a phase.

I went down the hall to the kitchen. Anne turned, smiling, already at the stove, already the hostess. 'Morning, Emmett, sleep well? What can I getcha? How about a one-eye?'

A one-eye is fried bread. Sweet-sliced Wonder Bread; you make a hole, crack an egg in the middle. Anne had been making me these, every visit, since I could talk. I loved one-eyes and, unlike my mum, I loved Anne. But I was sure she would not have been so keen to make me breakfast if she knew the truth.

'Thank you, that'd be lovely.'

She hummed, pulling the white middles out of two slices, pressing them to the hot fat. Smiling. I looked out at the paddocks, the baked red clay beyond. Anne's horses – Prinny and Barney, two proud, belligerent Arabs that only she could ride – stood against the fence, in early-morning conversation. Anne would not kick me out of the house – she was far too well-mannered for that – but she wouldn't be glad.

The sticky, slow days passed too quickly for me, though my mother visibly brightened as our flight home got nearer. Her father was easier to be nice to when he was only a voice, long-distance.

On our last night Anne baked a Key lime pie. She drove to Blockbuster, coming back with two pounds of gummy worms and two movies. I sat on the sofa between her and Francis. The first film was *The Gods Must Be Crazy*, a South African comedy. Francis enjoyed the candy more than the movie, but Anne laughed, insisting it was fun. I looked from one face to the other in the blue light of the TV, knowing that, after saying goodbye the next morning, I wouldn't see them for a long time – years, maybe. I was trying to fix each detail of their kindness, their relaxed, pyjamaed faces in my mind.

The second film was *Another Country*. The story set in an English school, like the one I had just left. I sat up straighter, watching Rupert Everett's chiselled loucheness. If anybody noticed, they didn't say anything. Two of the pupils were caught fumbling in a dark corner, when they should be singing at a remembrance for the school's war-dead. They pulled apart. The blond boy gaped in shock, his grey eyes wide, long underwear round slim knees.

My grandpa cleared his throat, stretched forward, his hand in the worms. 'Dontcha think you've had enough, pig?' joked Anne.

Grandpa beamed, happy to be told off. 'Yes, my pig, probably.'

He snapped the lid shut. My mother ignored them, pretending absorption in the film. Then, the blond boy was standing in the school chapel. He paused before the altar, looking up at the cross. The camera cut to his shiny toes, his hardly worn Oxfords, hanging from the bell-rope.

Francis said, 'That's enough for me, I think . . . I'm off to bed. Goodnight, my dears.' He rose, sighing. Steadying himself, a hand in my hair. 'It's probably for the best . . . I mean, it's a very lonely life—'

'Oh, Dad, must you? That's a bloody awful thing to say . . . awful. That poor boy.'

The next morning my mother, Anne and Francis went for a last ride. I waited until I saw them passing the fence into the paddocks. They'd be ages. At least an hour, maybe two. Anne had already put the films from last night on the hall table. Rewound, ready to be returned. I grabbed *Another Country*, lying on my stomach in front of the screen, clicking the tape into the old VCR. By the time the credits had rolled a second time, I understood that I wouldn't grow out of anything. For Ben, our friendship had been just that. A weekend pastime, nothing secret, or serious. Simply a detour on the road to somewhere less lonely. I knew then that I would probably be alone, gay, seven days a week.

Francis, Mum and I ate the leftover Key lime pie for breakfast, the three of us silent on the drive back to the airport. Francis waved us through the departure gate saying, 'Be good, both of you. Work hard at your new school.'

We waited until he had gone through the exit to the short-stay parking lot, until we couldn't see him any more. My mother started to cry, blinking back tears as soon as they came, rooting for Kleenex, embarrassed. 'Oh, Dad,' she whispered to herself.

The inflight movie was a stupid romance. A beautiful blond boy in love with a witty, complicated girl. You knew she was complicated because she was a brunette, chose dark clothes, even when the weather was bright, cloudless. Mum slept through it, while I cried, as quietly as I could. Love was the privilege of normal people. A language practised between a girl and a kiss-curled, white-smiling boy. Watching a big love on a tiny screen, I felt I'd always be alone. Living at home forever. Now that I knew what I was, I'd always be watching.

15

In Case of Emergency

Changing schools meant hiding again. The night before I left, my mother sat at the kitchen table, her mouth sharp with pins, sewing name tags into my new uniform. I loved her tools, her sewing basket. The cracked-leather needle case, soft with handling, that was Hilary's. The velvet pincushion, shaped like a strawberry. Her jade-handled seam-ripper. Even though I knew I'd be back the following weekend – five days, just five – I was silent with misery.

Mum pressed another pin into the velvet, balling a sock with its mate, adding it to the polycotton pile, saying, 'Buck up, Peach-face. It might be fun, you never know. Of course, we'll miss you. But it isn't forever.'

My mother wouldn't stop talking. Loud, falsely bright. She lifted my new boombox, a leaving present, my name in wobbling capitals along the handle, on to the single shelf above the pillow.

'Shelves!'

She said this as though she had made the shelves herself, as though she had invented them. The room was large, with tall windows, a view of fields, a church tower beyond the brick perimeter. I sat on one of two beds. Apparently, I had a roommate: the other bed had already been claimed. A Guns N' Roses poster – a grinning skull, joint smoking in a bony smirk – pinned over the pillow. In another, a footballer ran, arms wide, down a roaring pitch. I shifted back on the duvet cover, a

179

boil-washed pattern, pitching blue boats riding tall spray. There was a noise, the humiliating parp of a rubber sheet, which the three of us studiously ignored. My dad stood against the door, worrying at the skin of his thumb. It would bleed if he didn't leave it alone.

'It's only till Saturday, son. I'll come and pick you up as soon as I can . . .'

'You might help, Charlie, rather than just standing there with your thumb up your arse, for God's sake.'

He didn't respond; instead went to a bag, unzipping it. Pulling out handfuls of new clothes. I had left the towelling at home. At the last moment I'd stolen a dressing gown from my mother. An unwanted, unworn present from the back of her wardrobe, a friend she rarely saw. Cheap black silk with a red-embroidered dragon clawing its way up the back. It was delicate, would be ruined in a communal twin-tub, a flimsy act of rebellion. Seeing it, my father said nothing, but he didn't pull it out of the case, hang it up. He didn't say anything. But I saw he would rather have had a son who wouldn't stand out so much, who was content with cotton. He would rather have had a son who didn't need to board there.

My mother crossed to the wardrobe, hanging her carefully labelled shirts. The boy whose room this used to be had taped a pin-up above the inside mirror. A grinning Page Three girl whose professional smile didn't quite reach her eyes. A manicured thumb hooked into red briefs. Red *Sun* T-shirt knotted over huge, heavy breasts. I wondered who the boy was who saved her from the paper and then forgot her. My mother tore her smile down, looking for a bin.

The door opened and a woman entered. She smiled, a tray of tea in her hands. 'I'm Sue; you must be Mum and Dad. I'll be Emmett's unit leader for the first year, I'll help settle him in. I thought you might need these?'

'I'm Francesca,' my mother answered, her tone a deliberate line between coldness and warmth. 'And this is Charlie, Charles.'

Sue put the tray down on a set of scratched drawers. There were half-peeled stickers on the corners. Everything in the dorm was used, worn. Somebody else's. She handed me a mug and I forced myself to smile, thank her.

She had a tight brown perm; it fell round her kind face like a spaniel's ears. She was wearing a palm-printed T-shirt – *Florida: THE SUNSHINE STATE!!!* – across her chest. I sipped the weak tea. Sue took over. I pulled shoes from the bag, lining new toes under my new bed. As I leant forward, the mattress farted again. Sue laughed, glancing at my mother. 'Well, I can see he won't be needing that, so I'll change the bed. I'll get rid of it once you've gone.'

'We'll be off now, son. But I'll be here first thing, Saturday. We'd better get going . . .' Dad didn't move.

If I looked at my father, I knew the hard, fleshy lump of sadness in my throat would give way to tears, so I didn't. My mother kissed the top of my head, smiling. I wanted to leave with them. I wanted them to start laughing. To be in on the joke.

'Try to have fun, Peach-face. And ring me tomorrow. You've enough coins for the payphone?'

I nodded that I did, smiled. She reached into her bag anyway, slapping a handful of loose change on to the side.

And then they left.

Sue sat beside me on the bed, put an arm around my shoulders. We sat like that a long time. I wanted to cry, but didn't want her to see me. Finally, she got up. Soft-smiling, kind. 'I expect you'll want to be by yourself a bit . . .'

She gestured to a button on the wall I hadn't noticed. Orange, the tiny symbol of a nurse, her white-pointed headdress almost scratched off. 'There's your panic button, in case of emergency . . . if you need anything.'

A boy butted the door open with his footrests, pushing into the room. He whirred forward, stopping in front of my bed. He was wearing a blue Everton football shirt, listing slightly in his chair, like a scuttled ship. He had box-fresh, dazzling white trainers on his feet, and I understood that we had opposite problems. I wore out my shoes too fast. He didn't wear his out at all. He didn't get the chance, because his feet never touched the ground.

'I'm Joe,' he said, reversing on his wheels. 'We'll be sharing, at least for this term. I would shake your hand, but . . .'

One hand sat heavily over the chair's joystick, the other was a limp afterthought in his lap.

I wasn't asleep when the alarm sounded. A low, looping whine, like an air-raid siren, one of Peg's black-and-white matinees. There was the noise of fast-squeaking feet in the corridor, and the light was clicked on. I shut my eyes against the sudden brightness. A woman came in who was not Sue. Someone I hadn't met. She flung back my covers, all business. 'You're Emmett, aren't you? Up you get, please. There's normally a drill at the start of term, but the staff weren't warned, so it's unlikely, but could be for real. Move, please . . . I have to help Joe up. D'you know where you're going?'

I didn't have a clue, but nodded, hurried into my dressing gown. The hallway was blinking chaos. It looked like the aftermath of a bomb-blast. Carers carrying students, pyjamas covered by hasty towels. Staff running to get electric wheelchairs from overnight charging-points. Decanting their blinking owners into their wheels. I watched a girl get lifted into a long black chair. She had thin, stiffly twisted arms, her hands tiny. They looked more like fragile, translucent fins. Each suggestion of nail was varnished, pearly pink. The carer lifted a lever once she was strapped in, safe, and a joystick dropped down under her chin.

'Did naebody tell yae it's rude to stare?'

I couldn't understand the girl's broad Scots, but I could follow her anger. She fitted her chin to the stick, speeding through the automatic doors, out into the darkness. I clicked after her wheels, into a low brick colonnade. There were caged light bulbs, luminous intervals, fixed along the wall. Daddy-long-legs skittered over the bricks, hurling themselves at the glow.

There was nowhere to sit. Most of my school didn't need chairs; they already had wheels. I leant against the table, an awkward guest at a pyjama party. A girl came over, sliding smoothly on electric treads. She had a pink-dyed fringe; her ears were studded, bright silver that spiked her edges. She was not wearing a dressing gown, just a towel, draped over blue-mottled legs.

'I'm Rebecca, Becca,' she said. 'I like your dress . . .'

I looked down at the cheap, silk, tasselled belt. The stranger was right; I might as well have been wearing a dress. 'Emmett. My mum bought it for me . . . a leaving present.'

'Well, I wouldn't let her give you any more clothes. Of course, I know who you are, I've already seen you on the telly. I think my mother would prefer you to the child she got. Now I can tell her what you're really like.' Rebecca smiled, not happily.

A woman stood in front of a small stage, calling out names, counting off heads. I missed my own, and she called again.

'Here,' I said, wishing I wasn't.

I thought of my parents, asleep in London, snoring, hating them.

A boy smiled from the opposite wall. Tall, with close-cropped blond hair. Alert green eyes. He did not have a wheelchair, did not need crutches. Slouching against the peeling paint, he looked as though he didn't belong. As though his being here, in the middle of the night, was an administrative error. A shorter girl stood beside him. She was also blonde, also pretty. Also looked like she didn't belong. She reached up to whisper in his ear. They both laughed and I realized they were laughing at me.

After ten more minutes we were given the all-clear, allowed back to bed. Rebecca slid smoothly away, saying, 'Well, sitting in your pyjamas, at least it breaks the ice. Nice to meet you. See you at breakfast.'

I smiled back, but couldn't speak. My only thought, that I was surrounded. Breakfast, lunch and dinner, five days a week. This place, these people, was home now. The blond boy passed, the smirking girl in his wake. He was wearing boxers, and his muscled legs were still summer-tanned. His towelling dressing gown hung open over a baggy T-shirt. I noticed all this, and he saw me noticing. The boy stopped, smiling. His teeth were small, white and even.

'Faggot,' he whispered, just loud enough.

My mother needn't have bothered labelling my shirts, because I did not recognize myself. I had already been given another name.

16
Normals

Marie was Peg's very own miracle, born when my grandma was past forty, after Jim and Peg had retired to twin beds. My aunt was eleven, had just started at the local convent school, when Charles left home, and Newcastle, for good. She missed her brother, but not his records. Marie preferred the Bay City Rollers to Bowie. The radio-friendly glamour of Marc Bolan to Captain Beefheart.

I have a photograph of us: Marie in her prim school uniform. I'm on her lap, pink from the bath, wrapped in a towel and her smile. As I didn't have a sister, I grew to think of her as one, loved her laugh, her readiness for fun. Her shrink-to-fit Levi's, breathless hysteria when she had to lie on the floor after a night out to get them off. Jim bending over his daughter telling her that she was daft. Threatening to cut her out of them, a coat hanger in the zip of her precious denims. With Marie, I listened to Steve Harley and Cockney Rebel, 'Make Me Smile (Come Up and See Me)', or the Steve Miller Band, 'Abracadabra'. On the evenings she let me stay up, I loved my aunt almost as much as I did Peg.

The weekend before I was due to start at boarding school, my Aunt Marie took me out. We went for lunch at a red-checked Italian restaurant in Covent Garden. Paying the bill, she looked over her shoulder, pouring the rest of her carafe of house white into my glass. It couldn't hurt, this once, and she had her car at the station. We were celebrating. I didn't know what there was to be happy about, but clinked her glass, drank. Crossing Long Acre, Marie decided she wanted to buy me a present. Something useful for school. She had married, moved to Kent at nineteen. She had a good job now, a bigger house. Walking past the windows, blank-faced mannequins, I would have preferred clothes. Or a book. Something sentimental. Something Marie could write in. But she settled on a blue-enamelled cash box in the window of a stationer's. It had two flimsy keys. A lock that could have been picked with a paper clip. But Marie decided it would be useful, utility being the highest praise. I'd never lived with strangers before, might need somewhere to keep private things.

I didn't want to spoil our last afternoon, so smiled agreement. Standing in line to pay, Marie said, 'You know, I always fancied boarding school. It was quite lonely when your dad left, like being an only child. Peg was out at work, and when your grandpa wasn't, he was in the greenhouse. Your dad only came home in the holidays, sometimes not even then. I let myself in with a key round my neck most afternoons. I mean, it was all right . . . I had friends. But I'd read those Enid Blyton books, *Malory Towers*, I got them one Christmas . . . they were great. Apple-pie beds, pillow fights, a gang of girls to talk to . . . I loved them. I know it isn't what you want, but you might find you like it. It might be nice to be with other kids who understand.'

'Faggot,' the boy spat.

I turned round. That was my first mistake, answering to the name. It was the beginning of the fifth week, but a face I hadn't seen before.

'You heard me, faggot.'

The stranger tipped in his chair. The sides of his head were shaved short over sharp features, the rest gelled back in stiff lines from a narrow forehead. He had a large, long nose. Two heavy gold hoops in his ears. There was more gold on his fingers. I'd never seen a boy who wore so much jewellery, was confused by the contradiction. Surely, being so showy, he was the suspect, not me?

The boy next to him was on my table for meals. I'd thought we were becoming friends. He leant back in his wheelchair, smiling. Spitting another 'faggot' at me. It was loud enough for the teacher to hear, but he did nothing. Just stood with his back to the class, red pen squeaking across the whiteboard. Rebecca was sitting next to me. She hated maths, had been staring out of the window at the car park. The concrete troughs, leggy geraniums, mulched with the care-staff's break-time cigarettes. Suddenly, she said, 'Don't be a fucking mong all your life, Alex, just try.' She turned stiffly in her electric wheelchair, giving Alex the finger.

The golden boy laughed, more glass than amusement. 'You'd know all about that, you freak. You're the spastic, not me.'

The teacher was still writing equations, still pretending deafness. I looked at the board as though it were the only thing in the room. As though I'd find my escape in the quick red numbers. I wondered if the teacher wanted to leave as much as I did, whether his car was parked outside the window. Whether I could ask him for a lift, to anywhere but there.

'That freak your boyfriend, is he? I've seen him on the TV. He thinks he's better than us, but he's just a faggot, a stupid queer.'

I couldn't see, but the boy next to Alex thumped down on his wheels, clapping. Laughing agreement. Rebecca didn't speak.

Finally, the teacher put down his pen, turned to face the class. He had silver-thinning hair over a blushing scalp. A tired tweed jacket. The colour rose in his face, and I understood he was scared of Alex.

The teacher had been friendly until he understood that numbers were a hot-faced misery to me. He gave me a tight, apologetic smile, but didn't say anything. Looking at him, I understood I was on my own. I knew he knew the truth of what Alex had said. Perhaps he was gay too, silenced by the fear of losing his job.

I was eleven, already hoping I wasn't gay, in 1988 when Mrs Thatcher's Section 28 went on the statute books. The American teen movies I had watched, every Saturday with Ben, spat the word 'homo' in my face. I understood from them that to be gay was to be the punchline of a joke. An insult. A weird, weedy playground outcast. The new law banned any official mention of homosexuality in schools. Acknowledging the existence of a love less ordinary was forbidden. Any writers that wrote about queerness were removed from school libraries, in case their stories somehow turned you, made you gay.

According to Margaret Thatcher, being homosexual was a choice. A lifestyle, but not a life. A threat to heterosexual hegemony, Christian morality. A danger to true-blue family values, which made the Conservatives twitch.

The law meant I couldn't learn about myself in any classroom. It was a legal evasion, a brisk erasure. But pretending something, someone, doesn't exist won't make them disappear. My maths teacher couldn't answer my questions, even if I'd dared to ask them. Even if I was right, and he was queer himself. State-sanctioned silence meant I was terrified of the possibility of gayness, of being labelled a poof. My new teacher didn't defend me. He didn't send Alex out. I was the problem, not him. It was safer to ignore me. Maybe I was wrong, and he agreed with Alex? In any case, he didn't, couldn't, tell me I was normal. Nothing to be afraid of. No reason for shame. He said nothing. I sat under his nose, burning. Instead, the teacher smiled past me, saying, 'Are you all better now, Alex? We missed you.'

Alex spoke to the back of my head. 'Yes, sir. Pleased to be here.'

At first break, I went up to my dorm. It was empty. One of the most difficult things now was finding a place to be alone. I lay on my bed with my shoes on. I'd put the blue-enamelled box on my windowsill, next to my favourite paperbacks from home. I'd attached one key on my chain, sticking the other to the side of my underwear drawer with some Blu-Tack left behind by the last boy who'd slept in my bed. All these precautions were unnecessary, stupid. Anyone who'd wanted to could simply steal the whole box. There were no locks on the bedroom doors. No privacy anywhere. Anyway, it was still empty. I had nothing tangible to lock away. Only a secret that had already been guessed. I closed my eyes, willing myself to disappear.

As well as the box, Marie had given me her work number, for emergencies. I rang my mother most evenings, asking to come home. Asking to be home-schooled. She'd tell me she understood, but there was nowhere else to go. No other choice. I was miserable, she knew, but it was no fun for her either. I had to get some qualifications, GCSEs. Had to give myself a future, at the expense of my present. She'd put the phone down, telling me that she'd see me at the weekend, it wasn't long. Telling me she was sorry.

Looking at her gift, I wanted to ring Marie. I wanted to tell her she'd been wrong. That rather than her pillow-fighting fantasies, boarding school was heavy-metal hostility from breakfast to lights-out. My aunt valued conformity, hadn't guessed I was gay. I hoped she wouldn't care. That my double difference wouldn't make me too unusual, somebody she didn't want to know.

Marie was as good at numbers as I was bad. I wanted to tell her that, desperate in a maths class, I'd worked out that there were 120 hours in the five days I was required to spend there, 7, 200 minutes. I belonged, apparently, because of one diagnosis, and was picking spit-balls out of my collar for another.

Alex had understood, as soon as looking at me, that I wasn't like him. That I was queer. The school had been purpose-built to accommodate my physical difference. For the first time since being at Charlton Park, I was surrounded by disabled people. There wasn't a single step in the whole place. Just gentle brick ramps, smiling carers. But the place where I was supposed to belong also had loneliness built in. I was sure none of the other students were gay. It was just another place I was a stranger, somewhere I needed to hide.

Later that day, I was doing homework in the empty classroom when Rebecca found me. Her chair was so silent, I didn't realize until she was there. She smiled, a little shyly, pushing her pink-dyed fringe out of her eyes.

'This is where you've been hiding.'

'I'm not hiding . . . just homework,' I answered, lifting my book, wanting her to go.

Rebecca pulled out the chair beside me, pushing it to one side. Clicking neatly into the space left. She smelt sweet, a strong, musky perfume. I smiled at her, but tried to look as though I was busy. Rebecca inched forward, gripping the edge of the desk with long fingers. I noticed that each pale knuckle was scabbed, healing.

'The thing you probably don't know about Alex is that he's very ill . . . he's dying. The haemos, haemophiliacs – well, they look the most normal, they're at the top of the tree, they think. They can't stand being surrounded by us, because, out on the street, in the world, they can pass.'

Rebecca shifted in her seat, looking beyond me, out the window. 'But the irony is, they're the most fragile. They could fall, hit their heads, start a bleed, and that would be it. That's why

Alex's been off. There's a haemophilia centre here, that's why he comes. They get specialist care, it's supposed to be the best in the country.'

Until Rebecca had told me, I'd never heard the word 'haemophilia'. I didn't know what it was. I'd assumed Alex was at the school because he'd been thrown out of everywhere else, and that was why he was sharp. I put down my pen, turning to face her. 'What do you mean, "supposed to be"?'

'Well, they fucked up. Alex, all the haemos, they were part of the trials for a clotting factor: the thing we have, and they don't . . . factor VIII, it's called. Anyway, when he was eleven, before I knew him, he was given a dose that was infected with HIV. He's got AIDS now. They harvest the factor VIII from blood donations and this was given to him before the blood was routinely screened. The British government bought a lot of it from America and their blood supply was taken from junkies, drug addicts. People paid for their blood; they got donations from anywhere, weren't fussy. Not all of the boys here, not all the haemos, have it . . . but most do. They sued the government, and won, but they all had to sign something, as a condition of the settlement, that meant they couldn't sue again. Why do you think Alex has such nice trainers, good clothes? It's because he's rich. But he probably won't live to spend it all, poor bastard. He's angry; I would be too. If I was him, I wouldn't be bothering with school. I'd get out. See the world, while I still could.'

She smiled sadly, going on. 'If he thinks you're gay, then he's going to blame you. In his mind, they – the poofs – are the reason he's ill.'

I looked at her, my face hot, rigid with shame. If I was a fourteen-year-old who couldn't count on fourteen more, I knew I wouldn't be there either. I wouldn't worry about algebra, essays on *Hamlet*, imagined tragedies. I suddenly felt speechlessly sorry. Numb with sorrow for someone I disliked. For the first time since my parents had driven away, I felt lucky. There were worse things than this school. Worse things than having an awkward shadow.

'I've never lived away from home . . . never boarded,' I tried to explain. 'I don't have any disabled friends, don't even know anyone disabled. I feel like there's been a mistake, like I don't belong here. I don't *want* to belong here.'

Rebecca reversed back angrily, jerking the desks behind her out of line. She gestured to my sticks, splayed underneath my seat. 'I'm sorry, what are those? You don't know anyone disabled? How about yourself? Do you think anyone wants to be here? I used to go to a normal school too, but the girls there kicked the shit out of me. Teenage girls are vicious; boys too. They pulled me out of my chair, left me on the bathroom floor in all the piss. And I was the problem, I was the one who was asked to leave. I hated it here too, to begin with, but now it's home . . . a place where I'm not in the minority, where I've got friends. I don't always love it, but at least here I don't have to explain myself all the time. But then, I wasn't on the telly, breaking my legs, trying to fit in.'

She looked at me directly. I noticed her clear blue eyes for the first time. A look like Ben's. She clicked forward. 'But you're not really a poof, are you?'

I still thought of my friends at home as my real ones. London, and real life, was just fifty miles' drive. But Rebecca had been kind, understood I needed her. I wanted to tell her the truth.

'Of course not,' I lied.

Though the days of the week changed, they were all essentially the same. At seven-thirty, Amanda, one of the night staff, would bring Joe's chair from its overnight charge. She would bang through our door, clicking on the light, clicking on a smile. Getting Joe ready to face the day was her last job. She was impatient, eager to get home after a long shift. In the two years I shared a room, I never got used to dressing in front of an audience. I learnt to put clean pants under my pyjama trousers after showering; and I still pulled the duvet over my lap, edged away from Amanda's good-humoured briskness. She laughed off my attempts at privacy – had seen it all, a million times, more. Amanda assured me that mine was nothing special, I was nothing special.

My room-mate couldn't even attempt privacy, so I tried not to look as Amanda lowered the hoist, the sides of his hydraulic hospital bed. I tried to imagine what it must feel like to be lifted and prodded as though you weren't quite there. As though you were a doll. She would take each pale arm in turn, spraying deodorant. Turning on both taps of our shared sink, smarming down Joe's sleepy hair with a quick flannel. Joe dealt with the daily indignity by ignoring her. Like a king accepting necessary homage.

One Saturday, near the end of my first year, Amanda was kneeling at Joe's feet, forcing them into weekend trainers, when there was a loud alarm. A shrill scream. Amanda ignored it, tying Joe's laces in quick bows. 'There now. Not too tight?'

Joe just ignored her question. She smiled over his head. Standing, already ready to go. She folded his towel, put the cap back on his toothpaste. The noise carried on; a sharp, shocked misery. Seeing I'd ground to a halt, Amanda smiled. 'That's just Michelle. You know Michelle? Thankfully it's not every day, but something about the weekend sets her off. She forgets . . . and then when she wakes up, sees her face in the mirror, she remembers, and it upsets her. Such a shame, poor kid. It was a car accident. She could have been normal. You'll get used to it.'

I had seen Michelle, at the fire drill, my first night. I had noticed her slippers first. White rabbits, with pink, satin-lined ears. Seeing me, Michelle had smiled. She was younger than me, smaller than me. She had one quick brown eye. An uneven curiosity. The other eye was missing, the lid stitched shut, like a permanently drawn blind. She had black hair, loose curls. A scar, still angry, dividing her forehead. It ran down her temple, disappearing behind her right ear. I saw she had small gold studs in both. She had smiled at me, but I'd pretended not to notice her friendliness, the sad twist of her mouth. I'd turned away, taut with the shock of her face, my own shame. I'd avoided her ever since. Michelle was proof I couldn't belong there, that it had all been a mistake.

At weekends, we didn't have to eat on our assigned tables, so I found a space next to Katie. Katie was my best friend there, besides Rebecca. She had a blonde prettiness that had been slightly blurred by medication, the steroids she took for chronic arthritis. Her eyes were brightly blue behind thick-lensed glasses, her fingers crowded with rings. Katie's parents gave her twenty-four carats, more gold every birthday. Even though they bit into her swollen hands, she refused to take them off. Couldn't now, anyhow.

Katie looked soft, but I liked her sharp sense of the ridiculous. At eighteen, she was nearly three years older than me. We wouldn't normally have been friends, but she was still taking her GCSEs. Katie had lost time to hospitals, hip replacements. New knees. She wanted to be a social worker, but was struggling to catch up. She was, she laughed, already a granny, while still being a virgin. A miracle of her own. She leant forward stiffly, taking a careful sip of her overfull tea.

'I suppose you've got loads of plans?'

Her tone wasn't quite kind. I liked Katie. We had breakfast together every Saturday. Sat together in the common room most evenings. Watching whatever was on, eating the biscuits

I'd steal for us from the staff kitchen. But we sometimes felt more like colleagues than friends, our relationship one of proximity rather than choice. Like the biscuits we ate because they were there, not because we were hungry. Katie lived at the leafier end of the District Line, and every holiday we scribbled our home numbers down again, but neither of us ever called.

'Nothing much, just going home, back to London,' I said.

'Anything's better than this vegetable bin.' Katie smiled, sad.

When I'd first arrived I'd been surprised by the names everyone spat at each other. Katie's laughing names for me were Veggie, Spaz, Dribble, Ming-Mong, but I soon joined in. They were better than my private label, which still felt less than happy, like a synonym for loneliness. And if you used them on yourself, claimed them, they stung less. It was better to believe you were in on the joke.

'That's true. What are you going to do?'

She glanced towards the car park, leaning back in her wheelchair. I still couldn't drive, but Katie had got her licence as soon as she was able. She had spent her careful savings, her Disability Living Allowance, on a cherry-red Renault Clio. The metallic finish was extra, but fuck it, she grinned. It was going to be the start of big things. A whole new life. The first thing she was going to do, she told me, was go up West. Go clubbing. She parked the car outside her window. Always kept the tank full. I would watch her wheeling round it, a soapy bucket balanced precariously on her lap. She never wanted help, buffing the paintwork to a high shine. The trouble was, by the time it was legal for her to drive, there wasn't anywhere for Katie to go.

Before the onset of her illness, she'd been normal, she assured me. Katie had gone to a normal school. Had normal friends. But when her arthritis flared up she missed more days than she attended, and they had gradually stopped calling. The first weekend she'd driven home to show off her new wheels,

Katie came back quiet. Almost embarrassed. She closed her door. I finally plucked up the courage to ask.

Katie reddened, snapping, 'I just watched telly with my parents; was in bed by ten. My sister was going out with friends – she invited me to come with her. But they're all younger than me and I could tell she didn't really want me along, she was just being kind. I might as well have stayed here . . . at least it's company. What did I think was going to happen? I'm a fucking idiot.'

After that Katie stayed at school at weekends. Watching *Pretty Woman* for the thousandth time. The Renault always ready, parked outside her window.

Because it was a weekend at home, because he was driving me back on Sunday, because everything now was a kind of consolation for being sent away, my father took me shopping. There was a book I wanted that I didn't dare ask for back in Hampshire, at the single dog-eared bookshop near my school. Mrs Adams, my English teacher, often found me for a cup of tea before driving home. I don't think she knew she was my favourite, just understood I was lonely. Writing a title on a torn-out page of her notebook, she gave me a wary smile, said she thought I might enjoy it.

I spotted a copy of *Maurice* on the crowded shelves, next to Margaret Forster's *Lady's Maid*. I grabbed both books, hiding one under the other. Worried that the man behind the till would notice, guess. But it was a slow Saturday, the shelves almost empty of browsers. He rang them up, not looking at me, not caring. He put *Maurice* at the top, squaring the books against the desk. Sliding them into a brown paper bag, putting that bag in a plastic one. Handing me my change without a word.

That evening the three of us went out for dinner. Going to

the same restaurant we used to take Ben. It was full of week-end families like ours. Clattering talk, louder laughter. Adults debating who would drive home. Children buzzing with free-dom, too much Coca-Cola. I saw that Jenny was working. She was my favourite waitress. Her black hair shaved short, she had huge, amused green eyes, a bigger smile. Even standing on her feet all night, weaving between conversations, her thin arms stacked with plates, I never saw it slip. She must have been eighteen, certainly no more than twenty, but Jenny seemed a different species. A worldly, wonderful alien. Bringing the bill, she said, 'Emmett, I haven't seen you for ages. Your mum tells me you're away at school? How's it going?'

'It's great,' I lied, shouting slightly over the noise, feeling a rush of affection for her. The normality of a weekend at home.

Jenny tore off the slip. My father put twenty pounds on to the dish, beaming at her. She always wore a confusion of neck-laces over her white work shirt. She took one off. A jagged quartz crystal, wound in silver wire, on a leather thong. She put it round my neck, tucking the warm cord into my collar, kissing the top of my head. 'For luck,' she said.

When we got home I went straight upstairs, pretending a headache. I read *Maurice* in one sleepless night. The story was Edwardian, the love buttoned-up, illegal. Taking the risk of loving another man meant blackmail, two years' hard labour. But Maurice had dared, running away with his first lover's gamekeeper, their story finishing just before the First World War began, the two men vanishing into the green shelter of the woods. Hopefully they wouldn't be caught. Would avoid conscription, bombs.

I knew the ending was almost impossible. That a happy end-ing depended on where you stopped the story. It was a rose-tinted wish-fulfilment, but also the fantasy I needed. If Maurice and Alec were still alive, still together, they would be ancient. I was bullied, lying. But school couldn't last forever. I lay on my back, staring at the ceiling, the dim constellations of Glow Stars I was too old for now. Life might be possible, once I'd left classrooms behind. Love might be possible, somewhere else.

The dorms were separated by white sliding doors that couldn't be locked. After waving my father off on Sunday evening, I walked back. Daryl, my neighbour, was sitting on my bed. He was a gangling, blunt-cut boy, with chicken-pox scars on his forehead, a lazy eye. I never knew what his disability was, why he lived next door. Daryl smiled up at me. He was holding my copy of *Maurice*. 'You dirty bummer . . . you really are a fucking faggot.'

Daryl spat the word at me. Crashed back on my bed in an exaggerated pantomime of laughter. He rolled on to his side, throwing the book on the floor.

'I didn't know you could read,' I said. 'Get out! Go on . . . piss off!'

He rolled on to his other side, the laughter sharpening, clapping. I hated him, lunged for the book. Daryl grabbed it, ripping the cover off, tearing it, throwing the pieces on the floor. I felt sick. It would be all over the school by suppertime. Sooner.

'Fucking faggot.' Daryl pushed past me, shoving me back on the bed. He ran out into the hall, banging on every door as he went. I heard him shouting that I was a bender. A dirty poof. That I'd tried to kiss him. I stayed sitting a long time. The windows looked over the brick-columned quadrangle. There was a discreet memorial in one corner, a marble relief. The face of the school's founder, a Victorian industrialist, who had made his fortune in haberdashery: bombazine, button hooks, whalebone stays. He'd used some of his wealth to build a 'Cripples Hospital'. The institution had a small school attached.

It was intended as a refuge for barefoot children from the inner-city slums. Children born with ten fingers, ten toes, but disabled by osteal tuberculosis. The kids got another chance, and the founder got a knighthood.

The experiment was to strengthen the first pupils with fresh air, good food. Exercise and friendship. The hospital was progressive by the standards of the time, and it worked. The children thrived. They made the orthopaedic aids they needed in an on-site workshop, learnt a skilled trade, in order to be self-sufficient when they left the hospital's charitable confines. For most people, it was a kind place. A welcome, in a society that was generally unwelcoming, that preferred to shut imperfection away. I couldn't see the founder's face from my window, but queers had been illegal in his day. I was sure I wasn't included in his philanthropy.

I unlocked Marie's box, taking out the small tray meant for cash. *Maurice* just fitted. I put the tray back, locked it.

That night, I couldn't sleep, just stared at the orange glow of the emergency call button next to my pillow. It felt like an emergency. Wanting to talk, I said, 'Joe . . . Joe, are you awake?'

'I am now,' he answered.

'Do you actually like football?'

'You want to know that now, in the middle of the night? You idiot . . . Of course I like football, I love it. My dad always got us season tickets, before I came here. He used to drive us to all the games, miles. Every fixture, every weekend. I miss it.'

It was the most I had ever heard Joe speak.

'Of course, it was better when I could actually play. I wasn't always like this, you know; I used to be normal. Now I'm stuck here . . . stuck with you.'

He made a soft, disappointed sound. 'Night.'

The next day before breakfast, the housemaster, Ian – a

bluff, kind Northerner like my dad – knocked on my door. 'Morning, can I see you? It won't take a minute.'

I'd never been summoned to his office before. The desk was crowded with mouldy cups, spilling ashtrays, a chaos of paper. Propped on the windowsill were two school photos. Two girls, their uniformed smiles. Seeing me look, he gestured to them. 'My girls.'

Ian seemed embarrassed, wouldn't meet my eye. He swept some papers on to the floor, sitting on the edge of his desk, hands on his spread knees. 'Now, I'm not saying what Daryl did was right. He's younger than you, and between us, well, he can be a bit of a prick. But . . . if we do find out that what he's been saying is true –' he looked out the window '– if there's any truth in it, well, we'd have to ask you to leave.'

He turned, smiling, cautious. I guessed Ian was older than my father. His hair was thicker, but threaded with grey. There were deep creases, laughter lines, running to his temples. The whites of his eyes were smoked, yellowed with nicotine.

'We couldn't have it, Emmett, not here. We're responsible for too many other kids, and they're vulnerable. We're *in loco parentis* here; there'd be no way around it. Now, I don't want to know the truth, but my advice to you is to keep your head down. I know you're close to your parents, that you go home most weekends . . . that's good. Just keep your head down, get through it. You're a bright lad, and this place will be over for you in a moment. There's a much bigger world for you . . . just not today.'

He slapped his knees, standing. 'Righto, breakfast. My door's always open if you need a chat.'

I thanked him politely, not imagining a time when I would ever want to talk to him again.

The following morning, after cramming down too much toast, I asked Rebecca to go out with me. To be my girlfriend, my alibi. The white processed bread was a solid ball in my stomach. I felt sick with it, and with the lie. She looked at her knuckles for a moment, twisting the silver rings. She smiled, said yes.

17

Learning

The thing about going out with someone if you're at boarding school is that there aren't many places to go. You already live together round the clock. The only way to differentiate between school hours and leisure time is to change clothes. At four, Rebecca would disappear with the bell, coming to find me in the classroom, her hair loose over an angry band T-shirt. The heavy metal she loved and I hated: AC/DC and Iron Maiden. The closest to pop she got was Queen. Rebecca's favourite T-shirt was an image of Freddie Mercury at Live Aid, arm outstretched, proud, above the chanting crowds. Despite her telling me it would be all right, it was what she wanted, I never dared put my hand under it. We'd take out our books, but never looked at them. They were only an alibi.

She'd put on perfume, line her eyes. I liked her pink, floral smell; liked her. It bothered Rebecca, I think, that I never changed out of my uniform. But even with my tie off, I could never imagine myself anywhere else. Even with the door closed, I felt I was being watched, was always watching myself. We'd kiss. I knew I kissed as though I was being graded for it. But we still tried, every afternoon until November.

Then Freddie Mercury died. The twenty-fourth of November 1991. Rebecca and I were on the same table for all our meals. She had been crying all day, had missed the last period. English was normally her favourite lesson. Now she looked past me, still in her uniform; for once she hadn't changed. She pressed the ice-cream scoop of instant mashed potato into her brown stew without eating any, put her fork down, saying flatly, 'Can I talk to you, after? Can we go somewhere?'

I knew where she meant without having to ask. It was the place we always went. The only place to go, if you wanted to be alone, was the local churchyard. A square, squat Norman church, hard against the perimeter fence. Rebecca had to slow down for me, so that I could walk beside her wheelchair. We couldn't sit together, but I'd get as close as I could, perching opposite her on the low flint wall. Looking over her shoulder, Rebecca would reach under her seat cushion for hidden cigarettes. Her Bensons, gold Zippo lighter, a birthday present from a father she hardly saw. Who, she joked, had forgotten that she was only fifteen. Still too young to smoke. Smoking, kissing in the freezing graveyard were minor rebellions, but the only ones we had.

One weekend at the beginning of November, my second month away, Mum had bought me a jacket. It was another expensive consolation. Italian, navy wool, with a soft black suede back. A duck-down lining, furred hood. That night, even though Rebecca had her own – a cheap biker leather; she couldn't get the proper paint, so had Tippexed it with band names – I took mine off, wrapping it round her shoulders. A clumsy gesture borrowed from American teen movies, films I'd first seen with Ben, happy under his arm. *Pretty in Pink* or *Big*. I knew it was what normal boys did for their girlfriends, so I did it too.

Rebecca's smoking was another borrowed gesture. Normally, she'd blow smoke into the dark, watching as it curled upwards, mixing with our frozen breath. I was always amazed by how bright the stars were. How close they looked, and how many. It was comforting to feel so small, under all that glitter. What did it matter if I was really gay? Rebecca and I shared the same diagnosis: cerebral palsy, spastic diplegia. If I had not gone to America, I would have been in a wheelchair, like her. I felt guilty. Felt we belonged together.

Rebecca would usually say something about how romantic it was. Just us. We'd talk about the future. Imagined jobs we'd get. Houses we'd live in. I knew it wasn't likely we'd get as far as signing contracts, picking up keys, so heaped details on to the harmless fantasy. Dog or cat? How many kids? I was never sure whether she believed in it, but that night Rebecca didn't add any more. As soon as she'd lit it, she threw her cigarette into the grass. She turned awkwardly, looking past me to the high, starry hedges.

'I hoped we'd at least make it to the Christmas dinner. You've never been to one . . . it's the best part of the whole year in this dump. The Queen sends the turkeys from Norfolk, her estate. She sends the puddings too. It's so good . . . Everyone dresses up, everyone eats too much. There are candles, and we all get to celebrate together, have a happy Christmas, before we go home.'

I said nothing. I realized then that there was another difference between us. Home was where I was happiest. I didn't need Her Majesty's turkeys, royal charity. For Rebecca, school was more a home than anywhere else had been. But she knew I was counting off the meals, the minutes until I was able to leave. She lit another cigarette, taking a long drag, shifting in her chair. 'I even bought you a fucking present. Fucking aftershave . . . That's what you're supposed to get boys, isn't it? Even if they couldn't grow a beard in a competition.'

Rebecca stared at me. Even in the dark, her anger was bright, flaring. 'What a stupid cow I am. What an idiot. They all told me – Alex, Laura, everyone – they all told me you were bent. I don't know why I've only just figured it out. Maybe it's Freddie,

I don't know. Maybe I didn't want to know. It's slim pickings round here, not easy to get a boyfriend.'

I wanted to laugh. We were in the same boat. It wasn't going to be easy for me to get a boyfriend either. She took another drag on her cigarette, then threw it at me. It landed at my feet, hissing out on the damp grass.

'Did you ever really like me? Or was it just something to do? A way to look normal? A way to pass the time, take the heat off?'

'I'm not a bender,' I said, suddenly angry too. Spitting the word at her. 'And I did . . . I do like you. You're my best friend here.'

'Your best friend?'

In Rebecca's mouth it sounded tepid. Much less than she deserved. I thought of Freddie. I couldn't understand how a gay rock star was allowed but a gay schoolboy wasn't. Freddie could be pinned up over our pillows, his stadium chants shouted down the hallways, but I had to lock my books away. I hated his songs, but liked Freddie's humour. His sharp eye; his grand, grandiose swagger. Life was a great joke. He seemed so far above it all. Smiling down at grey routine, everything every-day, dull. Freddie lived in a glittering orbit, was famous, rich. So rich he was able to be himself, and not just at weekends.

Freddie's fortune had kept the world at a distance. I only had my Disability Living Allowance. A little from Peg. Washed pound coins Sellotaped into birthday cards, a swift pen line through the anniversary wishes.

Freddie hadn't publicly acknowledged he was ill, until just before he died. He'd retreated behind locked gates. It was nobody's business, and anyway most Queen fans chose to ignore how fragile he looked, the inconvenient truth that their favourite peacock was gay, dying of AIDS. The fact was his death made Freddie safe to worship. The only truly acceptable queer was a famous one. A dead one.

'Well, that just makes it worse,' Rebecca continued. 'That you just don't like me. Not like that, I can tell. It's like I'm homework to you. And we never go anywhere . . . never do anything. I don't want another friend. I don't need that.'

I wanted to shout at her: Where could we go? What could we do? We were fifteen, bored of waiting for our lives to start. Much too young to be sitting in the dark, playing with words like love. But I had loved somebody, or thought I had, once.

The truth was that I was ashamed. Of Rebecca, and of myself. On a school night, we were allowed as far as the local village. A sleepy, thatched place with one pub, which was forbidden, and one shop, which wasn't. The first and only time we'd gone there together, a woman posting her letters had looked at us as if we shouldn't be out, as if we were in her way. Her face a mixture of amusement and pity. With Rebecca, I felt more conspicuous, not less. We were disabled to the power of two. The square root of awkwardness. What made it worse was Rebecca seemed to accept herself. I liked her punky spectacle. Her loud insistence that it was the strangers who stared that had the problem, not her. But the fact I couldn't emulate her silver-studded attitude made me feel as though I was failing at being disabled. After that, we stayed in the grounds, or went to the churchyard, only when it was dark. Rebecca deserved someone better, someone braver.

'I'm sorry . . . really sorry.'

'Well, that's just great. Really useful, really kind. I don't need that either . . . I just need you to piss off, that's all. That's the one thing you can still do for me.'

She reversed, turning sharply, catching her front wheel on the low verge, then sped away down the unlit road. 'I'm keeping your bloody jacket,' she shouted behind her. 'I've earned it.'

That night, 'Who Wants to Live Forever' was loud behind every door. People who didn't like Queen had hurried to town, buying the equally hurried release, their *Greatest Hits*. Freddie sang in every room but mine. Surrounded by the song on all sides, I couldn't imagine anything worse than living forever.

18
Salt and Vinegar

The following Saturday my mother picked me up. She was early, already smiling by the car, waving, while we were eating breakfast. Her face was a small shock. Brightly made-up, even though it was the weekend. Before we'd even joined the motorway, Mum had pulled the car on to a verge, undoing her belt, folding over in great, gusting sobs. I was frightened by her sound, the unexpected reversal. I put my hand on her back, but the move felt clumsy, inadequate. Like throwing ice cubes at a forest fire. I felt like everybody was watching, didn't want the passing drivers to notice us, slow for my mother's despair.

Waiting, I thought of my sixth birthday party. The year my mother had given me an ocean, quick with swimming silver-foil fish. She had loved my surprise, scooped me up with laughing kisses. The fish had stayed up for weeks, long after the last guests had gone.

She stopped crying. Twisting for her handbag on the back seat, searching for a tissue. Briskly wiping away sad tracks of mascara, repairing the damage in her mirror. Mum cleared her throat, as if admonishing herself, tried a smile. In the long moment before she spoke, I imagined past-midnight telephone calls, mid-air collisions. Very sorry doctors with murmured, terminal diagnoses.

'Whoo . . . I hadn't meant to do that, Em. I'm sorry, I thought I was done. We agreed we'd wait, tell you when we're all together – your dad's making lunch – but I fucked that up.

We're splitting up, Peach . . . a trial separation. It's been coming for ages. I just can't do it any more, I'm sorry. You're here, your dad's always late, always working; I'm rattling around that big house, watching TV with the fucking cat. I don't think he even likes me much any more. He wants a bigger house, a bigger car, bigger friends. And I'm lonely; you know I've never cared much about any of that stuff – good times didn't use to be expensive. You don't need me to tell you that money isn't the answer. It's useful, but can't cure most things. Charlie still thinks it might, the stupid arse, or he thinks that if he keeps chasing it, he can ignore how miserable we are. Your dad used to be the most fun, but he's stopped playing, that's it. I'm sorry, Peach, it isn't fair of me to badmouth him, I'll shut up . . . I shouldn't involve you like this. And we both love you . . . that won't change. I've been looking at houses – I've found us one, smaller, in Hither Green. I hope you'll want to come.'

When we got home, Dad had roasted a chicken, but none of us were hungry, did more than pick. I couldn't meet either of their effortful smiles, tried to remember the last time I'd been an audience for their dancing, and couldn't. After lunch my father told me he had some work to finish. He kissed me on the top of the head before retreating to his office. My mother went to her room, closing the door. Turning up the radio. I spent the rest of Saturday shut behind my own door, George curled captive on my lap.

For the last few months, longer, the weekends had been like this. If the three of us did go out together now, it would be to places where we couldn't talk. The cinema, a matinee. Home was either loud with shouting, or too quiet when it finally stopped. I felt like an ignored referee at a football match. I used to dread Sunday nights. Would drag my feet towards the car, pretending to be interested in *Antiques Roadshow*. But lately I was happier to leave.

That Sunday afternoon, after a frighteningly cheerful lunch of leftovers, and much earlier than usual, Dad drove me back to school.

Normally, Dad always made five minutes for Joe. They talked football fixtures. Swapped the weekend positions of the Blues and the Magpies. My father was always telling me I should make more of an effort with my room-mate. He was a nice lad really. Just quiet, lonely. I should try to remember he was so much worse off. But when we arrived back that day, my dad ignored Joe. He put my bag down on my bed. Hands in pockets, awkward, wanting to go.

'Take care, son. Call me if you need anything. I'll be back next week to pick you up. See you on Saturday.'

'I love you, Dad,' I said quietly, not caring if Joe heard.

I saw Joe's slow smile, laughter twitching at the corners of his mouth. I wanted to be alone. Wanted to hit him. We weren't friends, just shared a room, a similar predicament, that was all.

'It's your mum who wants this, Em, not me . . . I wanted you to know. It might not be forever. I love you too. I'll see you at the weekend.'

It wasn't that we didn't, it was just that the word 'love' wasn't a part of our language. It was an everyday certainty between us, would never normally need to be said.

'I'll see you at the weekend,' he said again.

Joe reversed, letting my father out.

I've always been greedy. At home, food was time shared. Affection from chipped plates. Weekend wine, laughing conversation. Dad driving me mad, insisting I learnt to argue my opinions. At school we had breakfast, all our meals, in a long, low-ceilinged hall. We ate from brown shatter-proof plates. Brown shatter-proof meals, served quick and loud. Someone had painted a mural on one wall. A rainbow, intended to brighten our mornings, the blistered, institutional beige. I'd never really noticed it before, but looking at the curve now I felt trapped, felt my appetite disappear.

You could tell which day of the week it was by what you got for dinner. Monday was mince; Tuesday, the leftovers were turned into shepherd's pie with the addition of instant mashed potato. Wednesday was cheese and potato pie; Thursday, a chicken and mushroom pie. On Friday, we had a break from pie, plastic white bread and butter. We got the choice of flabby pizza or fish and chips. There was Coke to drink instead of water, or the usual tin-tasting tea.

It would be wrong to say that my parents splitting up was the reason, but it was a catalyst, the last straw. I stopped sleeping. Stopped being able to eat, whatever day of the week it was. I was still on Rebecca's table, but now she ignored me, talking too loudly to everyone, anyone else. School had never felt like home, and now home wasn't one either. After the fifth week of letting my chips go cold, Sue noticed. She stopped me as I was leaving the dining room. 'Not hungry again? What's going on, Emmett? Are you OK?'

Her face was as kind as always, her permed hair tied up with a flowered scarf.

Sue walked me back to the empty dorms. Sitting on my bed, she put an arm round me. This small gesture, the weight of it on my shoulder, let me finally cry. I could hear laughter outside the window. Didn't want any happier students to hear me. I wanted to tell Sue, though I'm sure she already knew, that I'd split up with Rebecca, but I hadn't expected that to mean silence. Rebecca and I had talked, joked, from breakfast to lights-out. And now I had nobody. It was my fault.

I wanted to tell Sue that my parents were splitting up too. That they had always felt like home to me. And in the months since they'd stopped talking, started shouting, I'd felt roofless, vagrant. I wanted to tell her that I was tired. Bone-tired of myself, the sweating effort of carrying myself around, standing on my hands. I'd found a picture of Cindy Crawford in a colour supplement the term before, torn it out. Apart from a photo of Joanna, it was the only picture on my side of the room. I liked Cindy's smile, her perfect American teeth, what I imagined was a perfect American life. She looked kind, not just beautiful. I thought that if I studied the photo long enough, I might see what other boys did. But we both knew she was only an alibi. Sitting next to Sue, I wanted to tear it down, to tell her I was gay, a liar.

I wanted to tell Sue that I was hungry. Starving. But that not eating, punishing my body, felt easier, suddenly, than giving it what it needed. It was stupid, I knew that. I wasn't fat, I knew that. But denying myself was the only way I'd found of letting my body know how much I hated it. How much I felt it had let me down, and how much I wanted to desert it, to walk away. There was satisfaction in my sharpening face, shrinking reflection. I'd found a way to take up less space in the world.

Sue waited for my noise to stop. She gave me a clean handkerchief from her sleeve, tucked under her watch strap.

We sat in silence. Then she said, 'You silly, if you don't tell me, how can I help you?'

All I replied was that my parents were splitting up, that it wasn't the end of the world, and that that weekend I was going to stay at school. When I rang to tell my mother, she agreed, seemed relieved.

The following Saturday, the others took the coach into town. My bedroom was next to the common room that separated the boys' and girls' wings. Later, I heard them watching movies: *The Lost Boys*, again. I could hear Rebecca's laugh through the open door. Her saying, again, how much she wanted Kiefer Sutherland to fuck her. Vampires were easier, more reliable, than any of the spazzers here. She always ate crisps in front of the TV, salt and vinegar. I was so hungry, wanted to share them, wanted to join her so badly. But except for mandatory mealtimes, I lay on my bed with my shoes on, stayed in my room.

After that, I ate most meals with Sue. The mornings she was rostered on, she watched every bite. I was given Nestlé Build-Up drinks. Every flavour, from chocolate to chicken. If I chose Weetabix with my toast, Sue gave me gold-top full-fat milk or single cream. At lunchtime, I was given seconds, thirds of Arctic roll. A treat. The ice cream tasted of nothing.

You only had ten minutes, fifteen at most, the break between morning assembly and first lesson. I would walk back to the dorms, shutting myself in the toilet, the only place with a lock. Forcing my fingers down my throat, trying to force up my breakfast. Even then, my body wasn't much help. Usually, my stomach stayed stubbornly full, so I'd use my toothbrush. Lathering the bristles with the shared, hairy soap usually worked first time. It was difficult to kneel on the floor, bend over the toilet, so I'd stand at the basin. I'd try not to see what I was doing, catch my red-eyed, retching reflection in the mirror. I'd try to convince myself that cleaning your tonsils with Imperial Leather after every meal was normal. That I was perfectly all right. It's amazing how quickly self-disgust can become self-denial, harm. An awful daily routine. I'd rinse my mouth out, scoop the food blocking the plughole into a paper towel, bin it. There was always a can of air freshener on the toilet cistern; I hoped the sharply synthetic lemon spray would cover the smell. Drying my hands, I'd tell myself that everything was fine. And at least my insides would be sparkling.

I queued for the spitty payphone, ringing Joanna almost every night. Talking about nothing, just to hear her voice. Peg still wrote to me every week, but her letters – her unchanging news, a cheerfully impatient jumble of capitals and lower-case, the cartoons she clipped from her *Daily Mail* – that usually felt so comforting now just made me angry. They felt like dispatches from a world I wasn't part of any more. I couldn't answer them. Didn't have the words. I knew that Peg would just tell me I was being daft, send me a fiver for some sweets.

I made another hole in my belt with the point of my nail scissors. And then another. Sue phoned home, and my mother, too busy with her own sorrow, snapped that I was fine. I'd always been hungry; greedy, in fact. Sue must be mistaken. I'd given up meat, yes, but my version of vegetarianism meant I seemed to live on crisps. I was a crispatarian. It was just a teenage phase, attention-seeking. I might get scurvy, but nothing more serious than that.

Sue made me an appointment with the school dietician, a plump, pretty woman I'd seen around but never really noticed before. She had a pink-lipsticked smile, a desk full of sweets. At the end of our first session, she explained that my walking burned so much more energy than normal. I needed calories. That my body was a machine that needed feeding even more than most. I was lucky, if I thought about it. I could have my cake, and eat it too.

Looking at her watch, she smiled more warmly. I could have anything I wanted, anything at all. She was sure she would like the same problem. Leaving, she put a lollipop in my top pocket. She agreed that the school food was pretty revolting, but said they were on a budget. I was just being picky and simply hadn't found anything to my taste. She smiled again, saying that boys couldn't really suffer from eating disorders, it was more of a girl thing. All I had to do was decide to eat. Easy.

After another month, whatever I tried to eat tasted of soap. I ate when I went home, but still forced most of my school meals down the plughole. Sue watched, sitting with me after breakfast, so I couldn't disappear. But she couldn't work, couldn't keep an eye on me, seven days a week.

One dinner-time, Rebecca finally broke her silence. 'I've never noticed it before, how big your nose is, massive . . . you could probably see it from space. You look like that little bird from *Charlie Brown and Snoopy* . . . Woodstock, I think he's called, yellow, all beak. You look awful. Really, like shit. Are you trying to leave by stealth?'

It was Rebecca's noticing that made me realize I had to stop, or rather start. I asked to see the school's counsellor. Because I was still only fifteen, still a minor, Catherine had to meet my parents before any sessions could begin. They arrived separately, still in their work suits, still barely talking. It was a heavy-raining afternoon; my father kept his coat on, could barely look at me. He stared at the clock instead, like a schoolboy summoned for something he was sure he hadn't done. The silence grew louder. Eventually, he broke it. 'Look, I don't really see why we're here. I don't want to be rude, but this is for Emmett, isn't it? He's requested to see you, not us. We're fine . . .'

Catherine was a tall, extremely neat woman. She had precise blonde hair, a precise manner. Looking at her, I felt painfully untidy. I wasn't at all sure that someone so pulled-together would be able to bear my chaos.

Watching my father biting at his thumb, his resentment making it bleed, I wanted to smile, eat. Walk out and take the next train back to London. Catherine drew back black polished loafers, explaining that the meeting was essential, school policy. An insurance. She couldn't see me without first seeing them.

My mother cut her off, angry. 'You're being so rude, Charlie. For fuck's sake, can't you simply be here . . . be where we are, even for a minute?'

She rooted in her handbag, wiping her eyes, smiling wetly at

Catherine. 'I'm sorry. You see the problem? He always wants to be somewhere else. I never see him any more, not without a prior appointment. It's for Emmett, and even then, he can't spare the time . . .'

'Fuck off, Fran. That isn't fair, and you know it. I mean it . . . just fuck off. All of you.' Dad stood up, belting his raincoat, leaving without saying goodbye.

My sessions with Catherine were every Wednesday at four-thirty. That way I wouldn't miss any teaching, would have time to change if I wanted. I was quiet for almost all of our first fifty minutes. Catherine smiled encouragement, assured me that my silence was OK. That she was there whenever I felt ready. It was my time, however I needed to spend it.

I didn't know where to begin. The borrowed office had a dusty African violet on the windowsill. Spare chairs stacked against the dirty magnolia walls. We both looked at the clock. At ten past five, Catherine told me I had ten minutes left. I liked her already, but this room was still school. I was still surrounded, could hear noises, shouts, on the other side of the closed curtains. It didn't feel safe to speak. I thought of my father, the look on his face as he buttoned his coat, stormed out, feeling sharply disloyal. Now I was sitting in front of the counsellor, I felt so hungry. My sadness felt too large, too ugly to talk about. Too small to take up Catherine's afternoon. I would be all right; I just had to keep my breakfast down. By the end of the session, I still hadn't opened my mouth.

'I'm sorry,' I said, feeling like I'd failed.

'I'll see you next week, next Wednesday; yes, Emmett? There's no need to apologize to me.'

When the bell rang the following Wednesday, I ran back to my dorm. Pulling off my grey school trousers, I swapped them for expensively slashed black jeans. They had been a mistake. The rips showed my scars, still pink, just above my knees. I didn't like them, didn't usually wear them. I had bought them for someone else. The person I wished I was. Catherine's door was open. She was early. Already sitting, hands crossed in her lap. She got up to close the door behind me. Smiled, saying, 'Now, those are extremely angry trousers . . .'

I laughed, then Catherine laughed.

'I'm sorry, I shouldn't have said that . . . started like that. But you learn, in this work, everything is a communication. I want to remind you that everything you say here is confidential, strictly between us. The only time I'd ever break it is if you were actively harming yourself or another student. Or if you had a plan to kill yourself, not just a suicidal ideation. I know it's a lot to take in, but you're safe here. Why don't you start by telling me why you asked to see me?'

I thought that starving yourself was obviously self-harm; whether it counted as suicide, I wasn't sure. I couldn't meet her eye. Instead, looking at my scuffed toes, I said, 'I just don't want to be here. I mean, I asked to be here, with you, but I hate this school . . . I hate it. I hate every day, every minute. And every weekend my parents ask me how I am, and I've stopped knowing how to answer, what to say. My dad . . . he made money . . . he used to be fun. But then he got too busy for that. Dad always tells me he did it for me, but it just isn't true; I never asked him to. And if it really was for me, then I wouldn't have been stuck here – I'd never have chosen to come. If I couldn't have stayed at my old school, then I could have had lessons at home. I wouldn't have had many friends, but I don't have many here. I might have been lonely, but not as lonely as I am here. Being on your own isn't always lonely . . . being where you shouldn't be is much worse, much lonelier. I hate it here, and I hate that this is where my parents have put me: a problem dealt with, shut away. They don't understand; they can't. I hate them for it.'

I looked at my hands, shocked at my own admission.

'I see them, Rebecca, Laura . . . they cope with this place, with themselves, so much better than I do. The only thing we have in common is a label I don't want, that I've never wanted. I'm jealous of them . . . want to know how they do it. Rebecca's happy here; it's home. When she goes out, she pretends not to see the stares, but I see them. She doesn't seem to have a problem; but, for me, my sticks, my walk . . . it is the problem. I just can't . . . Joe, my room-mate, he's much worse off than I am – I know I'm lucky. But that's worse: I feel shitty, guilty for being so unhappy. Being here . . . it's like a mirror I'm being forced to look at. And I don't, I can't, like what I see. And because I don't like it, can't see how anybody could, I feel like I'm failing . . . all the time. I mean, other people just get on with it. But who would choose this? Who actually wants it? All disabled people are different, right? As different as anybody else. But here, it's easier; the only way to treat us is as if we're all the same, a symptom, a diagnosis . . . a medical problem. I don't want it. Don't want to get comfortable here. This is my only life, my only time around. And this is how I'm spending it . . . I think I'd rather not.'

I stopped, surprised to have said so much, admitted it.

Catherine sat forward, slim palms on her knees. She smiled carefully. 'What would you rather not, Emmett . . . if you had the choice?'

'But I don't have the choice. That's the whole point . . . I don't have any choice. I could tell you I wanted to dance, but that wouldn't mean I could. I could tell you I wanted to leave, but to go where? I really can't talk my way out of this. I think . . . I don't think I want to die . . . I'm much too scared. But I'm not sure I can live like this either. I'm stuck. I need a miracle, not a conversation.'

★

At the end of term, both my parents came to collect me. My mother drove, singing along to *Dusty in Memphis*, 'Just a Little Lovin'', all the way to the exit for London, Dad quiet, smiling beside her.

I didn't know what had changed but it seemed like they were together again. I sat in the back, happy to be ignored, happy to be invisible. That night the three of us went out for dinner. We were the loudest, shiniest people in the silver-polished hum of the Mayfair restaurant. I was so thrilled that I forgot I didn't eat, said yes to pudding. Dad stopped at one glass of champagne, drove us home. My mother finished the bottle, closing her eyes on the back seat. The hotels lining Park Lane lit up the dark. I felt privileged. Safe. Stopped by a red light, Dad reached for my hand. 'You're my world, you and Fran. You understand that, don't you, Em?'

Catherine sat opposite me, in the fraying blue armchairs, every Wednesday for almost two years. She shared silence when words failed me. She let me cry. Listened. With her help, I did well, not brilliantly, in my GCSEs. Next year I'd still be sleeping at the school, but studying at the local sixth-form college. The promise of a new beginning made it easier to speak. At first, I still talked around my unhappiness, edged the possibility of my queerness, before one day just telling her. The sky didn't fall. Nobody outside the room had heard me say it. I started to eat.

19
Heavy Weather

It was a Sunday, the last day of the holidays. My father stood in the window, frowning at the sky, the rain drumming off parked cars.

'Christ, just look at it. There's nothing for it, Em, we should sell up . . . move to California, somewhere dry. What do you say to Death Valley? Your mum might prefer it.' He smiled over his shoulder. 'You'd better stay in, I think. Can't go out in that. Why don't you ring Joanna; she can come here instead, have lunch?'

Dad was just being kind, being careful. Like most people living in England, I am obsessed with the weather. But it isn't just small talk, finding something to say in bored corners at parties. Rain is dangerous. Caught out in it, my sticks will skid from under me on suddenly shining pavements. I'll go down, the ground lurching up to wind me. I'll bloody my knees. Once, I broke two fingers trying to break my fall. Whoever is with me will pull me up, put me on my feet again. I'll smile that it's all right, really. Stinging, more from embarrassment, my ruined trousers, than any injury. Wanting to be invisible. Because I live in London, not Death Valley, I'm often indoors, listening to the rain.

So I smiled back, rang Joanna.

Joanna always understood. Never seemed to mind the last-minute change of plan. Dad would drive to the video shop, stopping at the pizza place, grinning round the door, arms full.

We spent hours, whole listless days sometimes, in front of the TV. At seven, I'd felt like Joanna's equal; at sixteen, I could feel like a job. I pretended not to care. Listened to the rain on the roof.

Half an hour later, Joanna pressed the bell, darting a kiss at me. She was dressed as a teenage resentment: her dad's rusted Crombie, a no-colour jumper with holes where she'd forced her thumbs through the cuffs. Scuffed Cherry Reds. She called up the stairs to my mum, kicking them off. There were more holes in her socks; the boots' soles were cracked right through. They had been a grudging fourteenth birthday present from Madeline, who still wished her daughter would want something delicate. Looking at them, I was jealous that my friend's shoes lasted so long.

'Hello, gorgeous.'

Jo smiled, but it was wary, didn't convince. There were purple thumbprints, sleepless smudges under her eyes.

I hugged her, awkward. She smelt of cigarettes, tobacco. Golden Virginia, the rollies her mother hated. Underneath that the sour smell of wet wool, floral deodorant.

Jo pushed past me into the front room. She shrugged out of her coat, throwing it at the sofa.

'Are you all right, Jo?'

She didn't answer. Instead, pulled a CD from the coat, kneeling to load it into the stacking system. Pressing Play. 'You have to listen to this . . . it's just so good. I bought it yesterday, and you have to hear it.'

She was jagged, jangling.

I sat on the floor beside her, against the sofa. We listened to *Automatic for the People* twice. Jo sang along, softly, had already learnt all the words. I didn't want to listen to sad songs, already miserable to be going back to school. Heavy metal, blasting, angry, down the wings. The stewed, bleach-tasting tea, scoured melamine. The taunts I pretended not to hear, looks I pretended not to see. The professional comfort of care staff. But really, what could I expect? I didn't even try to blend in. I was the only boy on my unit who dyed his hair. Whose mother sent him back a different colour, drove him back to school with new clothes, every Sunday. You couldn't blame them really, kids whose parents only saw them in the holidays.

Joanna was a good friend, more. I loved her like a sister. When I wasn't hanging on the spit-smelling payphone, asking to come home, I was ringing her housemistress, asking if I could speak to her. But her sadness was contagious. All it took was the right look, the wrong song, and we could convince ourselves that the world was ending, that we might be happier if it did.

Joanna got up from the floor, locking the living-room door. Sitting down again. She was silent a long time, listening to the music, examining her fingers, forcing her cuticles back with a thumbnail.

'God, I hate it there . . . hate her. I've only been at home a week, and my mum won't stop picking at me. Everything I do is wrong. They're always fighting, always shouting, slamming around. I've spent most of the week shut up in my room. And now I'm going back. Fucking great holiday.'

I felt disloyal. Madeline was kind to me. Now that I was older, she always found time to talk. I liked our kitchen cigarettes, glasses of wine. Jo hated that I always stopped to say hello.

She was silent again, looking past me, out into the empty street. I reached for her hand, but she jerked away. 'I'm just going to disappoint her again. I know it, can't help it. What if I am gay? What if I really don't change, those bitches at school are right, I'm a dyke? I did things, sleepovers, but I thought it would pass. Well, it hasn't. I'm already the wrong daughter . . . we both know it. And now this. She'll fucking freak.'

Jo stretched for the remote, turning on to her back. Pressing

Play again. She sang along as though she were alone. Started to cry, tears sliding from the corners of her eyes on to the rug. The same threadbare Persian my parents had danced on, that we'd had tea parties on when we were six.

'It's the music talking, Jo, come on.'

I reached for her hand again, but Joanna brushed me off, unwilling, or unable, to be comforted. 'You don't get it . . . you can't. It's all right for you. Your parents love you so much, you know they'll support you. Your mum has always been so kind to me, I've always wanted to live here. She'll probably throw a party, bake a fucking rainbow cake. You're so lucky, Em.'

I knew I was lucky. That I could tell my mother, and she would probably make a cake. Dad would be more difficult, but he was still the same father who had built me Lego castles. Who had carried me on his shoulders until I had grown much too heavy, too tall. Who still joked that I was responsible for his shrinking. The same dad who, before I started singing, had taken me to the Saturday Cinema Club at the Barbican because he understood I didn't speak football, still wanted us to spend time together. Smiling in the dark, we had seen 20,000 *Leagues Under the Sea*, *The Thief of Baghdad*. Had travelled to the bottom of the ocean, the tops of mountains, without leaving our seats. I knew he wouldn't switch places now, wouldn't stop wanting to sit next to me.

But I also knew that I wasn't lucky. That I would have given anything to be able to walk, to not be nervous in wet weather. To take my body for granted, as Joanna did. From the morning we'd met in the playground, I thought she was wonderful, couldn't understand her tear-stained rejection of herself. Joanna could run up hills without breaking a sweat. She could dance, feeling the music in her feet. Because I had grown up with noise, laughter, I couldn't understand the loneliness of growing up in silence. A house where expressing affection was bad manners. Joanna was able-bodied, bright, beautiful. What was there to cry about? She would never understand the segregated loneliness of a special school. The walls weren't high, but I could never decide if they had been built to keep us in or the rest of the world out. Whether they were for our protection or to shut us from view.

I knew there was little point in trying to explain how caged I felt. Everybody I needed to hear it was so free, they couldn't possibly understand. It was like trying to explain colour to a person blind from birth. Music to someone deaf.

Joanna sat up, mopping at her eyes with ragged cuffs. 'I'd better go. I told Mum I'd be home for lunch.'

She ejected the CD, shoving it back in her coat pocket, her arms into the sleeves. She bent to kiss the top of my head, unlocked the door. Pausing, she smiled. 'D'you know, all the time you and Ben were mucking around, so inseparable, he told me we were going out. I thought of him as my boyfriend . . . Stupid, really, and all along you wished it was you.'

Joanna called up the hall that she was going, slamming the front door without waiting for an answer.

'Has Jo already gone? Isn't she eating?'

My mother was standing at the stove. She wiped her hands on a tea towel, flushed with steam from rattling pans, her cheek dusted with flour. She wasn't the kind of mother who made a sacrament of Sunday dinner. We always sat down together, but never normally had a roast. But as it was colder and I was going back to school, she'd peeled potatoes, made gravy from scratch. I burst into tears.

'I'm sorry, so sorry. I can't do it, I just can't be . . .'

She turned off the pans, looking at me carefully. Undoing her apron. 'Hey, come on, Peach. What have you got to be sorry for? What can't you be?'

She listened while I told her everything. That I'd hoped it

would go away. That I had even prayed about it, but the sky was empty. I told her how much I still missed Ben, that it was my fault we weren't friends. That I felt so lonely it terrified me. That everybody suspected at school, and that the housemaster had warned that if it was confirmed, if there was any truth in it at all, I'd have to leave.

Finally, I had nothing left. Mum put an arm round me, waited for my tears to stop. 'Well, I must have done something right.' She smiled.

'What?'

'I always wanted a gay son, and now I've got one. So, like I say, I must've done something right. And, while we're being honest, it's not the greatest surprise. All those trips to the Queen's House at weekends . . . drawing endless pictures of Elizabeth I. You insisted it was her house, even after we told you it was built for another queen. And there was something too intense about your friendship with Ben. I did suspect, but it had to burn out.'

I hadn't realized that anyone else had noticed. 'I still miss him, still think about him. I'm such a fucking idiot.'

I pushed the heels of my hands into my eyes, not wanting her to see me. Wishing I was invisible, that I'd kept my mouth shut. The word I'd finally said still felt like a label I didn't want, still felt like another word for loneliness, but I couldn't take it back.

'You're not an idiot, Em.' She kissed my ear. 'But I think you were the only twelve-year-old who asked his mother for a National Trust membership. I'm not an idiot either . . . I wasn't ever waiting to meet your girlfriend. I'm not as blind as your grandma. She still thinks you're going to marry Joanna.'

'Please don't tell Dad, not yet . . .'

'It isn't my news to tell. Of course I won't. But your father isn't blind; I really don't think he'll mind.'

In the car, driving back to school, we hardly spoke. I watched the road signs. Counting down the miles until I had to hide again. Coming up to the exit, the sign for Basingstoke, Mum said, 'I can't pretend I'm not worried, of course I am. I had gay friends at college . . . I do think it's harder. You're going into a world that seems to be obsessed with physical perfection and I want you to find kindness. You've always had such good friends, been such good friends with girls. I suppose I hoped that would carry on . . . I think women are kinder, generally. I hope I'm wrong.'

She reached for my hand. The car swerved. 'Shit, sorry. You've just got to live it, Peach, find out for yourself. But I'll be here . . . So will your dad, when you're ready to tell him.'

My mother carried my bags into the boarding house. People were already in their dressing gowns, gathered round a sitcom, the canned-laughter track shouted from the too-loud TV. Alex was there, his dressing gown open. Splay-legged in boxer shorts. A yellow T-shirt with DEATHBOX printed in peeling black letters across his chest. He hated me, and I hated that I still found him attractive, even when picking spit-balls from the back of my neck. Pretending they didn't sting. I wanted to turn the car around. To drive home to London, pretend I was just a visitor.

'The poof's back,' Alex spat, loud enough for my mother to hear.

20

A History Lesson

It was the spring term. The history teacher took his jacket off, hanging it on the back of his chair, rolling his sleeves. He knelt to plug in the wheeled television, sat on the edge of his desk, smiling down the rows. 'So, who can tell me anything about the National Socialists . . . the Nazis?'

I could. But I could also feel Alex's eyes on the back of my head, so bit my tongue.

'No one? All right, well . . . Before I start, I want to say that every year, when I teach this, it's difficult . . . in a situation like this, a school like this . . . it's hard.'

The teacher paused, looking out the window. Looking as though he'd rather be anywhere else.

'The truth is, if Hitler had crossed the Channel, if the National Socialists had won, then I wouldn't be standing here. There probably wouldn't be a school here, there wouldn't need to be . . . Because all of you would have been killed. At best, you would have been sterilized, institutionalized.'

He continued looking out of the window, staring into the car park, couldn't look at us.

'Hitler instituted a policy, Aktion T4. He called it *Lebensunwertes Leben* – "Life unworthy of life". It wasn't just the disabled, but anybody deemed degenerate, unworthy of inclusion in the Aryan race, the master race: Jews, homosexuals, the Roma people, criminals, people considered mentally ill. To call it a policy is to dignify it, but I think you're all old enough to know. And you might be asked a question on it in the exam.'

I was sitting in the front row, next to Rebecca. She was writing something in her exercise book. I tried to imagine the empty rows. My Grandpa Francis had been reluctant to tell me his story. Only my Aunt Vicky and I were really interested. He'd finally shown me his few photos. Posed sepia portraits he'd saved of his parents. They'd looked secure, smoothly prosperous. The end of their privileged world unthinkable. I'd wanted to see my face in theirs, pretended I could.

Sitting on his sofa in Greenville, the summer before my new school started, Grandpa had told me about being a child in Vienna. Cake, carriage clocks and carriage rides, creeping back downstairs, watching adult dances through the banisters. Francis wanted to remember the music, the gilded laughter, happier evenings. Initially, he'd been vague about how that music had stopped, but I asked him to tell me. He said that he'd been sent to school in England, was already there when the Anschluss began. It was considered smart then, for well-to-do families, and it was a fashionable decision that had saved his life. Franz was anglicized, became Francis. After war was declared, he was interned as an enemy alien. My grandfather, more used to daily, green-ribboned boxes from Demel's, got malnutrition in the camp. He lost his hair at sixteen, surviving on pilfered pots of marmalade. After peace was declared, Francis had begged his fare back to Vienna, but there was no home to return to. All of Franz's family had been murdered. He changed his name permanently. Franz Goldberger became Francis de Monterey. My grandfather was barely seventeen, and alone.

Back in school, I looked out the window, kept my mouth shut. From behind me, Alex said, 'You mean the Nazis, Hitler – he killed faggots, sir?'

He spat the word right at me. Normally, Alex didn't pay

much attention in class, but his voice was eager, bright. As if he hadn't understood that he wasn't exempt, that we would have both been killed.

The teacher stiffened, gripping the edge of the desk. 'Well, that isn't a word I'd use, not at all, but yes, as I said: anyone considered degenerate.'

He turned to put a tape in. Static gave way to a blue clock. A black-and-white Hitler, small, against a forest of flags, swastikas. He hectored the vast crowd, twitching with zeal. Electrified by fury, the ecstatic devotion of a sea of uniformed, uniform faithful. Watching, I felt sick, had to remind myself that Hitler was dead.

Walking back to the dorm, Alex was standing by the pool table, waiting. 'He'd have had you, you dirty poof. Fucking spaz . . .'

He looked sleek with malice, pleased. For once, I couldn't ignore him. 'What about you? Have you noticed where you are, where you go to school? You're just as much a spaz as I am, just as much of a target. We're the same . . . What makes you think you'd survive?'

'Piss off, I'm nothing like you . . . nothing like you at all.'

After supper that night, I went to sit in the churchyard. A woman I knew well enough to smile at was there walking her dog. Apart from us, it was empty. I couldn't speak German, couldn't understand it, but Hitler's speech was still loud in my ears, his hate still reverberating round my head. There were three reasons Hitler would have liked to murder me. I was Jewish, I was disabled, and I was gay.

I couldn't sleep a wink. The next morning I couldn't eat, let my toast go cold. Rebecca seemed to have forgotten the lesson, she laughed over the table, but I couldn't.

*

It was nearly Easter. All our assemblies ended with a song – 'All Things Bright and Beautiful' or 'Morning Has Broken' – but I didn't join in any more. Not many students did. The school chaplain waited patiently for our noise to stop. He was a man who wore short-sleeved clerical shirts, whatever the weather, but he wasn't as casual about his faith, God's ability to keep him warm. He walked to the front of the stage, pressing his palms together under his chin.

'Good morning to you all. I just wanted to remind everyone that we'll be going on pilgrimage as usual over the Easter break. I'll be taking a group of students from the college to France, we'll be going to Lourdes for a week. If nothing else, it's an excuse to travel, and it's free . . . usually good fun. Anyway, if anybody is interested, either come and find me in my office or there are sign-up sheets in each of the houses.'

The chaplain smiled again, more cautiously, before clicking down the steps, out through the doors.

After splitting up, Rebecca and I had a wary, teasing friendship. Careful as animals, caged together. At supper that night, I said, 'But you're not going to go, are you? You know it's all bollocks, right? Miracles . . . you can't believe in it, not really?'

She wiped her fingers on a napkin, balling it on her plate, uneaten beans. 'I might, what's it to you? I've been before . . . The water's freezing, and it's tiring having to be grateful all the time, smiling all day. But the volunteers are so happy to see you. They want to see evidence so badly, you almost want to give it to them. Of course, they're all mad, all loony, but it's only a couple of days. The rest of the time you get to yourself, go sightseeing, eat different food. It's better than being at home, better than sitting by myself, or sitting with my mum all day, trying to think of something to say. Worried I'll break something . . .'

She looked at me, her eyes hard. 'I'm sure you've got better plans, aeroplanes with Mummy and Daddy, but I don't. I'll bring you back a souvenir, a Virgin.'

Joe usually went home for the holidays, but that year he decided to join Rebecca at Lourdes. Always quiet, when I got back he was silent. Just sat in his chair, staring out the window, spending all evening in our room.

Following Peg to Mass, I had absorbed the idea that my body was imperfect. Father Miller had smiled over my head, talking of divine tests. The women in my grandma's congregation had prayed for me, stuffed my pockets with sweets. They thought they were being kind. Along with their sugar, I had swallowed the idea that my disability was somehow my own fault. A manifestation of sins I barely understood, that I was too young to commit anyhow. I had travelled to America, wanting nothing but to fit in. The operation had been a success. I was still pleased that Dr Gage had kept me on my feet, but had never questioned a medical model that wanted to correct me. I had flown thousands of miles to try to fix what was never broken.

Our school was nominally Anglican. But there was too much to do, looking after the students, to pay much attention to God. And, for all its care, the institution still allowed us to believe that our bodies were somehow sinful, wrong. Even if Hitler hadn't won, even if our school was still open, they thought we needed saving from ourselves. Sent Joe on smiling pilgrimages. It encouraged him to think that God, rather than science, might cure him. Now Joe sat, staring out of the window, silenced by his own hope.

21

Southern Comfort

I wasn't going to go. My name wasn't on the list. The coach already full when I changed my mind, ran to the car park.

The headmaster looked surprised to see me. 'A beautiful day for it, anyway. You can come with me if you like? I've got room for one more . . . front or back?'

'Front, please,' I said, wanting to change my mind, return to the boarding house.

He took the steps, rather than the ramp, crossing to his car. I watched him bend quickly, adjust his tie in the wing mirror. Run his hand over thinning grey. Today was, after all, official business.

The headmaster lived in a squat, ugly house on the other side of the drive. His bare lawn was separated off from the rest of the school by a low post-and-chain fence. The front door slammed, and Donna, his daughter, cut across the grass. I watched her hurry, step neatly over the boundary. Donna was older, a 'normal'. She went to the local convent school. After she had changed out of her uniform, she sometimes came to play pool. She would stand, waiting for her shot, the cue behind her back, thin arms looped over it. Watching the boys spin down the table's scuffed sides. Rising on their footrests to send the bright balls clacking over the green. She was a better player than any of them, but had the grace to lose more games than she won. I didn't play, so we had never spoken. Seeing her, the headmaster raised his arm, tapping his watch. 'Come on, Donna, it won't look good if we're late.'

He closed the car door after her, shutting us in. Starting the engine, he gave me a measured smile.

Donna reached round the headrest, her hand on my shoulder; her voice serious, soft. 'I'm so sorry, Emmett. So sorry.'

The crematorium was a silent hour away. We pulled in between tall hedges, down a short drive. It was lined with rose bushes, benches. Brass-plaqued acts of remembrance. The daffodils were already out. Nodding drifts stretched almost to the chapel door. They looked incongruously cheerful, their continuation brazen, hopeful. As if nobody had told them it was a funeral, not a wedding.

The college bus had already arrived. Mrs Adams was waiting at the bottom, ready to push Rebecca inside. But Rebecca didn't acknowledge either of us, just sagged in her chair, opaque.

Mrs Adams smiled to cover the silence. She was already an imposing woman, but her black wrap, smooth wings, seemed to add another foot. She was wearing the earrings she always wore. The ones Alex always teased her about. They were made from her daughter's christening spoon. The gilt bowl dangling from one ear, ornate handle from the other. Her daughter was twenty-two now, away at university, studying medicine at Bristol.

The first time Alex had asked her about her earrings, she had blushed with pleasure, pinching at the tarnished bowl. She had described them as a bit of 'sentimental vandalism', her daughter wouldn't miss it. When she had turned back to the blackboard he had gestured to the class, winding his finger at his temple. The second time he grinned the same compliment at Mrs Adams, her eyes widened in irritation. She understood the mockery in his bright, upward inflection.

'Just open your book, Alex. Who knows, you might even learn something?'

★

The crematorium chapel was packed. The mourners from school couldn't slide into the polished pews filled with Alex's other life. Mrs Adams and Tony, the bus driver, worked to park the chairs as fast as they could. Rebecca was wheeled in last. Mrs Adams knelt to apply her brakes. She whispered, 'You might help, Rebecca, you've still got arms.'

But Rebecca didn't respond, just looked straight ahead. As passive, as angry as a doll. A man in the front pew looked round. He seemed embarrassed to be there, embarrassed that we had come. I saw a girl on the other side of the aisle stare at Rebecca. Her hair a neat, blonde cap, her eyes red. The vicar nodded, and the music began, Jon Bon Jovi singing 'Always'. The polished box, quilted with roses, was all that was left of Alex.

I looked out of the tall windows at the bright nearly-spring. I tried not to look at Alex, his coffin. I tried to picture his still hands. The gold on his fingers. Who had the rings now? His mother, probably. I remembered my confusion when I first saw his earrings. Jewellery, any kind of brash individualism, was strictly forbidden at my old school. Even the hair on your head didn't really belong to you. The masters would demand you got a cut, pinch at your hair if it wasn't squared off, shaved close to your neck. There were break-time debates about whether earrings were queer. Was it the left or the right ear that let the world know you would bend over?

My mother had bought me a new coat for the autumn term. Another expensive consolation. Alex had taken it from the back of my chair as the bell rang for break. I found it in a shit-smeared toilet, left it there. I had wished Alex was dead then, never imagining that he would actually die.

I could hear that the vicar was still speaking, but not what he said. Then two men came forward from the pews, with a fixed look, professional sorrow. They lifted the roses from Alex's lid, placing them gently between their feet. The coffin rolled forwards, disappearing behind automatic velvet. Mrs Adams stood, dabbed at her eyes quickly, before stowing the tissue in her bag, getting ready to help with the loading. The only time Alex had ever really noticed her lessons was when we were studying *Hamlet*. Normally he refused to read, tipping back in his chair, but Hamlet's fury chimed with his own, made him sit up straighter.

There was a silent traffic jam at the end of the service, while the wheelchairs filed out. The blonde girl paused to let me go ahead. She smiled, but it felt like blame. If Alex wasn't disabled, if he hadn't, in some angry, hidden way, belonged on my side of the pews, then she would never have seen me, never had to wait for me to pick up my crutches. Her friend would not be dead.

The last time I had seen Alex had been the previous September. I had just started at the local sixth-form college. Alex was doing vocational courses instead of A levels, so I wouldn't see him any more, didn't have to drag my feet round corners at the sound of his voice. I was sitting in the classroom, doing homework, when he noticed me through the open door.

'Emmett, I've not seen you for ages. How's it going?'

I put down my pen, moving back in my seat. Stiffening, alert.

His narrow, not-quite-handsome face was even thinner, the whites of his dark eyes yellow. He picked up my headphones. His signet rings clicked, loose on his knuckles. He wedged an earphone in his ear, pressing Play, nodding along. I could hear Michael Stipe's voice, 'Everybody Hurts', the sad song tinny through the other hanging plastic bud.

'I'm good, thanks. Life's good . . . college is good.'

I needn't have mentioned the college, the fact that I had escaped. But a part of me wanted to pay him back, to remind him that I was moving on. That my life was beginning, and he wasn't a part of it any longer.

He sat on the desk, pulled out the headphone, handing it back. 'Will you make me a tape? It's not my kind of music, usually. But I love this album.'

Alex grinned, sliding off the table, picking up his bag, squeezing my arm as he left. It wasn't an apology, but that weekend I made the tape, filling in the track-listing in my neatest capitals, tucking it carefully into my bag. Alex never came back to school, but I kept the tape for years, long after it was obsolete. Long after I had donated my boombox to Oxfam.

Alex's parents stood in the weak sunshine, shell-shocked with sympathy. As I filed past with my head down, his father pulled me into a hug, crying into my shoulder. He was older than I imagined, with greased-back grey hair, a silver clip on his black tie. He held me a long moment. That morning I had tried to cover the spots that blurred my mouth with some foundation, the wrong shade, stolen from my mother. As he set me on my feet again, gripping my arms, I saw the orange tideline on his suit and squeezed his shoulder, trying to rub away the make-up.

'You're Emmett, aren't you? Alex told me about you. You have the same birthday as my son . . . March. He'll turn seventeen soon.'

We followed the coach on the journey back. I sat, silent, behind the headmaster. Their duty done, he and his daughter chatted in the front. Weekend plans, what was for dinner. I listened, biting back tears, the anger fleshy in my mouth. The school was supposed to keep us safe, and it had failed Alex. It had given him the transfusions of infected plasma that had killed him. The government had continued buying contaminated

236

blood products from America, long after the advent of AIDS, after Mrs Thatcher's tardy, admonishing leaflets. And now Alex was dead, at sixteen. Never mind what's for dinner?

I stared out the window at the passing cars, trying to tune out the headmaster's talk. And I thought, well, this is it. Your one chance. You've got to grab it. Even if life isn't the shape you want, your body isn't the shape you want. Alex couldn't any more. I still could.

That night we got drunk. Robert agreed to buy us the booze. A volunteer, staying for a year before going on to Durham University, Robert enjoyed being a big fish, how we competed for his attention. Gathered round him, laughing too easily at his bad jokes, exaggerated worldliness. He came back with two bottles of Southern Comfort, hidden, obviously, under his coat. The permanent staff turned a blind eye. We closed the common-room door. The place was an afterthought, mismatched sofas pushed against scuffed walls. A sideboard, spider plant, dusty CD player.

We listened to 'Always' for hours. Rebecca stationed herself near the music, hitting Repeat before the song had faded. Robert sat on the arm of a sofa, next to Laura's chair. She needed assistance to break the rules; her own rigidly uncooperative hands couldn't lift the bottle, so he put it to her lips. Tipping it carefully, wiping the spill with his cuff. I watched her, watched Robert. When Laura wanted another swig, all she said was 'again'. Between drinks she kept saying Alex's name, as if it might bring him back.

Rebecca got so drunk that she slid out of her wheels, slumping heavily between the metal footrests. Alex had stolen the computer disk with all her GCSE coursework on it. He had given it back, useless. The edges blackened, melted with a lighter. She had pinned him against the wall with her wheels while he laughed, dangling it over her head. She had called him a fucker, but forgiven him.

Rebecca understood that he was looking for ways to hurt anybody who was going to survive. He had more problems than retyping essays about *Hamlet*. Less time than he, or any of us, could imagine. We drank until there was nothing left, listening to Jon Bon Jovi's stadium angst, boastful pain. We cried for Alex, and for ourselves. I never touched Southern Comfort again.

22

Heaven

Joanna was late. Or I was early. I still wasn't used to starting a night when I'd usually be getting a cab, going home. It was summer, the end of term. I stood at the top of Villiers Street, waiting in new trainers. Watching people spilling up from Embankment. It had been a hot day; the pavement was still crowded, had a thick, sour smell. It was long after ten, but not quite dark. The sky just a heavier, airless blue.

Three women, their arms linked, swayed happily up the middle of the road. They wore identical black going-out dresses, identical smiles. A demob-happy man walked quickly past, his tie at half-mast, suit jacket slung between the handles of a sports bag. I must have been staring, because he noticed, smiled. I sat on the bench, looking towards the Strand, checking my watch.

'Hello, gorgeous!'

Joanna put her hands over my eyes, bending to kiss my ear. We'd planned this a week ago, when I arrived home, sprawled on my bedroom floor, a copy of *Time Out* between us. We should do something, she said, to celebrate the end of school, the start of summer.

My parents kept old copies of *Time Out*, long after the advertised events had passed, stacked on the hall table. It sometimes meant we turned up too late, on the wrong day. I often took one, wedging it into the top of my bag before the too-short drive back to school. The gay listings were three pages, between the Film and Cabaret sections, before Rock and Pop. I had a room of my own at school now, but no lock on the door. I would close the curtains, listening for sounds in the hallway, as if the magazine was illicit, pornography. I would memorize the gay section, knew that Fruit Machine was every Wednesday at Heaven, and Trade was an all-nighter, Saturdays, in Clerkenwell. Kinky Gerlinky at the Empire Ballroom in Leicester Square. I didn't know if a disability counted as a kink, but liked the suggestion in the names. Hoped that one day I'd dare to join a queue. I'd lie in my narrow bed, imagining a wider, brighter world. It was only sixteen stops away.

At the back of the magazine there were personal ads. Terse columns of Men Seeking Women. Women Seeking Men. Women Seeking Women. Men Seeking Men. The ads were sandwiched between others for yoga holidays, chat-lines, holistic healers. I learnt the abbreviations quickly. *M, 24, VWE, seeks older, 30–50, to show him the finer things. M, 40, seeks same for no-strings fun, clean, with GSOH.* I committed some of them to memory. The loneliness between the words was louder than the assurance of a good sense of humour, no strings. I wanted strings, romance, but already had a sense that this was taboo. Turning off the light, I tried to picture the strangers behind their ads. Their faces, rooms. Their own single beds.

I stood, leaning in to kiss Jo. She was dressed for dancing, in skate trainers, combat trousers, overlapping vests. A hoodie knotted round her hips, long plait pinned up. A new piercing winked painfully in her right eyebrow. I didn't like it, was momentarily sad that she'd not told me. The large silver ring made her look aggressive, like somebody I didn't quite know.

'D'you like it? Cool, isn't it? I'll have to take it out again when term starts. Of course, Madeline hates it. Which isn't why I did it, but a total bonus.'

Now Joanna was grown up, away at school herself, Madeline wasn't Mum any more.

'Does it hurt? I mean, it's great . . . suits you.'

'You don't have to like it, it's all right.'

She put her arms round my neck, laughing. We almost looked like a couple. A Friday night. An ordinary start to the weekend. I thought how easy it would be, how much easier it would be, if that were true. Pulling back, Joanna grinned again.

'I'll just go and get some drinks, to put the stuff in.'

The stuff was speed. Joanna had arranged some, as a gift for the start of the holidays. From a friend of a friend. When she told me she was going to get us a couple of grams, knew someone, I half-hoped she would forget, but also understood that I couldn't stand on my hands all night without it. I knew it would keep me up.

There was a tourist kiosk across from the bench. Union Jack flags. Unofficial football shirts. Postcards of the Queen and Princess Diana, their dutiful, disapproving smiles.

I watched Joanna pay for the drinks, pocket her cigarettes. I suddenly wanted to catch the train. To be watching television while my dad snored on the floor, his Friday-night Guinness tins lined in the fireplace. Drugs made me dry-mouthed. But as soon as my friends started to prefer all-nighters to a night at home, video rentals, I had to join in.

If I wanted to keep up, and I did, then the only way to stay standing all night was speed or E. My father asked me never to do it in the house. He had a contract with the Home Office now. A pilot project, tagging offenders. If I was found to be one, he'd lose his welcome in Whitehall, the discreet, storied institutions of Pall Mall that had proposed and seconded him. My mother knew I was taking drugs. I think the weekend rebellion of it secretly pleased her. The only bit of advice she ever gave me was to never drop acid in a club. If I was going to do it, and she knew I would, could I please take it at home, where she could keep an eye out? She had grinned before going upstairs. 'Or else, do it in a field somewhere. A sunny day, naked, with your very best friends.'

Any kind of rebellion was impossible with her. She was much more worldly, so much cooler than I was, had done everything before.

Joanna came back, balancing bottles of Snapple. Sitting on the bench, she felt for the wraps in her wallet, peeling open the tight packets. Tipping them into our drinks, as casually as spooning sugar in tea. I looked over my shoulder for the police.

'Nobody's watching, for fuck's sake. Don't worry so much, nobody cares.'

She replaced the lids, licking traces of powder from her fingers, shaking the pink liquid.

'We'd better drink it here, before we get to the queue. We don't want to get searched.' She grinned, moving up the bench. 'Here . . .'

Joanna unscrewed both lids, handing a drink to me. We clinked bottles. The artificial sweetener, pink lemonade, didn't quite mask the bitterness of the speed. I drained it, wondering what I was doing. Wondering if the powder was cut with bleach. I wondered, briefly, if I might die, if I would mind if I did. I was living now. Everything else could take care of itself tomorrow.

We walked round the corner to the arches. The short, early queue. Joanna's friends, two girls I hardly knew, were meeting us later, inside. The bouncer, a blocky, broken-nosed man, his hair just shaved shadow, smiled at us both. 'He can come to the front . . . no worries.'

We looped back around. The bouncer stuck out an arm against non-existent shoving. He wore many-holed black boots. A black satin bomber jacket. A red AIDS ribbon pinned to the sleeve. Thanking him, I wondered if he had it, or if he was just being charitable. Joanna was behind me. As we passed he grabbed her shoulder. 'Are you his guest? He does know it's a gay night, doesn't he?'

'Why don't you ask him? He can speak. We both know where we are, thanks, though.'

'You'll look after him, yeah?'

Joanna pushed past, ignoring him. I followed, thanking him again. The narrow black corridor smelt thick, stale. It was a blank darkness, disorientating after the brightness of the street. I searched for the glow of the emergency exit. There were hand-painted neon arrows pointing in one direction. Booths, seats, carved out of black-brick arches. The low-ceilinged space suddenly opened on to a galleried dance floor.

That's when I saw him. The boy was dancing by himself, at the edge of the room, next to a tall speaker. There are people you see that you always remember. They probably don't notice you, running for a train, standing in front of you in a bleary morning queue for coffee, but you never forget them. In the spinning lights his hair shone like spilled petrol. He was wearing combats, of course he was; they were the overlapping Venn of lesbian and gay clubbing style in 1994. We might have had opposite desires, but we all looked the same that summer. The boy was in a sleeveless black T-shirt that exposed shining skin, smooth-muscled arms. His heavy boots were unlaced. It was like the moment at a wedding after the speeches, but before most people are drunk enough to dance. The boy was dancing for himself, with the music. Not in the self-conscious way that wants an audience, but just for the sheer joy, the lithe pleasure of it. As I watched him move, his fringe fell over steep cheekbones. He pushed it back with a quick hand. It wasn't only that he was beautiful, though I could tell that the men hovering at his edges thought so too. It was that he looked so free, so much like himself.

I was suddenly aware of my crutches, their weight in my hands. Watching him was both a thrill and a sharp kick. I might wear combats; I might buy gay magazines, if the shop wasn't too crowded. Take amphetamines from strangers, friends of friends, so that I could keep up with my own. Grinding my teeth on the night bus home, after the club staff had swept us up and out. But my jerky movements had none of his grace, and never would have.

Finding Joanna, I shouted over the busying floor, louder beats, 'I'm sorry, Jo, I need to go. I'll call you tomorrow.'

I leant to kiss her. Didn't wait for a response, and for once she didn't follow. As I walked up the corridor towards the exit, I felt a hand push into the back of my combats, cupping my arse with a rough, digging entitlement. I didn't try to turn. To see the man's face. He started trying to slide his fingers between cotton and skin. To squeeze my penis. His fingernails were sharp. If I tried to bolt the stranger could easily pull me over.

'Get off me! Let go . . . Let go, now!'

The man removed his hand. I still hadn't seen his face, had no idea who he was.

I swung hard for the exit, not looking back. Not wanting to see him. The stranger's shout followed me.

'Like you're ever going to do any better. I felt sorry for you, that's all.'

23
Pilgrims

For days after the night at Heaven I thought about the stranger. I was more shocked by what he'd shouted after me than his hand in my pants. It was a slap. A stinging dismissal. Like being a child again. Sent to my room for something I hadn't done. If I'd had the words then, I would have called it depression, but really it felt like panic. His was the first voice I heard, opening my eyes; the last when I closed them.

I'd hear my father leave the house, turn over. But I'd smile through breakfast with Mum, list the ways that I was going to spend my day, that were mostly lies. Listen for the receding click of her heels, wait five minutes in case she had forgotten something, ran back for it, swearing. When I was sure I was alone, I'd take all the dusty bottles out of the sideboard. Lining up holiday souvenirs, so delicious by a pool, suddenly undrinkable, unthinkable, back at work. I'd drink anything, I didn't care. Yugoslavian plum brandy chased with Italian grappa. Kirsch, a Christmas gift from Grandpa Francis. Green-glass gin swigs before ten. I'd mix thick, sticky cocktails of the dregs. I hated the taste, but liked the sting.

I'd hand myself along the walls to the living room, lying on the threadbare Persian rug, next to my parents' records. Too drunk to pull them from their sleeves. Too sad to enjoy sad songs. Sitting in silence. I liked the way drink blurred my edges. For a few hours I didn't hear the stranger's shout in my head, or if I did, it was like hearing through a door, somewhere beyond me. I still answered the phone when it rang. Still saw friends when they wanted to see me. Sat on Joanna's roof, or in Grace's garden, but I felt disconnected from everyone, behind glass again. Smiling through Saturday nights, the lead-crystal chatter of my parents' dinners. I would hear myself talking, falsely bright, as if listening to a stranger. I stopped queuing for clubs. Stopped pretending I liked the music. I stopped pretending I could dance.

In the last week of August, we travelled to Cape Cod. My mother and three of her four siblings had rented two large, salt-weathered houses on a bluff overlooking the beach in Wellfleet.

The trip had been my mother's idea. She could never quite reconcile herself to the humid greyness, the thunderstorms that passed for summer in London. She missed the dependable East Coast sun. The sandy-footed casualness of her childhood memories. Being part of a garrulous noise. Her brothers and sister had had children she hadn't even seen. And her dad wasn't getting any younger.

I'd been given the only bedroom on the ground floor. The first morning, too early, I heard him opening cupboard doors. Slamming round the unfamiliar kitchen. Hearing me come in, Francis smiled. 'Good morning, my dear. Did you sleep?'

'Yes,' I lied. 'Morning, Grandpa.'

He was already dressed for the day. Plaid shorts, belted high over a low paunch. A spreading seventies collar, a shirt older than me, loose on thin shoulders. A trucker cap I remembered from the last time he'd dropped me at the airport, jammed on his head. I had hated it then. He smiled that it had come free, as part of a promotion on horse feed. I had walked five paces behind him, ashamed of the safety pin where a button had gone missing.

The only thing that was new was his moustache. Stiffly silver, the waxed curl exaggerated his smile. An exuberant flourish, at odds with his frugal appearance. It made him look like an Austro-Hungarian general, as if he had never left Vienna. As if his American family, and I, had never happened.

He had always told me that vanity in men was suspicious. Proof of a trivial mind. I bit my tongue. It didn't matter. I was happy to be there. Suddenly so happy to see him.

He came to sit at the table. Looking out of the brightening window at the flat sea. 'Lovely here, isn't it?'

He had already lined up his medicines. Pills for diabetes, blood pressure. Illnesses real and imagined. Daily doses for high cholesterol, and hypochondria. He popped the caps, counting the pills on to a plate.

'It's great to see you, Grandpa,' I said, surprised by how much I meant it.

'Your mum tells me it's not going to be just us . . . that you've got a friend coming.' He looked up from his counting. 'Is she someone?'

I laughed, hoping to sound cheerful, unconcerned. 'What does that even mean, Grandpa?'

I felt myself smiling, automatically. Looked past him, at the ocean. Close to shore, I could see a large white bird, too big for a gull, too small for an albatross, perched on the swell. Francis was bound to know what it was. He liked animals, all animals, better than people.

'You know what I mean. Don't pretend . . . I mean is she *someone* to you?'

'I like her a lot, Grandpa, but it's nothing like that. She *is* somebody to me, but not in the way you'd like. She's a friend . . . just a friend.'

As if a real friend wasn't a rarity.

Francis said nothing, pushing the pills into an orderly row

on his plate. 'Your mum told me she's coming all the way from New York on the bus. Nobody takes three buses out here, in August, if they just want to be friends.'

'She wants a holiday, not a boyfriend, Grandpa.'

The bird was still coasting on the water, smoothing its feathers. I wanted to tell him that Rachel was queer, like me. That our difference was the reason we were friends. She was older than me. Rachel didn't usually bother with people her little sister Olivia brought home, but as we were both off the straight and narrow, I had become hers too.

Her parents had thought themselves liberal until they found love letters to another girl in her year. Lesbianism in other people's children was a talking point, but in your own kids it was something awful. They had threatened to kick her out from under their roof until she got accepted by Cambridge. Oxbridge made queerness almost respectable, as long as it was never mentioned at home.

'I think you'll like her,' I said. 'She's very clever, very funny – at Cambridge.'

He knew I wanted to go to art college, but didn't approve. Francis thought art was a nonsense, only liked books, opera. The only clothes he ever cared for were his tailor-made tuxedos. They still fitted. He'd shown me them proudly, the summer I was fourteen, unzipping moth-proof covers. Grandpa only aired them for occasional first nights at the Met. Music was important, but the rest of art was just a waste of time. Nothing that you might make money at. That could provide for a family. At best, it was something for after dinner, a hobby.

'You should try for it too. Maybe join her there?'

'I doubt I'd get in, Grandpa. And anyway, I don't want to go.'

Just then, my mother appeared at the top of the stairs. Barefoot, in a creased linen dress, her face still rumpled with sleep. 'Oh stop it, Dad, honestly. Why be in such a hurry? Rachel's a lovely girl, but it isn't at all like that. Let Em apply where he wants.' She came down, bending to kiss her father. 'Drop it now, hey?'

He smiled at us both, abashed. 'You're my first grandchild, Emmett, that's all. I'd like to see you doing well.' He gestured across the table at my sticks, propped against an empty chair. I'd never noticed his hands before. His fingers were long, elegant. The skin on their backs thin, brown-spotted with sun, age. 'And things have been difficult for you. It might not be so easy for you to find a woman who'll take you on.'

The green-striped Peter Pan Bus Line dropped Rachel in Wellfleet later that day. She jumped down the steps, shouldering a bursting rucksack. Seeing her smile, her sun-browned ankles, dirty plimsolls, a blue-flowered cotton dress, I nearly shouted with joy.

She put the bag down, her arms round my neck. 'Eight hours on the bus! And then when I changed at Hyannis, I realized I didn't have the address, or a number, so I'm very glad to see you.'

I couldn't speak for a minute, her familiarity strange, thousands of miles from London. 'I'm so happy you're here. So happy.'

I kissed her quickly, on the cheek.

That night, Francis took us all to dinner. Soft-shell crabs, at a starched-linen tourist restaurant. My grandfather beaming round the table at his family, his holiday largesse. The following morning, while the houses were still sleeping, Rachel and I went for a walk. The early sun was screened by sea mist, the horizon a tentative pencil-line. The only other people on the beach were a couple being walked by their dog. A smiling, tail-chasing Labrador that ran yards ahead of them, stopping occasionally to check they still followed. We were both quiet, looking at the sea, then Rachel said, 'If it's really what you want, I'll marry you. I'm going to be a journalist, and your name would make a great byline.'

I didn't look at her. 'You're not serious? What about if you wanted to get married, to somebody you actually loved? You've always said you're bi, not gay . . . There might be someone, one day.'

'Unlikely,' she smiled. 'I don't think I want to be loved like that. I think I'd prefer not to be.'

'You can use my name without marrying me – just take it, I don't mind. I'm not very good at this. I thought that coming out to myself would be the tricky part, but my mum warned me that clubs would be difficult, that it might be hard to meet someone. I thought it would be a beginning, but it isn't.'

'There are other places than clubs, other people. It's hard for everyone, not just you.'

The couple with the dog were coming back; they waved behind sunglasses. We waved in return.

'You could walk into a club, anywhere, any night of the week, and someone would want to know you – I've seen it. I'm so tired of never feeling like I fit in anywhere, I never see any-one who looks like me . . . I'm too disabled for the gays, and I went to a disabled school, and was too gay, too ashamed of my body, to fit in there either. I have no disabled friends, no gay ones. Can't dance . . . and I was shit at wheelchair basketball. I feel like my nose is always pressed to the window; whatever else happens, I'll always be watching.'

Maybe it was the strangeness of Rachel standing next to me on a beach in Cape Cod. Maybe it was the fact she was leaving the next day that let me speak.

It was the most I'd ever told her about how I felt. Jokes were our usual language; we were careful to talk about hurts as if they didn't. She was quiet, looking out at the glinting swell, letting me talk. She altered her pace to match mine, scuffing sand in front of her, her shoes in her hands. I told her about Heaven, that was actually hell, but stopped before I got to the man. His attention an unwelcome shock, but still a sharp proof that I wasn't invisible.

'I can't even knit . . . my hands are too fucked. Peg tried to teach me, but I drop all the stitches, end up with holes.'

Rachel stopped, her eyes widening. 'What the hell has that got to do with anything?'

'Isn't that what you're supposed to do? If you have to sit things out? It's what Peg does. She pretends she isn't disappointed, doesn't mind being old, doesn't mind that her children moved hundreds of miles away . . . and every few months I still get a lumpy parcel. All the things about being young, I can't do. So I'll just watch. I'll be the dependable friend. Make bloody awful jumpers.'

Rachel started to laugh. Then I joined in.

'If you knit me a jumper, I won't wear it . . . I'll fucking kill you.'

Later that day, we piled into four cars, driving to Provincetown. The mist had burnt off, leaving a cloudless afternoon. Francis sat in the back, his long legs round his ears, complaining. I was beside him, trying to tune it out.

'Why d'you want to go? Whale-watching is just for tourists, too expensive.'

My mother turned round from her front seat. 'Because we *are* tourists, that's exactly what we are, Dad. Try to enjoy it, and if you can't, don't spoil it.'

As we drove down Commercial Street to the harbour, I looked out of the window. Rainbow flags hung in every doorway, every shop. Pink triangles stuck to every window. As if gayness was something you could wrap up and charge, simply another consumer choice. A place where we were an overwhelming majority. It was nearly five, and it seemed as though the town was on unofficial parade. There were men, couples, unhurried on the narrow sidewalks. Short haircuts, short shorts. The traffic moved slowly, locals shouting to one another from opposite sides of the street. I saw a shirtless man, his skin a varnished mahogany from weeks in the sun; he was wearing a baseball cap with a red AIDS ribbon on the crown, sitting at a pavement table with a younger, buzz-cut man. As we moved past, they kissed lightly, as if it was nothing. As if they did it every day. I decided, then and there, that I wanted to move to Provincetown. The main drag was exactly that. There was a cheerful whoop behind us. Scattered claps, whistles. I turned to look. Two women in identical aviator shades, greased silver quiffs, were driving a bubblegum-pink Cadillac convertible. It was almost a block long, the fins sharp, chrome bright. A car from the movies. America's widescreen fantasy of itself. They waved right and left, making sure that everyone had time to see them. Serene, queenly, granting an audience. At four miles an hour, there was no danger of crashing. The woman driving, the older of the pair, took her eyes off the road, kissing her girlfriend.

'Wonderful, so good,' grinned my Aunt Vicky, climbing up the seat for a better view.

My father was behind the wheel. He slowed, smiling over his shoulder at me. 'Isn't this great, Em?'

Before arriving I'd bought a guide to Provincetown and the Cape. I'd read that when the Mayflower Pilgrims sailed from England in 1620, they finally made land in November, anchoring in Provincetown Harbour after three days unable to dock because of rough seas. The first settlers were Puritans, fleeing religious persecution under James I. There was a section on

Gay Travel, which told me that an artists' colony had been established in the twenties. A theatre, the Provincetown Players, that staged early works by Tennessee Williams. A loose community of artists thrived on a narrow spit of land curving into the wide Atlantic. People seeking freedom of a different kind.

The pink Cadillac was still on its progress. Francis snapped, 'Do they have to make such a show of themselves? I mean, everybody knows they're happy, queer, but why shout about it?'

He slapped his bony knees, gesturing at nobody in particular. I tensed, staring out the opposite window. We were approaching the harbour. The grey granite monument looked down on us, an Edwardian memorial to *Mayflower*'s crossing. Francis gestured to it. 'It's unnecessary. Back home, of course everybody knew if people had certain tastes, proclivities. And it was tolerated, if it was kept private . . . conducted behind closed doors . . . with discretion. It wasn't something discussed by polite people, decent people. What you did was your own business. But in America, everybody has to know; they have to shout about it all the time. I know you're gay – so what?'

Vicky reddened with the effort of biting her tongue. Her daughter Amy lolled, not listening, in her lap.

Francis went on, loudly oblivious. I was glad Rachel had chosen one of the other cars, to ride with my uncles. I wanted my dad to pull over. To leave the car, my family, and fly back to London.

Vicky clapped her palms over her daughter's ears, snapping, 'For Christ's sake, Francis, why shouldn't those women do what they want? Why shouldn't they be happy, and want to show it off? Not everybody gives a damn what you think. I think it's great . . . terrific.'

I was surprised by the tears in her eyes. Vicky turned away from her dad, staring determinedly out of the window at the passing parade.

'All I'm saying,' Grandpa huffed, 'is that it isn't natural.'

Nobody spoke.

The following morning, Rachel left. It was only a flying visit, a weekend escape from sweating Manhattan, her summer internship. My Uncle Sev was going back to New York too, and offered her a lift. While he gathered up toys and children, cramming them into the rear of his dented Datsun, we went for a last look at the ocean. Returning to the house, Rachel said, 'You know, families love you, if you're lucky, because of their relationship to you . . . *because* you're theirs. Why does he need to know? You hardly see him, he's old. Let him think what he likes. Lie.'

She grinned, putting an arm round my shoulder.

It was kind. It might even have been true, but I couldn't hear it. I kept turning over what Francis had said. The contempt in his voice was still ringing in my ears. I wouldn't say anything, and it would become another reason not to call. I suddenly wanted Rachel to go.

'Thanks for coming. I'll see you when we get home.'

'I'll be back at uni, but Christmas, for sure.'

She smiled, already somewhere else, wedging her rucksack into the boot.

After supper that night, I excused myself, walking down to the beach again. The tide was in, the sand a silver, narrowed ledge. The moon just visible; an indefinite thumbprint. I didn't believe in God; I'd shrugged him off, finally impatient with silence. Peg had stopped offering to take me to Mass when she visited. But watching the water I asked him once more to make me normal, or if he didn't want to do that, to just let me dissolve where I stood. I thought about the pink Cadillac. The thrift-store drag queens, kissing men. The weekday carnival, slightly defensive hilarity. I was sure most of them were tourists like me. Did they save all year, for a week of not having to look over their shoulders? Changing their lover's pronouns during office hours? Or did everybody know, summer and winter? I thought about walking into the sea. My crutches were hollow, would sink in seconds if I let them go. Finally, I wouldn't need them.

There was a voice behind me. 'You going home tomorrow?'

I started, surprised.

'Sorry, I didn't mean to do that. I don't want to disturb you.'

The man was around fifty, wearing a windbreaker over faded shorts, Docksiders. He had sparse, greying-blond hair. A stranger, but I was suddenly glad he was there.

'I'm not leaving for a few days. I'm with my family . . . we've been here two weeks already.'

'I've seen you with the blonde little girl, your mother?'

'My aunt. That's Amy, my cousin . . . they're American. My mum's American too.'

He laughed. 'If her sister is, then that's usually how it goes.'

He lived near the beach, alone now, after his partner died. It was cancer, not AIDS, had taken four years. They'd made money at jobs they didn't like. They'd come to Provincetown one summer and fallen in love with it. The noise; the salty, barefoot freedom of the place. He told me they'd retired out there as soon as they could, running a jewellery shop on Commercial Street, living above it. When Jack had died, he'd sold up. He didn't need the money, but the noise they'd sought was too raucous now. He'd bought a place in Wellfleet, and it was OK. He was getting used to it.

'So, are you gay?' he smiled, hands in pockets.

'I am.'

The simple truth still shook me, even though there was no one to hear us.

I went on, avoiding eye contact with the stranger, 'I'm not

sure I'm very good at it, I'm not sure it matters what I call myself, if it's always theoretical, if I'm always on my own, always watching. We went today, whale-watching, and then there was a sort of parade through town. Everyone looked so beautiful, so confident. And my grandpa told me that they were unnatural, but I'd never seen anything so natural in my life; I thought it was wonderful. But awful too, because it isn't for me . . . I can't join in.'

We'd been standing a long time. My arms ached. I wanted to sit on the sand, but was worried if I did the stranger would see how awkward it was, pity me. I wanted him to stay, so stayed standing.

He listened, gazing out at the ocean. 'The thing is,' he said, when I'd finally finished, 'if something is in nature, then it can't be unnatural . . . it's impossible.' He gestured at the darkening immensity of water. 'You, me . . . everything.

'You'll find someone, you will. I thought I never would . . . I was this skinny kid, picked last for everything, bullied. And then in college, I did. The best thing that ever happened to me. I've had that . . . and you will too.'

I suddenly wanted my someone to be him. Pictured myself living there. Running a hobby shop on the Cape.

He kissed me, clumsy, unexpected, our teeth butting. His mouth was sour with coffee, cinnamon gum, Big Red. It felt like a blessing, an awkward benediction.

He pulled back, smiling. 'Well, goodnight. Safe trip home.'

The man walked away, up the beach, before I had a chance to speak. Watching him go, I realized I didn't know his name.

24
Daytime Drinkers

Back in London, on a Monday, the day stretching ahead of me, blank. I don't know why I chose that day to go to a gay bar, except the sense of time running out. The following Sunday, I'd be back at school. In hiding again.

I decided on a blue button-down shirt, something I'd bought in Provincetown. A pair of jeans, and my battered, beach-stained Converse. Casually anonymous, like the kind of man I hoped might be waiting. Catching sight of myself in the carriage window when the train pulled into London Bridge, I nearly stood to get off, crossed the platform for home.

The bar was opposite Charing Cross. I'd first noticed it, or rather heard it, the half-term before. To celebrate, my parents had got us tickets to a matinee, *Becket* at the Theatre Royal, Haymarket. We walked back to the station. Loud dance beats, thumping from open glass doors at the corner of Adelaide Street, as we waited to cross. Men spilled out on to the pavement, T-shirts stretched tight over expensive muscle. They were laughing, smoking. Swigging imported beers, ignoring the grey passers-by. Looking left, instead of right, I had almost tripped over my feet.

Crossing now, I could see the bar was almost empty. Only a few daytime drinkers in the window. Next to the entrance there was a women's clothes shop, a stationer's. I spent nearly ten minutes, longer, pretending absorption in a pink cashmere jumper that wouldn't have fitted, a back-to-school pack of highlighter pens, before going in. Music bounced round the metal walls. Insistent Euro-disco that made the place seem emptier. There were high stools lined along a zinc-topped bar, too high.

The sleeveless barman smiled at me, understanding immediately. 'What can I get you?'

'A gin and tonic, please. Double, thanks.'

'Take a seat at one of the tables, and I'll bring it right over.'

I wasn't old enough to drink what I'd ordered. At seventeen, I wasn't legally old enough to sleep with anybody who might buy me a drink. The barman put down the gin. He had bleached hair, a bleached smile. A heavy silver chain, tight round a gym-thickened neck. Watching him, I regretted my cautious shirt. I didn't look as though I belonged there, still didn't know where I did belong.

Taking a sip, I tucked my crutches under my chair, rolled up my sleeves. There was a neat stack of magazines on the empty table next to mine. I took one, trying to look as though I was waiting for a friend. At the back, between ads for club nights, underwear, there were escorts. Pages of hairless, by-the-hour muscle. Tanned, sleekly identical torsos. Identical boasts of being *VWE*. There were a few oddly shy smiles, but most of the advertisers, happier to show their cocks than their faces, were cut off at the neck. I closed it. These strangers' explicitness was both exciting and deflating. Any intimacy for sale in the free pages was too expensive for me, and so much less than I wanted.

I swallowed more gin, noticing a grey-haired man on a table further away. He didn't look up, absorbed in the same magazine, making his pint last. I wondered if he had a boyfriend, or if he ever called the numbers.

Another man came in. He took a seat at the other end of the bar. I must have looked at him too long, because he stood, came over. He was maybe forty, in faded jeans, a rugby shirt stretched over the beginnings of a belly, but he had amused eyes, a ready smile. He wasn't who I had dreamt of. I probably wasn't his fantasy either, but it was a September Monday, a slow afternoon. A start.

'Can I get you another? What are you drinking – G&T?' He gestured at my empty glass.

'Thank you.'

Putting the drinks between us, his pint frothed over the glass, the man looked at me frankly, but it was the same kind of bored everyday appraisal you'd use scanning aisles.

I have never greeted my own face with much enthusiasm. My mother assured me I'd grow into it, but I never did. In any mirror, the gap between it and the Gillette-men on TV was too wide for my liking. Jo was always quick to tell me I was gorgeous to her, that it didn't matter. I had an eager smile, kind eyes. But my shoulders had broadened, bearing my weight; I was slim with the effort of walking. In the years to come it became a pattern I recognized. Sitting down, men sometimes looked at me twice, bought the drinks. Standing up, they never did.

Nick told me that he was a banker in the City, but he was on three months' gardening leave before starting a new job. He said that what had begun as fun was now dull. Being paid to sit at home wasn't all it was cracked up to be, was it? I didn't tell him that I had no idea what gardening leave was. That I pictured it as some kind of mandatory horticulture scheme, National Service in the Royal Parks. He told me that he had thought of going on holiday, Mykonos, or somewhere in the Balearics, but he couldn't face it in the end, on his own. His immediate, incautious intimacy rushed me. I didn't know how to respond, so just listened.

Finally, he stopped. 'And what about you?'

The only lie I told was that I was twenty-one. Everything

else was the truth. I was newly out. Wasn't it awful, that phrase, as though it was a confession of something criminal? I lived with my parents, but it was still a secret from my dad. I told him that I'd never had a boyfriend.

His eyes widened at that. He took another sip of beer, wiping the foam from his lips with a large hand. 'This probably isn't the best place to go looking for one.'

I wanted to ask him where I should go, then, but didn't.

Coming back a little while later with more drinks, Nick saw my crutches, paired on the floor under my seat. 'What are those? I mean, why d'you need them? Have you busted your leg? Are you positive?'

I didn't want to tell him that I was a virgin, but neither did I want to lie any more than I had to.

'I'm not HIV positive, I'm careful.'

'Then, why . . . ?' He gestured at my sticks.

I told him the truth. That I had cerebral palsy. Couldn't get far without them, but that otherwise I was fine. It was beginning to feel like work. An interview for a job I wasn't sure I wanted.

Nick straightened, blowing out his cheeks, leaning back in his seat. Exposing an inch of pale-furred stomach. Looking through me, out into the street, he said, 'You should be at home. You shouldn't be in a place like this, wasting my time. Two drinks . . . two.' He stood heavily, slapping his knees, turning back to the bar.

It took me more than a year to dare to go to a gay bar after that, and I didn't go alone. But it wasn't the last time I saw the look Nick had given me on some other man's face.

25

French Tips

I take taxis everywhere. Taxis if it's raining. Taxis if I am tired. Taxis home, often without a bean in my pocket. Praying as I stop at the cashpoint in the dark. It was a Saturday, a weekend in October, and I was on my way to Soho again, meeting Jo. The meter ticked, £25 already, even in light traffic.

I had received the first payment of Disability Living Allowance a month after my fourteenth birthday. The £244 felt like some kind of win, a jackpot. The money was for help with getting around. A brown-enveloped acknowledgement that disability was expensive. I usually spent it by the middle of the month. Peg, always frugal, was quietly horrified. She told me I must have holes in my pockets, it went so fast. If my grandma was visiting, she would fold an extra tenner into my jeans, whispering for me to go out, enjoy myself.

Watching the meter tick upwards as we turned on to Shaftesbury Avenue, I counted my notes. Wondered if my difference would ever stop costing me, or if I'd ever learn not to care.

The driver caught my eye in his mirror as we drove into Wardour Street. He had green eyes, a recent haircut. An easy smile. He jerked his chin towards my crutches. 'D'you mind if I ask what happened? I mean, what happened to your legs?'

I returned his smile, roughened my accent. 'Course not.'

Looking again, I guessed he was only about ten years older than I was. One hand sitting lazily on the steering wheel. Polo shirt, brown arms. He seemed at ease, inhabiting his body, driving his cab on this bright, ordinary afternoon. I liked the stranger, was conscious of a sudden need to impress. I so wanted to be a man like him. A man who took his body utterly for granted. A body that could run after a Saturday football in the park, could casually hold the hand of a girlfriend as she stepped off a train. A body that was everyday-beautiful, that hardly crossed its owner's mind.

'I broke my back . . . in a skiing accident.'

I held his look, but could already tell he didn't believe me. Something in the stiff way I had approached his cab, thrown my sticks on the floor, exposed me. For a moment I wanted to turn back, admit the lie. One weekend, when I was about nine, my mother had taken me to a dry slope in Kent, with an organ-ization called the Uphill Ski Club, skiing for the disabled. You were strapped into a sledge, launched towards the smiles at the bottom. I never went again, wanted to really ski. The lie was ridiculous. If I had broken my back, would I still have been able to walk, even in my own clattering way?

But the driver just nodded. Told me he was sorry. He smiled, careful. Pocketing my fantasy, along with his tip. Being more kind, more understanding of my need than he knew. It was a revelation, felt fantastic.

For years after that, it was a game. Every time I hailed a cab, thumb up, crutch dangling from my wrist, I used the journey, the black-polished anonymity of cabs, to explore possibilities. As a respite from the awkward daily rhythm of myself. There was one rule: I never initiated the conversation. I have been a soldier injured on my second tour, a student hit by a car while in Paris celebrating A level results. Once, more wildly, a dancer with the Royal Ballet who had been hurt in a fall. He still taught, but would never perform again.

I was ashamed. Shocked by the ease of my own deceit. But more than that, I felt liberated.

Sometimes I was believed, sometimes not. What was true about these encounters was the sadness. Not only mine, but theirs. Sitting in traffic, drivers told me how lonely they were. Most fares didn't want to talk. It was all right, but you could go a full ten hours, a whole shift, in silence. Something about my crutches, my perceived vulnerability, meant they could trade their own. Cabbies told me about divorces, partners who had left, finally bored of being alone in front of the TV while they worked nights, weekends. Girlfriends tired of always coming second to a fare. There were others who confided their affairs, passengers they'd swapped numbers with. They'd been kicked out, were crashing on a mate's sofa. Drivers who spent any money that was left after renting the cab, child support, on cocaine and drink.

I didn't lie the afternoon I met Christine. Getting out to help me in, the driver asked me what was wrong. I told him I was disabled, just that. He apologized, as though it was somehow his fault. I offered him the usual too-bright assurance that it was OK, really. Telling him I'd never been able to walk like he did anyway; that you couldn't miss what you'd never had, right? He apologized again, looking away. Back behind the wheel, going up Charing Cross Road, he told me that he still loved his wife, even after being married thirty years. They had met right out of school. But he knew she wouldn't accept Christine. It wasn't an affair, understand? It was him. He was also *her*. Drove to a flat in Essex every spare moment to shave her legs, paint her face. Pull a dress on. To be herself. By chance, he had met a drag queen, up from Ilford. A journey from Liverpool Street, after last trains. Good fare, £70. And a life-changing moment thrown in for free. They had become good mates, not lovers; he wasn't gay. Not his thing. 'I couldn't put in the hours,' he smiled.

So now Christine was allowed out sometimes, with the blinds drawn. As we pulled up to the kerb he handed me a crumpled photo from beneath the cab's visor, pushing it through the glass partition. There was Christine: tight black dress and shoes, sophisticated, on a battered lounge chair. Blonde-bob wig, nude mouth. Ankles tucked one behind the other; straight-backed, watchful as a hostess. This secret self weighty, somehow ineffably sad.

What had I done to deserve this confession? What had he sensed in me that meant he felt free to tell all? Maybe it was just the fleeting intimacy of the fare? Christine was certain never to see me again, so maybe it was safe to speak.

I was so moved by her trust that I told the truth. 'You are beautiful.'

I blurted it out. It was less than I wanted to say. Sounded dismissive, a greeting-card sentiment not worthy of Christine's confidence. He smiled, his eyes crinkling, holding my gaze. For a moment, behind his thinning, sandy hair, the softening jaw, Christine was there.

I passed him the fare, and the photograph. He had large, broad-knuckled hands with no trace of the French-manicured tips that Christine favoured. I slammed the door behind me and the driver sped away, shouting, 'Be lucky, son.'

He rounded the corner, disappeared from view.

26
Pride

It was a soft grey Saturday in June. I was eighteen. The last summer before university started, and life began. The night before, the weatherman had smiled, confident of blue skies, sun. But waiting for the Charing Cross train, I was cold, wished I'd brought a jacket.

Buying the clothes had been fun, had felt like a secret mission. I'd gone up to Covent Garden, walking down Neal Street through dazed shoals of tourists.

Hanging in the busy, brightly lit shop, the T-shirt had seemed right. Had seemed to promise a transformation. A buzzing neon future of parties, clubs. Of lovers. Yawning early mornings, another head across my pillow. I had bought a pair of navy combats to go with it, stupidly expensive Japanese trainers. The last pair they had. Pinching, half a size too small. Doubly painful, as I knew they wouldn't last me the week. But I didn't care. Handing my card to the professionally bored girl behind the till, my mouth dried. After a long moment, the sale went through. In the cab back to the station I'd felt light, imprudently happy.

Trying the clothes on at home, their promise had evaporated. I stared back at myself, floored. The reflection was still me, after all. These vulgar, foolish purchases couldn't change that. How could I really have expected them to? The T-shirt was too tight, too short. I couldn't live up to the trashy confidence of the outfit. I pulled at the hem, stretching it, angry.

Catching sight of myself again in the ticket-office window, I had nearly turned for home. I looked ridiculous. Felt naked, exposed. A wary animal. I didn't know the grey-haired man behind the counter beyond a cheerful good morning, but pocketing my change, I wanted to tell him I was going to Pride. Returning his smile, I decided to keep my mouth shut. Suddenly not proud at all.

There were only three other people on the London-bound platform. A straight teenage couple and a single, silver-haired woman. I was sure they were looking, laughing. Who did I think I was, anyway? Stupid bender. Brown-Nose. Batty Boy. I could almost hear their shouts, stinging spits of disgust. The couple leant against a dusty ledge, peeling paint leaving traces on the boy's jeans. Toe to toe, arms loosely round necks. They pecked soft kisses, like grooming birds.

I looked away, aware I was watching. Suddenly angry. They didn't have to be publicly proud, they could simply live. They didn't need protests, parades; didn't have just one day, out of 365. They didn't need to shout their right to exist. They could hold hands in the rush of Saturday shoppers on Oxford Street and nobody would turn a hair. If they were noticed at all, the watcher might smile, misty at young love, might recall their own dimly remembered affections. Before mortgages and children made them forget. This couple were prosperous with love, oblivious to their everyday freedom.

The boy slid his palms into the girl's back pockets, pulling her closer, kissing her again.

The third person was a woman of about seventy, in a worn floral dress. Comfortable chemist-shop sandals on her broad feet. She busied herself with shopping bags. Checking and re-checking her tickets. Finally satisfied, she patted her handbag shut. Nobody noticed me. Nobody cared.

The 12.03 was tight-packed with weekend families. I found a

free seat near the window, holding my crutches between my knees so the space next to me was empty. It stayed empty, despite parents standing, already hot, harassed. Already regretting this day out, they looked pointedly away.

I turned to the window. I loved the view you only saw from the tracks; it was like flipping a picture, examining the underside for clues, forgotten traces. The graffiti-sprayed sidings, stupid daring. The old, painted advertisements, TAKE COURAGE bleaching on bricks. The low-rise tower blocks crowding Tower Bridge. Balconies spiky with satellite dishes, stacked with bikes. Others were bright with flowers, carefully tended geraniums. Ordinary lives, normal lives. I imagined myself sitting on one of those balconies, watching the fast-passing trains, having nowhere I needed to be.

At London Bridge the train emptied. Two men boarded, taking seats across the aisle from me. They laughed, legs spread. Fear made me sit up straighter, twisted in my stomach. I was far too obvious, too conspicuous in my stupid clothes. The train moved off. I stared out of the window, half-listening to their conversation.

'Does your better-half know where you are? What did you say, about today?'

'I told her I was meeting you, told her I wouldn't be back until late. Course, I didn't say what we were actually doing. Her brother's bent . . . She thinks I like him, but I hate the dirty little fucker. Makes me sick.'

I fixed my eyes to the smeared glass. There was a smile in the older man's voice. 'We'll have to see how many we can get.'

I was sitting in a half-deserted carriage with a pair of weekend queer-bashers. I stared at the view, not taking it in. The blood running coldly to my feet. Charing Cross was a long stop away. Plenty of time to start their tally with me. I tried to tune them out, listening to the pulse in my ears. My fear was so

267

loud, I was sure the men must hear it. I tried to ignore their beery laughter. Hoping that if I stayed still, I'd be invisible. The way I used to imagine I was, pulling my hood over my head in the playground, watching Simon crash his planes, but it was a childish magic, long outgrown.

The men got louder, sounded excited, talking over each other, trading boasts. Unabashed descriptions of the sexual violence, the harm they were looking to inflict. They'd love it, the filthy bastards. They'd absolutely beg for a kicking.

The train slid into Waterloo East. More passengers got on. I hoped this would silence the men, but the larger audience just made them louder, drawing anxious glances. I looked at my hands, the thin white-gold ring my mother gave me for my last birthday. Crossing the river, the train stopped. We sat there. After a long-held breath, we pulled into Charing Cross. I stayed sitting, head down. The men gathered their cans, standing. The older one shrugged on his jacket. The younger turned, seeing me. I looked at him, accepting the inevitability of a punch. Waiting for it to connect, with a sharp-blossoming pain.

Instead, he smiled. 'You all right? Got someone meeting you?'

I was still holding my breath, clenched for his anger. A laugh. Too shocked to respond. The man smiled again, widely, warmly. I saw him wondering if I might be deaf too, finally managed a 'yeah, thanks'. It wasn't my voice; it seemed to come from somewhere beyond me. He pulled me to my feet, patting me easily on the shoulder. The stranger handed me my crutches. He had blond hair, shaved into an undercut, the rest gelled into a sharp fringe, above quick blue eyes, a neat, blunt nose.

I guessed he must be twenty-three or -four, not much older than I was. The blade of a Charlton Athletic tattoo just visible under short sleeves. I was disturbed to find him handsome; more than that – sexy. He would have killed me if he had guessed. The older man passed, ignoring me. But his friend turned, looking back a last time to check I was safely on the platform, before being absorbed by the fast crowd.

Watching him go, I understood I was invisible. For all my careful, costly preparation, I was a ghost. The handsome queer-basher didn't see a target. I was no threat. He only saw someone disabled. A cripple he was happy to help. A good deed.

My disability rendered me sexless. It protected me from his bruising hate, kept me safe. But it also kept me apart, under glass. Waiting for Joanna, the others, outside Tie Rack on the station concourse, I was shocked to understand I would rather have been punched. I would rather have been picking my teeth up off the floor, my eyes starting to purple. Would rather have been unable to march, if it meant that the stranger had seen me. If he had seen that I belonged.

I saw Jo before she spotted me. Speeding up, she beamed, raised an arm. Kissing me lightly, she said, 'We made it, then.'

Rachel was already standing in the cobbled forecourt. Waiting by the taxi rank, wearing fishnet tights under a metallic plasticky mac, a sweep of liner over smiling eyes. Scuffed Dr Martens. She embraced me, her arms round my neck, pulling me close, her joy almost tipping me off balance. 'Em, how brilliant is this? Look at it all . . . just look. I wasn't sure about coming today, but I'm so glad I did.' Grabbing my shoulder, she turned me. 'Someone's keen . . .'

One arm still round my neck, Rachel gestured towards Jo, who was talking to a slight, smiling Indian girl. I'd heard of Sophie, Jo's phone calls bursting with her for weeks. The girl's blue-black hair hung below her waist. My friend laughed at a joke, throwing her head back, roaring. Suddenly conscious of being watched. I could see the fillings, the silver, in her teeth. She bent to tie a lace. Something about the gesture reminded me of hopscotch grids – Joanna, not Jo, jumping after stones.

Rachel undid her shoulder bag, lifting the flap. Inside, there were stickers, a neat row of pink triangles, covered in small, strident capitals: LESBIANS ARE EVERYWHERE!

There were hundreds of us, thousands of gay people massing in Trafalgar Square, particles in motion. More queer people than I had ever seen, ever imagined. Everything was colour. Glitter and noise. I felt tears start, blinked them back, overwhelmed by the rising clamour, the pushing crowd. The huge, irrefutable fact of it. Rachel darted away, shouting over her shoulder, 'Stay put, darling, don't move. If you do, I'll never find you again. We need supplies.'

She disappeared, and was back almost before she went. Some paper cups in one hand, a bottle of Asti Spumante in the other. She bent, popping the cork between her knees. Wine frothed, bubbling up, spilling over the rims of juggled cups, down her slender wrists. We both laughed, were suddenly hooting, hysterical. Doubling over with the absurdity of it all; the grinning, surging relief of us being there together. Standing in the middle of that carnival, drinking bad wine on the street.

'Sorry, it's warm as shit, but it's all they had left. Vile, really, but fuck it. Cheers!'

Rachel licked the sticky wine from her fingers, handing me a cup, I took it, awkward, balancing on one stick. The square was now so full, surging with people, I could probably have been held by it, lifted my feet off the ground. Too nervous to eat breakfast, I now felt sick, dizzy, panic tightening in my throat, because I'd lost Jo, couldn't see her anywhere; she had vanished into the noise, the insistent, one-note shriek of whistles.

Next to me, a trio of black drag queens in matching red sequins, redder lips, polished as a Motown girl group. Taller than the rest of the crowd on patent six-inch heels, their faces precise masks in the brightening afternoon. One returned my smile before pushing ahead, carried by the sea of people. I wondered where they had travelled from, whether they'd dared the train in all their shine, or ducked into a toilet to change?

I noticed a larger woman, topless except for an open leather waistcoat. She had close-cropped silver hair, a tufty Tintin wave; her breasts fell comfortably to her waist, each nipple jewelled, bristling with multiple piercings. Catching my stare, she grinned at me. 'Enjoy yourself, honey,' she shouted. 'It's our day today.'

The woman gave me a quick thumbs-up before turning back to her friends. A ripple moved through the crowd. Marshals in loose high-vis vests scanned the perimeter, waiting for an unseen signal. Rachel reached for my cup. I felt gratefully for my crutch handle, the ground solid, stable again. There was a blast of gas horns, louder cheers, an outraged cloud of pigeons.

Because there were so many of us, we moved off slowly, snaking round Trafalgar Square, up towards Piccadilly. Rachel stayed right beside me, craning her neck to take it all in, her bright beam fixed. It felt wonderful to be there with her, and white-knuckle terrifying. I hoped the jostling elation, the thousands of strangers, would finally silence my fear.

Looking at the marchers, I understood I wasn't alone. No longer a joke. Not lying any more, hiding in the school library. Reading everything for any mention of what I might be. I wasn't sitting in bed, the volume turned right down on my push-button portable, images of longed-for men shining in the dark. I thought of my afternoons with Peg, watching Gene Kelly dance in glorious Technicolor. I wasn't watching any more. I was there.

I felt a hand on the small of my back. A chin fitted neatly to my shoulder. 'I found you,' Jo shouted. 'I can't believe we're actually here, Em, that we did it.'

Jo looked thrilled. She smiled so hard, her cheeks pinking, her delight almost painful. Somewhere behind us in the throng, I could hear drums. A steadier beat fighting with more hectic, bossy whistles. Jo caught the tail of a rhythm, dancing, head back, eyes closed. Suddenly alone in the crowd.

A whistle screamed in my ear. I turned, ready to shout. A shyly smiling face. Large brown eyes, framed by strong brows, black wire-rimmed glasses. The dark V of an already retreating hairline. The stranger was ordinary-handsome, still gripping his rainbow cord. Baggy black T-shirt; a cotton jacket, its arms knotted round narrow hips. Discreet, confident. The boy saw my hands were full, so rather than shake, he touched my shoulder, his thumb resting a moment on my neck. This almost invisible gesture, tiny intimacy in the huge mass, sent a low volt right to my feet.

'Sorry about your eardrums. I'm Michael, Mike . . . I just wanted to get your attention. I like your T-shirt.'

I heard myself thanking him. Saying how nice it was to meet him. Formal, nervous as a dinner-party guest. Someone invited to make up numbers, who didn't really know anyone else. I could feel the colour rising on my neck. I'd wanted to be polite, to downplay the sparks I felt; instead I'd sounded chilly, uninterested. But Mike just smiled, his eyes lively with amusement. He bowed slightly, teasing. 'It's a pleasure.'

Mike stayed by my side for the rest of the afternoon. I kept expecting him to peel off, to disappear into the straggling marchers. But he was in no hurry, made a discreet effort to match my pace. He told me he was a student, in his first year of a design course at Warwick; he loved it. Eighteen months older. Most of his friends were already on holiday, away, but he didn't want to miss out, so he'd come by himself. It was his first Pride too. He'd been bricking it on the train down, but what a day, what a brilliant day.

Sometimes I didn't really hear what he said. I was too busy looking, trying to commit him to memory. His dark-furred arms, jaw already blueing with stubble; the friendliness of his frank, open face. I wondered what it might be like to kiss him.

We sat on the beer-sodden grass in Brockwell Park; by the time we arrived, the post-march party was already winding down. Rachel left, reluctantly, for a family dinner. I watched her walking away, stepping lightly over kissing couples, passed-out drunks. The sun had finally given up, and it was cloudy, cold. The grass a mess of lost clothing, plastic cups, cigarette butts.

Jo sprawled happily in Sophie's lap, smiling up into her face. Batting at the long strands of hair that hung over her, like a cat. Watching them, I thought quietly of this girl, my best friend. The almost-sister I was lucky enough to find on my first day in the mainstream. Everything had changed. My palms now stinging, red. New blisters forming from standing so long. That morning, and all the numberless grey days before it, suddenly seemed a long time ago.

Mike asked if I had plans. He suggested, if I'd like, that we go to the Popstarz Pride Party, pulling a crumpled flyer from his jeans. 'It started at ten-thirty, in a railway arch near London Bridge. Did I fancy going? If I was tired, we could get a cab?'

At seven the next morning, we were sitting in a branch of Upper Crust at London Bridge Station. I caught sight of myself in the window. Sallow, sagging with fatigue in the flat, fluorescent brightness. My ears still ringing. I had borrowed Mike's jacket. He had found a Duffer hoodie on a banquette, after the lights came up, and had taken it, delighted. 'These go for eighty quid back home.'

If he hadn't, then the bouncers, the club staff, would have

thought nothing of swiping it for themselves. He grinned at me, shrugging. It might as well be him. Already, anything Mike did was fine with me, but I'd only known him a few hours, so bit my tongue. He leant back, stretching, the hood bunching at his neck, T-shirt rising over a dark fishbone of hair. I was so tired, almost beyond speech. My feet were aching, blisters burst, but I couldn't remember ever being so happy. I'd met this boy.

He took a sip of the scalding, burnt coffee, his fingers an inch from mine over the bolted-down table. Grabbing a napkin from the dispenser, he wrote down his number, his parents' address. He was home for the summer. Folding the thin paper, he reached across the table, tucking it into my breast pocket, the pocket of his jacket.

'Keep it,' he said. 'I'll see you soon.'

Epilogue

It was a normal day, almost twenty-five years after my first Pride. A bright, late-September afternoon, the very last of the summer. An errand, just a pint of milk, some bread for the morning. Crossing the street in front of my building, I noticed a homeless man on the corner. He was chalking a huge flower on to the pavement, absorbed in his drawing. Yellow petals spreading under fast, indifferent feet. I felt for some change, bending to drop it into his palm. His fingers were long, fine, the nails edged with dirt. He smiled, thanked me, before continuing with his work.

I suddenly felt so lucky. For my flat, a private bed, soft pillows. Enough money to buy whatever I wanted for dinner. Work, friends. A boyfriend. Someone who cared where I was. Who I needed to ring if I was going to be late. A relationship I had looked for hard, in bars and behind smiling online profiles. Talking up every infrequent, fleeting possibility with friends in noisy pubs, returning home to clock-ticking silence. He was the only man I'd ever met who I didn't feel I had to change shape for, who had never asked me to try. It wasn't what I'd imagined, but his face, when I finally found it, was a relief. We didn't really use words like love, but that was what it was. The kind of ordinary, extraordinary affection I'd begun to believe I'd never find. We made dinner together, shared the bills. We took holidays, had a dog. I didn't have many disabled friends, but the ones I had hadn't been so lucky. Most were still looking, still alone.

Walking towards the shop in the warm sun, I noticed my

shadow, still pinned to my feet. So much had changed, but not that. I picked up a basket, looping it over the handle of my crutch. The security guard smiled. Did I need a hand? I thanked him, as I did almost every day, but I'd manage. Standing in line to pay, I looked at the bouquets of hothouse flowers – irises, pink tulips – flown in daily from Amsterdam. They were positioned near the expensive chocolates, ready-made apology kits for forgotten birthdays, anniversaries. Two worlds – destitution and everyday extravagance – separated by a busy street. I was lucky, didn't hear the cashier's shout: 'Next please.'

She reached for my basket, smiling. As I let go of it, sliding it into the silver gap next to the till, my crutch fell off my arm, landed behind me, just wide of the next customer. I turned, ready with apologies. The apologies for existing that still sit just under my tongue, tight behind my teeth. The man was conservatively dressed, sixtyish. Mirror-polished loafers, a panama. A man like my father had become.

'Fucking spastic,' he spat.

It was like being punched. I pretended I hadn't heard him, just picked up my other stick, my shopping. The cashier caught my eye, smiling again. Shaking her head, she tucked the receipt in the top of my bag. Everything had changed, and nothing had. There was no choice but to keep walking.

Acknowledgements

To Mitchell, my best friend and biggest support. I run out of words to thank you. And for Oliver and Edmund, with love, always.

For my mother, who said, 'I feel sorry for children who don't skin their knees, it means they aren't having any fun.' Thanks for encouraging all the joy, and the risk. You are still the best time.

And for my father, who listens more than he speaks, and is always there to catch me. Thank you for never taking me to Newcastle United again.

To Andrew Solomon, who first gave me the idea.

To Isabel Wall, my wonderful editor and friend. You are simply brilliant, and spot what I often miss. I couldn't do without your guidance, patience and endless enthusiasm.

To Sarah Rigby, who first told me I could, and should. This book wouldn't exist without you, and I cannot thank you enough. And to Mary Mount, who believed in this story and told me it was important. Your taste and good-humoured support are invaluable.

To Sophie Lambert, super-agent, just thank you, so much.

For Rebecca Sinclair, Siena Parker, Louisa Burden-Garabedian and Ithaka Cordia. It is no exaggeration to say that WriteNow, and all of you, have changed my life. I will always appreciate your many kindnesses.

And to Markus Zuzak, who stopped me from falling on my face, and told me it was all right to want it.

Thanks to Sarah-Jane Forder: your eagle-eyed suggestions

have made this book so much better. I hope we get to do more.

To Marie Heesom and Vicky de Monterey-Richoux. Aunts near and far, but never less than loving. To Hattie and James Heesom, with love.

To Caitlin Albery Beavan and David Charles: friends like you make even rainy days a joy. To Paul Ibell, with thanks for your good eye, listening ear, and many breakfasts. To Charlotte Fox Weber. Thank you for pushing me, gently, over the finish, and for everything else; I cherish you. To Joanna Green, an early reader of this book, brightest and best. To Naomi Dawson: from Notting Hill Gate to Walthamstow Central, I'll always adore you. To Annika Caswell: thanks for all the laughter, and the quiet. To Kala Simpson: thanks for all the shows, and more than twenty years of conversation. And to Kristi Kouchakji: you make me smile as much now as the day we met. To Laura Sandelson, kindest, most beautiful of friends. Thank you for all the long, laughing lunches. To Helen Thomas, who talked me through lockdown, when this book felt impossible to finish. I won't forget your practical kindness. Jenny Knight, wonderful writer, wonderful friend. I'm so glad to have met you. To Laura Kay, the very best thing about WriteNow; I'm so delighted Penguin brought us together, here's to more queer evenings. And to Katharine Weber for her good advice and boundless curiosity.

Thanks, too, to Penny and Gareth Steele, Georgiana Dacombe, Helen Batten, Mazzi Odu, Martha Aldridge and Anil Sharma. John Betts, one of the kindest men I know. Tom Lau, Nicolas Howells, Roger Tatley, Catherine McCoy, Rachael Tremlett, Rebecca Parkin, Gareth Mason. Harry Burton and Jai Morjaria, Grace Williams and Charu Grace, Imogen and Emma Wall. I'm so grateful for your friendship, and all the years we've had. To

Naomi, Trevor and Julia Smith, with fondest love. To Stephen Baker, Sara Pritchard, Tiffany Watt-Smith and Augusta Annesley. And to Sarah Beal, Julia Robins, Bron Quilter, Stephen Savage and Gianluca Antonelli.

And lastly, for Sam, who would rather eat books than read them, but is essential.